The 39 Articles in Contemporary Anglicanism

Defining Convictions and Decisive Commitments

Michael Jensen and Tom Frame

The 39 Articles in Contemporary Anglicanism:
Defining Convictions and Decisive Commitments

First published in 2010
by Barton Books, Canberra

This edition published 2025
by Broughton Publishing Pty Ltd
32 Glenvale Crescent, Mulgrave, VIC 3170

Copyright © Michael Jensen and Tom Frame 2010

All rights reserved. No part of this publication may be reproduced, stored in a retrieval system or transmitted, in any form or by any means electronic, photocopying, recording or otherwise, without the prior written permission of the publisher.

ISBN: 978-1-922441-18-8

Foreword

The 39 Articles in Contemporary Anglicanism first appeared in 2010 under the title *Defining Commitments and Decisive Convictions*. The project was conceived with Tom Frame, who was then in Canberra, while I was in Sydney. Our first meeting was in the rectory at Bowral – a convenient halfway point, but also a symbolic one. For this was not just a joint book but an unusual collaboration across diocesan lines, bringing together two Anglicans from different contexts to reflect on what unites us. We discovered that the Articles of Religion offered precisely such common ground, and the book bears witness to that conviction.

Our hope was, and remains, that the Articles might resurface as a reference point for Anglican theology and polity in the twenty-first century. Too often Anglican identity is described as little more than a broad inclusivity – as though the only defining feature of Anglicanism were a refusal to be defined. The suggestion is that Anglicanism is a church with no firm commitments, where conviction itself is suspect.

Yet the only alternative is not a brittle fundamentalism or an arid traditionalism. The Articles provide a better way: boundaries wide enough to give genuine liberty, yet firm enough to give substance. They shape Anglicanism as a reformed and orthodox expression of Christianity – Scriptural, creedal, liturgical, and deeply spiritual. They remind us that the formal principle of Anglicanism is the supreme authority of Scripture – not the episcopate, not tradition, and not human 'reason' (so often indistinguishable from cultural fashion). And they insist that the material principle is salvation by grace alone, through faith – the heartbeat of the Reformation and the note that resounds through all the sixteenth-century formularies.

Since 2010, the trajectory of Anglicanism in Australia – indeed, across much of the Western world – has only become clearer. Compared with our brothers and sisters in the Global South, we are far from vibrant in spirit or zealous in mission. Our numbers decline, our public voice diminishes, our congregations grow older. If the second quarter of the twenty-first century is to look different, it must be marked by a renewed passion for mission: above all, the proclamation of the good news of Jesus Christ. The 39 Articles call us back to the gospel we are entrusted to share, and to the kind of churches we are summoned to be.

Michael P. Jensen
September 2025

Contents

Introduction		1
1	The Articles in Anglican history	17
2	The Articles and Anglican belief	33
3	The Articles in Anglican life and witness	95
4	Assertions, arguments and articles	117
5	Conviction and consensus	135
6	Alternatives, amendments and additions	159
Closing remarks		191
About the authors		194
Index		195

Introduction

We live in an age that is suspicious of anything resembling ideology. Doctrinal systems and political theories have led to conflict and violence that have divided communities and caused bloodshed. The modern tendency is towards disdain for great schemes and distrust of those who propose them. Insisting that there is a right way appears to be antithetical to personal fulfillment and a prescription for discrimination. The great 'isms' of the past century – Marxism, Stalinism, Maoism, Fascism, Nazism and Nationalism – engulfed the globe in war and appeared to bring nothing but misery. For their part, the major world religions have been indicted for inflaming sectarian tensions and for their complicity with terrorism. Most right-thinking people in the West distrust doctrines claiming to be an answer for everything. They disavow any system of belief asserting its ability to make a complex world neat and tidy by imposing a grid of ideas that every man and woman must embrace. It was almost 90 years ago that the Irish poet WB Yeats (1865–1939) wrote:

> The best lack all conviction,
> While the worst are filled
> with passionate intensity.[1]

His words speak to our times with clarity and we are left asking: might it be better to 'lack all conviction' and just get on with others regardless of their beliefs? Surely, 'passionate intensity' has wreaked enough havoc and caused enough death and destruction? Haven't we seen sufficient evidence that certainties are inherently dangerous and that some are literally explosive? Aren't convictions effectively 'prisons' as the German atheist philosopher Friedrich Nietzsche (1844–1900) contended more than a century ago?[2]

We also live in a deeply sceptical age. There is widespread doubt that a person can be asked to have confidence in what cannot be experienced first-hand. Many people doubt anything that cannot be appropriated with their senses. This partly explains the shift from traditional religion to spirituality and that the individual is content to be referred to as 'a spiritual person'. This form of spirituality is beyond critique because it relies upon a unique experience that others have not had and cannot possibly share. If it is real to the individual who experiences it, then it is real in a profound sense; no-one else is in a position to deny it. But to speak confidently of things that are beyond oneself – to say that there is one God who is known as three persons, for example – must be beyond our capacity. To make statements, particularly in the form of public declarations, about one's belief is, at best, little more than the wishful thinking that characterised another age and, at worst, an attempt to persuade others to have confidence in notions that might be alien to their experience.

But however much we might imagine a path to a saner and safer world, *it is simply impossible to live without convictions.* Believing – that some things are true and that some other things are false, and that some things are good and beneficial and that some other things are bad and detrimental – is a part of what it is to be human. Even the person who loves peace and whatever it takes to achieve harmony between people is saying something about what they believe to be most important in life and their preparedness to give everything in order to achieve it. These kinds of personal beliefs may be carefully discerned and articulated; they may be merely what everyone else thinks. They may be 'gut reactions' expressing things of which we are aware at an instinctual level; they could be merely statements of preference or admissions of prejudice. But at some level these are all 'convictions' about how things are and how they ought to be. So, the question is not 'do I have convictions' but rather 'about what am I convicted'?

Christians are people with a particular set of convictions. Primarily, they are convinced that in Jesus of Nazareth, a human person like one of us, God the Creator took on human form, died for the redemption of sin and rose again. They believe Jesus is alive and can be known today through his Spirit.[3] Contrary to some suggestions, this is any-thing but a dry-as-dust set of propositions put to prospective believers in a manner resembling a philosophy tutorial. These convictions flow from a personal encounter with the very source of life itself – Jesus of Nazareth. Jesus, and their encounter with him, transforms their lives in a continuing way. For the earliest Christians, the depth of their encounter explained why they were worshipping this Jesus – a man – as the only true God – something previously unthinkable. These convictions were not a matter of ticking boxes in some survey. They were a life-transforming reality; something that many of them would be willing to give all to preserve – even their lives.

This cluster of convictions plainly requires careful explanation and sustained reflection. And there are, it must be conceded, a number of cogent and compelling questions that one could put. Conscious that their beliefs required explication, the first Christians and the earliest Churches attempted to put some flesh on the bare bones of their particular understanding of God and this world. They recognised that the political, social and economic consequences of their convictions had to be clarified, even defended. Further, they had to say what they *weren't* saying as well as what they were. As the circumstances required, they produced detailed statements of the faith in order to set out, as clearly as possible, that 'these are the things which we are convinced *are* true (and, incidentally, here is what we know *isn't* true)'. One of these statements, developed over the course of the fourth century, was known as the Nicene Creed. In this creed, the churches asserted, among a number of things, that the Jesus they worshipped was both fully man and fully God. The statement sought to end, within and beyond the Church, the controversy over the nature of Jesus.

Our aim in this book is to present a contemporary interaction with another statement of faith. Leaders of the Church in England in the sixteenth century assembled a set of convictions: *The Articles of Religion*.

The Church of England – known today as the 'Anglican' or 'Episcopal' Church in many parts of the world – had its beginnings not with high-minded theological convictions but with more mundane considerations. In 1534, King Henry VIII of England (1491–1547) broke from the Church of Rome by rejecting the temporal and spiritual authority of the Pope and making himself supreme governor of the Church in England. This action served a number of ends. Most immediate was his desire for a divorce from his Spanish wife,

Catherine of Aragon, in order to marry his mistress, the young English noblewoman Anne Boleyn. But there were concerns of genuine theological conviction in play. The break with Rome was more than a matter of serving the temporal and passing needs of a ruling dynasty. The movement we know now as the Reformation had begun to sweep Europe in the 1520s under the influence of thinkers such as Martin Luther (1483–1546) in Germany and Ulrich Zwingli (1484–1531) in Switzerland. Their influence had certainly been felt in distant England, so much so that Henry had written a tract staunchly defending the Pope's position against the claims of Luther!

In brief, the Reformation made a two-pronged attack on the form of Christianity being practised in Western Europe. The first substantial issue concerned authority. The leading Reformers believed they were reinstating the Bible to its rightful position as the supreme authority in all matters connected with Christian belief and custom. Scripture was ultimately authoritative. The Bible, rather than the Church or its traditions, defined belief and settled disputes. The Church, including the papacy, needed to be *under* the authority of the Bible and to be shaped by its teaching. The task of translating the Bible into modern languages and distributing copies for people to read were vitally important tasks that the Reformers undertook with vigour and enthusiasm.

The second substantial issue was answering the critical theological question of how someone might be saved (what theologians call *soteriology*). All were agreed that the death of Jesus for sin was a necessary component of human salvation. But how did the whole scheme fit together? In the medieval period, various theories had been suggested as to how salvation was effected. How much was God's doing and how much depended on human response?

One theory popular at the time demanded that a person 'do whatever was within them' (*facere quod in se est*) to please God and, having done their best, God would graciously accomplish the rest in Christ. By their close and consistent study of the Bible, the Reformers concluded that no human effort was required for salvation. In fact they were adamant that no human effort could achieve salvation. It was beyond human reach and required divine initiative. A person is justified only by faith in the work of Christ on the cross, and not by their own efforts to win divine favour. Doing good is a response to what God has done in Christ. Good works do not contribute to salvation. These two dominant themes, as we shall see, underlie the attempt to provide a summary of the Christian faith that we find in *The Articles of Religion*, commonly referred to as the 'Thirty-Nine Articles'. Through the agency of the Archbishop of Canterbury, Thomas Cranmer (1489–1556), and others, Reformation ideas shaped the faith of what became the Church of England.

The Articles are mainly the work of Cranmer, who was Archbishop of Canterbury during the reign of Henry VIII (1509–1547) and then under his son Edward VI (1547–1553). It was during Edward's brief rule that Cranmer began to create a list of doctrines that would stamp the English Church with the indelible mark of Reformed theology. It was not until Elizabeth I (1553–1603) acceded to the throne in 1558, however, that the Articles took their final form and present number, with a little help from Matthew Parker (1504–1575), the Archbishop of Canterbury after 1559.

The Articles are, in many ways, a statement of faith for the sixteenth century. They reflect the controversies of their day, not ours. For example, the Articles feature an extended statement on the Lord's Supper, which was a real point of contention between the Reformation Churches and the Roman Church (and between the Reformers, too, it has to be said). The Articles are certainly not a complete or perfect list. They leave out what may seem to us important. For instance, they are almost silent on the origins of the created order and the return of Christ. We might also be surprised by their emphasis on what seem to us unimportant. For instance, a whole article is given over to Jesus' descent into hell, another is concerned with the swearing of oaths. At several points they appear to embody the necessary evil of compromise rather than present a unified vision of what is true. It is obvious even to an uninformed reader that the Articles are the work of a drafting committee that could not agree on every word or phrase. The Articles are, in places, rather verbose and repetitious.

We are, then, well justified in asking: are they worth studying today? The answer is not an unqualified 'yes'. Very different issues confront Christian believers in the twenty-first century. Anglicans disagree on matters that are not even dealt with by the Articles. Contemporary Christians are asking: what is the right way for Christians to behave sexually? How can we reconcile our faith with the scientific knowledge on which so much of modern life depends? What is the best way to order our churches and what should our public services look like? How should Christians relate to the political world? Should the Church cooperate with civic authority when it appears determined to prohibit Christian witness?

Although the Articles have remained unchanged for nearly 450 years and debates between Christians have moved on to some new subjects, many of the concerns and convictions outlined in the Articles have a timeless quality and a universal application. The Articles, far from being an embarrassing skeleton in the Anglican closet, are the fruits of careful listening to the Bible and its teaching. They are an attempt to understand God's self-revelation and what this means for the Church and for individual believers. In the Thirty-Nine Articles, the Church of England declares itself subject to God's Word in scripture and acknowledges that it is not free to do anything other than to listen to what the Bible says and to respond in humble obedience. Those who drafted the Articles were well aware that times would change. They anticipated different customs and cultures in which Christians would have to declare and express their faith. They themselves had lived through turbulent and difficult days. Societal beliefs were in a state of tremendous flux with individual men and women enduring enormous pressure to change their beliefs to suit the mood of the times.

Our times are no less complicated or coercive. The national churches that identify with the Anglican tradition currently face a crisis of identity. People calling themselves 'Anglican' spend time and energy arguing over what precisely it means to be Anglican and who has the right to deem that certain ideas, practices or people are not 'Anglican'.[4] The Thirty-Nine Articles – along with the 1662 *Book of Common Prayer* – are still regarded by many as a touchstone for authentic Anglicanism. And yet, even the status and the function of the Articles is disputed. There are leading Anglicans, bishops and theologians among them, who consider the Articles an historical relic without any real place in modern church life or contemporary Christian living. Some have insisted that the Articles have no entitlement to authority and should be accorded none. They argue that an understanding of Anglican theology is best served by ignoring them. There is, we would contend, more than a touch of intellectual arrogance and spiritual pride present in this attitude. It suggests a feeling of superiority over the past and an inference that it was acceptable for people to subscribe to such crass and unsophisticated beliefs four centuries ago but that we now know better.

In our view, those seeking to be ordained into the Anglican ministry and those preaching and teaching on its behalf should be prepared to subscribe to the Church's formalised beliefs on matters affecting the salvation of souls. At the very least, they should be aware of what those beliefs are, and able to give a defence of them against the counter-claims of, for instance, Roman Catholics and Pentecostal Charismatics. We fear that some ordinands and some licensed clergy are not sufficiently aware of the Church's doctrine before they are invited or encouraged to preach doctrines that accord with their own convictions and commitments. No Christian is ever free from the obligation to listen to the voices of brothers and sisters from the past. The Articles remind that, for Anglicans as for all Christians, convictions do matter. They remind us that Christians in every time and place have a duty to proclaim the Gospel in ways that are faithful to the words and works of Jesus but also speak to the hearts and minds of a rising generation. Stating one's beliefs is not an easy task. Finding the right words is not always straightforward. Nonetheless, Christians are called to give an account of the hope that is within them and this includes their core convictions.

We need, then, to be clear about what the Articles attempt to do and what lies outside their point and purpose. The Articles are not intended to be a creed or a catechism. They do not try to give expression to the Church's sense of mission and ministry or outline the basis upon which other Christian communities might be received into the Anglican Communion. In 1660, John Pearson (1612–86), the Bishop of Chester, famously explained that the Articles are not nor were ever intended to be 'a complete body of divinity … but an enumeration of some truths, which upon and since the Reformation have been denied by some persons; who upon denial are thought unfit to have any cure of souls in the Church or realm'.[5] It would be wrong to contend that the Articles embody or promote something called 'Cranmerism' in the same way that Lutherans can speak of 'Lutheranism'. The common charge, that the drafters of the Articles meant them to be vague and ambiguous, is simply wrong. Their aim was to avoid making any statement that said either too little or too much. They were keen to arrive at inclusive statements that reflected the comprehensiveness of view then deemed acceptable within the Church of England. There are, of course, many things that we might wish the drafters had said, such as the steps to be taken and the facts to be weighed in determining that any belief or custom was agreeable or repugnant to the Word of God. While convinced that this distinction needed to be made, the drafters did not proceed to explain how it was to be made or by whom.

The Articles are a highly nuanced and thoroughly considered theological position that points to the implications of professing a living faith in Jesus Christ. Agreeing to the content of the Articles is not, however, the same as having a saving faith in Jesus Christ. But they help to protect and shape the preaching of that same Jesus Christ by some of those who would follow him. There are those, such as Archbishop Cranmer and Bishops Hugh Latimer of Worcester and Nicholas Ridley of London, who died for these very beliefs, pointing as they suffered martyrdom to the greater reality those beliefs represented.

Many books have been written on the Thirty-Nine Articles over the past four centuries. Their principal readership has been theological students, obliged to study the origin and standing of the Articles as part of their preparation for ordination and service in the Anglican Church. In most instances, the texts have followed a predictable pattern. After a brief historical introduction, most authors explained that the Articles are grouped together in sections relating to particular subjects which are discussed individually and collectively. For instance, Articles I–V contain teaching on the persons of the Trinity, Articles VI–VIII deal with the character and exercise of faith, Articles IX–XVIII are related to personal dimensions of belief, Articles XIX–XXXIV cover duties and responsibilities within the Christian community, and Articles XXXV–XXXIX are focussed on religious and civil life in England. There would have been some comment on the formal requirement in canon law for clergy to subscribe to the Articles and the relationship of the Articles to the other historic formularies, the 1662 *Book of Common Prayer* and the Ordinal.

The vast majority of published works on the Articles originate from the Church of England. This is to be expected. The Articles were devised and drafted in England to deal with questions of belief and order in that country. The Articles presumed the existence of monarchy and the legal Establishment of the Church. As subscription to the Articles has been required of English clergy and a select group of laity since 1571 (the requirement for lay subscription has since been dropped), it is not surprising that the Articles have been the focus of a great deal of English thinking and writing. And because most of the major movements within the Anglican Communion were initiated or gained momentum in England, it is to be expected that the Articles have been cited or quoted to either support or oppose new ideas and novel practices. The liturgist and historian Peter Toon observed that:

> expositions of the Articles from the seventeenth to the twentieth century have fallen into four types – i) Evangelical and Reformed ii) Broad Church and Latitudinarian iii) High Church and generally Arminian, and iv) Anglo-Catholic. Of course, some expositors have had their feet in two traditions of interpretation. That there have been different traditions of interpretation is generally acknowledged.[6]

The dominant theological tradition in Australian theological colleges has been reflected in their choices of prescribed textbooks. The Evangelicals preferred *The Principles of Theology*[7] and *The Catholic Faith: A Manual of Instruction for Members of the Church of England* by WH Griffith Thomas, an English cleric who taught at Wycliffe College in Canada. This work first appeared in 1904 and was revised in 1952.

The Anglo-Catholics tended to use *The Thirty-Nine Articles of the Church of England*[8] published by ECS Gibson, formerly Bishop of Gloucester, in 1897 and revised in 1910. Those of more liberal Catholic sentiment much preferred EJ Bicknell's *Theological Introduction to the Thirty-Nine Articles*[9] which was released in 1919 and updated in 1955. There have been few recent treatments of the Articles that could claim to be a substantial advance on extant works. Perhaps the best is the English theologian Oliver O'Donovan's concise study, *On the Thirty-Nine Articles: a Conversation with Tudor Christianity*, which first appeared in 1986.[10]

While the English Church continues to engage in conversation about the Articles, in some of the national churches comprising the Anglican Communion, the Articles have no formal status. Accordingly, little attention has been paid to them. The Articles passed by the September 1801 convention of the Protestant Episcopal Church of the United States contained some notable commentary. Only the titles of Articles XXI and XXXV of the 1571 Articles are included but these are followed by bracketed statements to the effect that their contents do not apply to the American Church because they relate to England and its legal and political conditions. The Homilies are not to be read in American churches 'until such a revision of them be conveniently made, for the clearing from them, as well from obsolete words and phrases, as from local references'. In a society that had won its freedom from Britain and wanted to assert its independence, this action was not surprising. The 1888 Lambeth Conference of bishops declared that newly founded Anglican provinces need not be 'bound to accept in their entirety the Thirty-Nine Articles' although they were required to give 'satisfactory evidence that they hold substantially the same doctrine as our own, and that their clergy subscribe to the Articles in accordance with the express statements of our own standards of doctrine and worship'.

Within the Anglican Church of Australia, the Articles have an important place in defining the Church's beliefs and customs. They have been incorporated into the Church's Constitution and every candidate to be ordained deacon, priest and bishop must assent to the doctrine they contain. The Articles also appear at the rear of the two locally authorised prayer books: *An Australian Prayer Book* (AAPB) which was published in 1978 and *A Prayer Book for Australia* (APBA) which first appeared in 1995.

The Articles receive varying levels of attention at Australian theological colleges. In some places, the Articles are taken very seriously as an essential statement of Anglican belief. They are discussed in classes dealing with doctrine, ecclesiology, liturgy and church history. Ordinands receive lectures on the intent and content of each Article and come to understand where and why Anglicans have held specific views about a range of subjects. Before being required to indicate their assent to the Articles, they are invited to indicate any difficulties they have with the meaning of the Articles and are made aware of the latitude that exists within the Articles for divergent views. Those being ordained are, then, fully acquainted with this particular formulary and have a sense of the force and effect of the Articles on their future ministry.

In other theological colleges, the Articles are treated with disdain and virtually ignored. Ordinands are not required to study the content of the Articles or obliged to come to their own mind on whether they accept or reject their teaching. In many dioceses, the only time ordinands are made aware of the Articles is immediately before their ordination when the diocesan registrar invites them to make the necessary oaths and declarations. The assumption is that the ordinand is able to make the requisite declaration relating to the Articles, but what it means legally, ethically and spiritually to assent to the Articles remains unclear to most. Indeed, a number of clergy have reported being directed to make the requisite declaration and being instructed not to ask questions about its intention or its consequence. A brief survey of Anglican clergy reveals significant differences in opinion. Some say they assented to the Articles because they personally professed the doctrine they contained. Others say they believed that the Articles accurately portrayed what the Church of England believed in 1571 rather than what they personally believed. Some clergy thought they were being asked to affirm their assent to each and every Article; others thought they were declaring their general assent to the Articles taken as a whole.

There is little to commend the perpetuation of this kind of diversity. Anglicans ought to be familiar with the Articles, whatever their attitude towards them. But neglect of the Articles among those obliged to subscribe to them is not new. Reflecting upon the period before his ordination in 1638, the great English poet, pastor and Puritan, the Reverend Richard Baxter (1615–91), remarked:

> [When] I thought of ordination, I had no scruple at all against subscription. And yet so precipitous and rash was I that I had never once read over the book of ordination [the Ordinal], which was one to which I was to subscribe; nor half read over the Book of Homilies, nor exactly weighed the Book of Common Prayer, nor was I of sufficient understanding to determine confidently in some points in the Thirty-Nine Articles. But my teachers and my books having caused me in

> general to think the Conformists had a better cause, I kept
> out all particular scruples by that opinion.[11]

It is not surprising that the status of the Articles is unclear when ordaining bishops, diocesan officials and theological faculty have vastly different attitudes to the need for emerging leaders to declare what they believe. And it is far from surprising that the Church is accused of doctrinal incoherence when a document that is intended to serve as the benchmark for Anglican belief and custom is treated with cavalier indifference or casually dismissed as a relic of the past. Only slightly less concerning is the lack of attention to the Articles in discussions about the way ahead. By way of example, there were only four brief references to the Articles in *Facing the Future: Bishops Imagine a Different Church* which appeared in 2009.[12] Reading this book tends to confirm our view that the Articles do not have much of a profile in contemporary Anglicanism in Australia (or elsewhere in the Anglican Communion) and are not considered useful to the continuing life of the Church. The book does not focus on the sources of theological authority or dwell on the importance of orthodoxy to mission and ministry, although a link is asserted by Bishop Stephen Hale.[13]

In the many conversations we have shared as authors of this book, we anticipated that there would be substantial differences of opinion between us. Indeed, we presumed that each chapter would need to carry one of our names because we would not be able to secure agreement to the extent that we would both be prepared to defend the contents of the entire manuscript. But we have been surprised by the convergence of our thoughts and words as to the content and status of the Articles.

The drafting of this introduction was a shared affair with approximately half the material originating with each author. Michael Jensen singlehandedly produced the largest single section of the book – chapter two – which deals with each of the Thirty-Nine Articles. Some of this material was prepared initially for his well-known website 'The Blogging Parson'.[14] He also contributed most of the section in chapter six identifying topics for additional articles. Tom Frame drafted chapters one, three and four. The remainder of the book is an amalgam of ideas and insights from both authors. The full text of the Articles is spread throughout chapter two.[15]

As theological educators and vocational trainers, we have written this book to assist ordinands who want to know what the drafters of the Articles intended to say, why certain words and specific phrases have been used, the matters of disagreement and points of controversy they tried to settle, and how the Articles have shaped Anglican belief over the past four centuries. This book will also help the laity to gain a firmer grasp of historic Anglican belief and to acquire some insights into debates over distinctive Anglican customs. We hope our words might revive interest in the Articles among the Australian Bishops, the General Synod and its Doctrine Commission, diocesan synods and academic theologians. We want to inspire them to reconsider some of the enduring debates over the Articles and perhaps to ponder afresh the possibilities and prospects that might exist for devising contemporary statements of Anglican belief. We intend that our words, and desire that future statements, should honour the Church's history and respect its continuing efforts to preserve and promote the Gospel of Jesus Christ.

We do not expect that everyone will agree with our descriptions of the Articles or enthusiastically embrace our suggestions for revision. In fact, we expect strong disagreement and spirited criticism. But it seems to us that the Articles ought to be the venue for a conversation about Anglican belief because of the place of the Articles in the evolution of Anglicanism and because many Anglicans still believe that the Articles define Anglican belief and confirm Anglican commitments. The Articles certainly touch on the character of God and the state of fallen humanity, the origins of sin and the fact of death, the work of Christ and the offer of salvation, the means of grace and the hope glory, authority and leadership within the Christian community, and the means by which the mission and ministry of Christ is preserved and promoted in the world. These are matters of life and death and the Articles treat them with a seriousness and sincerity that deserves our close attention. There is no point in those who can adhere to the Articles demanding that those who cannot, and those who are content to subscribe to the Articles telling those who resist, that they should leave the Anglican Church. The better and more commendable strategy is not to issue anathemas but to engage in dialogue and then debate. There is more to this than a mere refusal to profess certain beliefs because they are incompatible with personal conviction. It is contrary to the modern Anglican mindset to demand compliance. If a person cannot believe they must be assisted in their unbelief rather than damned for it. If, however, a member of the clergy finds they can no longer subscribe to the Church's formularies in good faith, they ought to consider relinquishing any leadership post they might occupy.

We firmly believe that the Articles have a continuing place in the life of the Anglican Church of Australia because they deserve such a place. In our view the Articles are a treasury of wholesome doctrine and ought to serve as the basis for assessing new thinking and novel customs. We are convinced that the Articles point to a distinctly Anglican approach to theology and ecclesiology, and are worthy of close attention and sustained study. Rather than have the Articles overlooked in the hope that they might quietly fade from view, we argue that Anglicans ought to pay closer attention to the Articles. In relation to disagreements about their meaning, Anglicans ought to engage in discussion about where and how they might be amended. Ultimately we might achieve a new consensus or see new articles added in relation to matters that presently divide Christians – and even Anglicans. Pretending the Articles do not exist is not a long-term solution or an attractive option in any sense. The longer the task of reviewing and revising the Articles is delayed, the more imposing will be the scope and substance of matters requiring clarification and codification.

This small book is part of our effort to revive interest in the Articles. It reflects our commitment to an expression of Anglican mission and ministry that honours the past, engages with the present and anticipates the future, for the sake of Jesus Christ and the coming Kingdom of God.

Michael Jensen
St Mark's Anglican Church, Darling Point

Tom Frame
Tarago, NSW

Notes

1. WB Yeats, 'The Second Coming', first printed in 1920. For the text and a commentary see:
   http://www.thebeckoning.com/poetry/yeats/yeats5.html
2. Friedrich Nietzsche, *The Anti-Christ, 1895*, translated into English by HL Mencken, 1920. The entire text can be accessed at http://www.fns.org.uk/ac.htm. See p. 54 for quoted idea.
3. There are a couple of early summaries of Christian belief in the Bible itself. See, for example, 1 Corinthians 15:3–5: 'For I handed on to you as of first importance what I in turn had received: that Christ died for our sins in accordance with the scriptures, and that he was buried, and that he was raised on the third day in accordance with the scriptures, and that he appeared to Cephas, then to the twelve.'
4. The label 'Anglican' is frequently used to mean a more formal style of church service, as in 'that church is more Anglican than this (usually more laid-back) one is'. As we shall see from the Articles themselves, liturgical flexibility was already in place in Anglican thinking in the 1500s.
5. John Pearson, *Minor Theological Works*, vol. II, edited by W Churton, 1844, p. 215.
6. Peter Toon, 'The Articles and Homilies', in Stephen Sykes, John Booty and Jonathan Knight (eds), *The Study of Anglicanism*, revised edition, SPCK, London, 1999, pp. 147–48.
7. WH Griffith Thomas, *The Principles of Theology: An Introduction to the Thirty-Nine Articles*, Longman, Green and Co, London, 1930.
8. ECS Gibson, *The Thirty-Nine Articles and the Church of England*, Methuen, London, 1897.
9. EJ Bicknell, *Theological Introduction to the Thirty-Nine Articles*, Third Edition, Longmans, London, 1955.
10. Oliver O'Donovan, *On the Thirty-Nine Articles: A Conversation with Tudor Christianity*, Paternoster Press, Oxford, 1986. In the same year as O'Donovan's study appeared, WCG Proctor, an Irish cleric and theological lecturer, published *The Teaching of the Church of England Following the Thirty-Nine Articles*, Churchman Monograph No. 2, Churchman Publishing, Worthing, 1987. This book does not cover the historical context in which the Articles were drafted, debates about subscription or continuing controversies about their content and

interpretation. Most of the narrative is devoted to generalised discussion of the theological intention of each Article.

11. JM Lloyd-Thomas (ed.), *The Autobiography of Richard Baxter*, Everyman's Library, JM Dent, London, 1931, p. 16.
12. Stephen Hale & Andrew Curnow (eds), *Facing the Future: Bishops Imagine a Different Church*. Acorn Press, Brunswick, 2009. Archbishop Jeffrey Driver notes that the Articles do not have the same status throughout the Communion (p. 166); Bishop Godfrey Fryar suggests that the Thirty-Nine Articles and the Prayer Book have achieved something approaching canonical status (p. 242) and, in so doing, have bound the Church too tightly to particular teaching (p. 243); and Bishop Peter Brain simply notes that Article XXXIV allows local variation in liturgy, something he welcomes (p. 107).
13. Stephen Hale, 'A new style of leadership', *Facing the Future*, p. 188.
14. See http://mpjensen.blogspot.com/
15. The full text of the Articles can be accessed electronically at the 'Anglicans On-line' website: http://anglicansonline.org/basics/thirty-nine_articles.html

1 The Articles in Anglican history

When Jesus called his first disciples, they struggled to understand his message and to grasp its significance. Even though the coming of the Holy Spirit at Pentecost made him known to them with a new clarity, the early Church had to deal with disagreements about how believers were to express Jesus' teaching in both their private lives and corporate gatherings. The fourth and fifth centuries of Christian history were a time of controversy over key beliefs and core convictions. The Christian faith was subject to novel ideas and new interpretations that created anxiety and caused upheaval. There was a pressing need for the Church to clarify its teaching and this provided an opportunity to codify authentic doctrine.

There was another such period a thousand years later when the ideas and insights of the Reformation brought about the collapse of a unitary ecclesiastical authority – the Roman papacy – and establishment of national churches. National churches needed to assert their identity and determine their belief. For the greatest part they retained the creeds that were devised a thousand years before. These statements were foundational and no effort was expended in trying to either revise or replace them. But each of these national churches felt the need to explain their position with respect to the great doctrinal controversies of the day.

Their positions were outlined in documents like the Westminster Confession, the Confession of Augsberg and the Decrees of the

Council of Trent. The English Church declared its faith in the Thirty-Nine Articles of Religion. Like all historical documents, the Articles can only be understood in the context of the times in which they were devised. They are principally an attempt to define the doctrine of the Church of England in the midst of deep dispute and continuing controversy. They reflect the main concerns and highlight the key beliefs of the English Reformers. They are not, and were never intended to be, a holistic account or even a detailed inventory of the Christian faith. This was the role of the Creeds. The Articles are a succinct statement of belief in matters where there was controversy. In effect, they clarified the Church's belief but only where there was dispute and controversy. What, then, were the matters that promoted the tumultuous upheaval that was the Reformation?

The origins of the English Reformation

The English Church had long cherished its distinct character and ecclesiastical autonomy. Following his conquest of the Anglo-Saxons near Hastings in October 1066, the Norman king William I (1028–87) initiated a reform of the Church, establishing himself as one of the key reformers of Europe. Although adhering to its national independence and demonstrating a reforming tradition, the *ecclesia Anglicana* (usually translated the 'Church of England' when the phrase entered common use in the middle of the twelfth century) continued to acknowledge the special prominence of the Roman papacy. The administration of the civil and ecclesiastical courts was based on papal decrees and Roman canons.

In the later Middle Ages (1000–1400), a succession of corrupt and worldly popes used their position as Pontiff to gain temporal wealth and administrative power. The Church, the most important religious and political institution in Western Europe, accumulated great wealth and territory while many of the leading clergy became preoccupied with civil affairs and political intrigue. To many in the English Church, the Pope in Rome bore little resemblance to the Chief Shepherd of Christ's Flock, possessing instead the likeness of a greedy and oppressive foreign monarch. A desire for reform began to stir among some of the English people. They wanted the Bible available in their own language and senior clergy made more accountable for their actions. John Wycliffe (1320–84), sometimes referred to as the

'Morning Star of the Reformation', translated the Bible into English in 1382. His theological outlook almost anticipated the work of the early Reformers, with whom he had much in common. His followers, known as the Lollards, were itinerant preachers who inspired a spiritual revival in Britain. But Wycliffe, whose views were seen as heresy by Church authorities at home and abroad, was expelled from his position at Oxford University and Lollardy was brutally suppressed. However, English objections to official Church teaching did not end when Wycliffe's bones were exhumed, crushed and scattered in a river by order of the Pope. Others were to take his place despite violent opposition from Rome. More than a century later, the conditions for major reform were developing.

On the European Continent, the reform movement led by the German Augustinian monk Martin Luther (1483–1546) produced upheaval and created chaos. Luther had encouraged defiance of papal authority and repudiated much of the Church's dogma. His ideas reached England as early as 1521 and immediately caused controversy. His books were burned in front of St Paul's Cathedral in London. The ideas of the leading Swiss Reformer Ulrich Zwingli (1484–1531) were apparent in the translation of the Bible into English by William Tyndale (1494–1536). The uproar and confusion in Europe demanded a response from the Church in England. There were those, like Bishop Stephen Gardiner (1493–55) of Winchester, comprising the 'Old Learning' party who wanted independence from the Pope but overhaul of existing doctrine. And there were those, like Archbishop Thomas Cranmer (1489–1556) of Canterbury, comprising the 'New Learning' party who wanted independence from the Pope and a thorough overall of existing doctrine. The English were well aware of what was at stake. When the Continental Reformers attacked religious structures they disturbed the social order upon which political settlements were based. In Europe there had been riots and rebellions as the promotion of new theological convictions were pressed into the service of ideological causes. The confusion and uncertainty that had followed these spontaneous reformations were exacerbated by the existence of disagreement between and among the Reformers.

When those allied with Luther issued a public statement of their position, it was not just Roman errors that they sought to correct. They also wanted to show where and why their beliefs differed from the Swiss reformers and the Zwinglians. The 'Schwabach Articles' were devised in 1529 to distinguish the 'Lutherans' from other reforming parties. The 'Confession of Augsberg' was produced in 1530 to confirm the Lutheran position. Containing twenty-one articles on doctrine and seven on discipline, it remains a defining document for contemporary Lutheranism. At the same time, Zwingli developed a statement of his own which served as a basis for the 'Confession of Basel' which appeared in 1534 and the 'First Helvetic Confession' of 1536. All of these documents were widely-known and examples of the custom that had developed in that period: statements of belief were routinely drawn up to establish a particular theological position, to identify its specific outlook and defining beliefs, and to correct the errors apparent in rival positions. They were for the sake of brevity and clarity dominated more by assertions than arguments. Because there were so many conflicting opinions and so little apparent consensus, dialogue was usually conducted on the basis of declarations and formularies that allowed the parties to know what their opponents believed and to have some confidence that they were actually opposing their accepted belief. In order to converse with Lutherans and Zwinglians, the English were able to say they at least knew what they believed and, to a lesser degree, why they believed.

For his part, King Henry VIII (1491–1547) was publicly hostile to ecclesiastical change until personal circumstances led him to exploit calls for structural religious reform to achieve his own political and dynastic ends. The jurisdictional and financial relationship between the English Church and the Papacy was ruptured and then severed between 1532 and 1536. Henry claimed, among other things, that English fealty to the Pope had been signed by King John under duress in 1213, and was thus invalid. He argued that throughout history it was apparent that England had been an autonomous body distinct from Rome, and that he was simply officially recognising its independence. The progress of reform movements in Europe, coupled with King Henry VIII's need for a healthy male heir to ensure a stable and uncontested succession to the throne, led to major rethinking of biblical doctrines and religious customs in England. These pressures altered, among other things, the social and political standing of the Church in England. The reformers demanded that the Church be purged of the 'heretical teachings' and 'unbiblical practices' that had been introduced during the previous millennium, asserting that these accretions and novelties obscured Christ's teaching and deformed his Church.

Political aspirations and theological principles

The 'reformation' of the English Church reflected two key principles. First, the national church was independent and, as a consequence of the royal 'takeover', subject to civil law. The English monarch became 'Supreme Head of the Church' and the subjection of English Christians to Papal power was rejected. The English Church claimed the right to order its own life. This included altering the forms and patterns of corporate worship, with liturgies that used words ordinary people could understand. The Archbishop of Canterbury, the senior English cleric, was already *de facto* Primate of the official or 'Established' Church of the Realm of England. As his formal authority was limited to his own diocese, however, his position and role was nothing like that of the Pope. He did not 'govern' the Church nor could he settle doctrinal disputes with authoritative pronouncements. The English Reformers believed, like the Eastern Orthodox Church, that it was possible to be genuinely Catholic without bearing allegiance to the Bishop of Rome and the Holy See. They also denied Papal claims that Rome could define for everyone the true character and constitution of 'Catholicism'.

The second Reformation principle held that the Church could be reformed and still claim for itself historical continuity with the teaching of Jesus, together with the community and order of ministry he founded. Only those things which were deemed plainly contrary to Scripture were abandoned. The reformed Church retained the canonical Scriptures, the historic Creeds, a threefold order of ministry (with bishops, priests and deacons) together with a corporate life shaped by the sacraments of Baptism and the Eucharist. The ancient Church *in* England became the reformed Church *of* England and still claimed to be Apostolic and Catholic. As John Bramhall (1594–1663), Archbishop of Armagh, later remarked in his celebrated essay, 'A Just Vindication of the Church of England from the Unjust Aspersion of Criminal Schism':

> I make not the least doubt in the world, but that the Church of England before the Reformation and the Church of England after the Reformation are as much the same Church, as a garden, before it is weeded and after it is weeded, is the same garden; or as a vine, before it be pruned and after it is pruned and freed from luxuriant branches, is one and the same vine.

The consolidating work that was led by Archbishop Thomas Cranmer of Canterbury and reforming bishops such as Nicholas Ridley (1500–55) and Hugh Latimer (1485–1555) was stalled with the death of the young King Edward VI (1537–53) and the accession to the throne in 1553 of Henry's daughter, Mary Tudor (1516–58), who was a fanatical Roman Catholic. Mary's early death in November 1558 ended the so-called 'Counter Reformation' and all subsequent hopes of reviving papal supremacy in England.

After the religious and political turmoil of the previous three decades, the enthronement of Elizabeth I in the place of her half-sister produced a religious 'settlement' that reflected the temperament of the English and the spirit of the Reformation. On Pope Pius V's realising that Elizabeth would not submit in any way to papal authority, the Queen was excommunicated in 1570, thereby confirming formally and finally the breach between the papacy and the Church of England. By way of reply to Elizabeth's excommunication, the 'Articles agreed upon by the Archbishops and Bishops of both provinces and the whole Clergy in the Convocation holden at London in the year 1562 for the avoiding of diversities of opinions and for the establishing of consent touching true religion' were ratified a year later.

Debates and declarations

The Articles promulgated in 1571 were the products of an exercise that had been underway for more than three decades. The 'Ten Articles' were devised in 1536 at the behest of the King. This document was intended to establish 'Christian quietness and charity among us and to avoid contentious opinions'. These very long, specific and detailed Articles mark the beginnings of reformed theology in the Church of England. They affirmed the primacy of the Bible in settling disputes over Christian doctrine, the existence of three sacraments – Baptism, Penance and the 'Sacrament of the Altar', that justification is attained by 'contrition and faith joined with charity', that images may be retained as representations of virtue rather than as objects of virtue, the permissibility of seeking the intercession of the saints in heaven, the legitimacy of a range of spiritual and devotional practices mandated by the Church, and the encouragement of prayers for the dead and the relief of their suffering in purgatory.

The 'Ten Articles' were followed by the 'Bishops' Book' of 1537 which was used by King Henry to gauge the mood of the people. Drafted by a committee of bishops and theological scholars chaired by Thomas Cranmer, the 'Bishops' Book', subtitled 'The Institution of a Christian Man', contained summary teaching on the creeds, the sacraments (which numbered seven although Baptism, Holy Communion and Penance have an elevated importance), the Ten Commandments, justification, purgatory, the Lord's Prayer and the Ave Maria. It also sought to offer a broader explanation of justification, purgatory and the English rejection of papal authority. The last two sections were taken directly and without amendment from the 'Ten Articles'. The 'Bishops' Book' was drafted hastily and did not impress the King who did not impart his authority to it although it was printed by his press.

The 'Six Articles' of June 1539 accompanied the *Religion Act* passed earlier in that year and were an attempt to halt the progress of some specific Reformation doctrines. These Articles upheld the doctrine of transubstantiation; approved the reception of communion in one kind; upheld clerical celibacy; preserved monastic vows; endorsed the offering of private masses; and reinforced the requirement for regular auricular confession. A number of bishops, including Thomas Cranmer, opposed the legislation and the Articles, neither of which was rigorously enforced before as the *Religion Act* was repealed in 1547.

The 'King's Book' of 1543 carried a preface allegedly written by the monarch himself. The text reflected King Henry's criticisms of the 'Bishops' Book', including its imprecise language and mundane prose. In contrast to the 'Bishops' Book' this statement placed greater emphasis on the King's supremacy in religious matters. Commonly known as 'A Necessary Doctrine and Erudition for any Christian Man', it represented, in some respects, a reaction to the more advanced Reformed ideas, after conversations with Lutheran thinkers had lost their impetus and Cranmer's personal influence was at a low ebb.

However, the importance of purgatory was diminished, transubstantiation of the elements was denied and there was a more Reformed treatment of free will and good works. A stronger statement on faith, probably penned by Cranmer, amplified its relationship to justification and sanctification. Scholars contend that the 'King's Book' was probably intended to be a permanent statement of the Church's doctrine. It certainly remained so until the King's death in 1547.

The accession to the throne of Henry's young son Edward heralded a new beginning for the Reformers. The new monarch supported the publication of two new prayer books in 1549 and 1552, the second being shaped predominantly by Reformed ideas. In effect, the prayer books were effectively the standards of doctrine in the Church of England. In May 1553, the '42 Articles', which were drafted by Cranmer during the previous year and numbered 45, were issued with a Royal Mandate and designed to serve as a test of orthodoxy. All ordained persons together with schoolmasters and university graduates were required to subscribe to these succinct statements of Christian belief. Despite the contemporaneous claim that the Articles received the approval of Convocation, the Articles only ever existed in draft form. There is clear evidence that Cranmer was inspired by the 'Confession of Augsberg' when he drafted an unpublished statement – the '13 Articles' in 1538 – that he later expanded to become the '42 Articles'. Edward's death in July 1553 at the age of sixteen and the accession to the throne of Mary Tudor led to the restoration of the Catholic faith. The '42 Articles' were never enacted or enforced by the English Parliament. Archbishop Cranmer and many of the leading Reformers were tried and imprisoned or executed.

Despite her fanatical loyalty to Rome, personal delight in everything Spanish and determination to undo the work of her father and brother by restoring the realm to papal obedience, Mary's death in November 1558 ended the so-called 'Counter Reformation' and all subsequent hopes of reviving papal supremacy in England. The experience of the previous years had tied Roman Catholicism, in English thinking, to popular persecution and political domination. With the accession to the throne of Elizabeth, the embrace of Reformed theology was revived. The 1552 Prayer Book, subjected to a conservative revision, was issued for use throughout the realm in 1559. The new monarch sought to include rather than exclude as many of her subjects as possible in a highly nuanced religious settlement that tried assiduously to avoid any unnecessary alienation of any shade of opinion or belief. She was also adamant that the Church should not be prescriptive on matters that ought rightly to be the subject of prudent judgement and individual liberty. As part of the 'Elizabethan Settlement', Cranmer's '42 Articles' were revised in 1563. There is clear evidence of Lutheran influence in the form of the 'Confession of Würtemberg' which had been presented to the Council of Trent in 1552 as an official statement of Lutheran views.

When presented to the Convocation for consideration in 1563, four of the old articles had been removed and four new articles were added. During discussion, the number was reduced by three before promulgation as the first edition of the 'Thirty-Nine Articles'. Shortly before they were printed, however, the text of Article XXIX ('Of the Wicked which eat not the Body of Christ') was removed, perhaps to avoid a diplomatic rupture with the Lutheran princes of Germany, and a preamble was added to Article XX ('Of the Authority of the Church') acknowledging the Church's right to decree rites and ceremonies. It is not possible to be precise in explaining the reason for these late changes nor is it possible to prove that they were made at the direction of Queen Elizabeth, as is widely thought. But in 1571, Article XXIX was restored, the list of Apocryphal writings was finalised and the whole document gained strong synodical approval. The Articles were subsequently printed at the rear of all prayer books authorised for use within the Church of England.

The Articles and apologies

Despite the criticisms of those Catholics who thought the Church of England had gone too far and those Reformers who thought it had not gone far enough, the Elizabethan Church claimed that it remained truly Catholic as well as being thoroughly Reformed. The earliest assessment of the 'Reformed Catholicism' that was at the heart of the Church's self-understanding was *An Apology of the Church of England* by John Jewel (1522–71), Bishop of Salisbury, published in 1564. He insisted that the Church of England had 'returned to the Apostles and the old Catholic fathers. We have planted no new religion, but only have preserved the old that was undoubtedly founded and used by the Apostles of Christ and other holy Fathers of the Primitive Church.'

He stressed the continuity of the Church's beliefs and customs with antiquity, and its continuing catholicity:

> this lawful Reformation ... is so far from taking from us the name or nature of true Catholics ... or depriving us of the fellowship of the apostolic Church or impairing the right faith, sacraments, priesthood, governance of the Catholic Church that it hath cleared and settled them on us.

But this did not mean that everyone was content with the governance and organisation or the doctrine and customs of the Church of England.

The 'Elizabethan Settlement' was resisted by those who could not assent conscientiously to every element of Anglican doctrine and prescribed practice, by those who could not accept the notion of an Established Church on theological grounds and by those who philosophically opposed the principle of the State prescribing religious belief and demanding compliance. Theological and political objection took extreme forms. The Roman Catholic dissenters who acted on behalf of the Pope came from Europe and often combined their religious objectives with political intrigue and sporadic acts of violence. Those committed to continuing the reform agenda became known as 'Puritans' (the term being first used in 1573). Although they differed among themselves on theological questions, the more voluble demanded explicit scriptural justification for every aspect of belief and custom, believing that anything not clearly mandated by Scripture was either Popish, superstitious, idolatrous or anti-Christian. They attacked the episcopate, which they believed lacked scriptural support, and advocated presbyterian forms of church government based on the Geneva model pioneered by John Calvin (1509–64). Presbyterian polity was based on the authority of local 'elders' rather than on bishops, with those advocating this system of Church government insisting that it was a rediscovery of the apostolic model found in the New Testament. Many Puritans advocated the abolition of confirmation, contending that adult baptism provided a sounder basis for membership of the Christian community and allowed a more rigorous spiritual discipline to be applied. Most opposed clerical vestments, church ornaments and all symbolic ritual acts or gestures during worship, such as kneeling to receive the consecrated bread and wine during Holy Communion, and the giving and receiving of rings during the service of holy matrimony. They also emphasised preaching and Sabbath observance, denounced ecclesiastical courts and resisted parliamentary interference in congregational life.

In contrast to foreign papal agents, it was much more difficult dealing with internal dissenters who were less easily recognisable until their religious intrigues took the form of political objectives. While Roman Catholics wanted to overthrow the polity of the Church of England and restore Papal jurisdiction, many Puritans wanted to transform the Church so that it would reflect their own narrow vision of the Christian community. The Calvinist system of belief being introduced into Scotland by John Knox (1505–72) was attractive to those of Calvin's English disciples who had returned from exile after Mary's death. But Queen Elizabeth opposed Puritan ecclesiology and refused to sanction any reforms to the Church of England to accommodate them. Although Archbishop Edmund Grindal (1519–83) was sympathetic to elements of Puritan pastoral practice, his successor at Canterbury, John Whitgift (1532–1604), was a vehement opponent. The 1583 'Articles Touching Preachers and Other Orders for the Church' were Whitgift's attempt at suppressing Puritanism, while the intention of the *Act Against Puritans* passed in 1593 was 'the preventing and avoiding of such great inconveniencies and perils as might happen and grow by the wicked and dangerous practices of seditious sectaries and disloyal persons'.

The foremost theological (as apart from legislative) response to the more extreme Puritan arguments (although its overall scope and purpose was much broader) was *The Laws of Ecclesiastical Polity*, published by Richard Hooker (1554–1600). The first four volumes of the planned eight appeared in 1594 and, according to many within the Church, form one of the finest analyses of faith and practice ever written. Hooker found a common basis of law for both church and state, and provided a defence of the Church's claims to apostolicity and catholicity. Hooker rejected the Puritans' argument that scripture is the only test of what is correct in terms of belief or custom, insisting on the Church's right to make its own laws as long as those laws are not contrary to the tenets of scripture. He was adamant that the Church of England should not be reduced to servile submission to the religious movements gaining prominence in Geneva owing allegiance to Calvin. Being neither leader nor legislator, Hooker was not, however, the authoritative theologian to whom the English could turn to settle points of dispute, as Luther had been in Germany or as Calvin was to Presbyterians. He was an intellectual and a pastor who believed that right thinking would be reflected in right practice. Nonetheless, by 1605, the Church of England had its own statements of faith, forms of public worship and a body of canon law. It was also episcopal and by law 'Established'. This reflected the indissoluble bond between the Crown and the Church that was embodied in the slogan attributed to King James I of England: 'No Bishop, no King!' These two features – episcopacy and Establishment – and consistency with Scripture were critical expressions of Anglican self-understanding.

As a consequence of Establishment, the Church of England became, in theory and also in effect, the spiritual arm of the English State. Parliament possessed authority to appoint clergy, settle debates over doctrine and regulate public worship. This presumed that every person within the realm was a member of the Church of England and that there was one religion under one monarch, a presumption that was the foundation of Bishop Robert Sanderson's theory of ecclesiastical laws:

> In this, as in many other debates, the mean between the two extremes seems to be the truer opinion and safer to follow – Romanists who would exempt the clergy from all jurisdiction of the civil magistrates ... and the Puritanical Reformers ... who take away all power, authority, and ecclesiastical jurisdiction from the Crown and confine it wholly to their own classes and conventions.[12]

Could religious pluralism be allowed or tamed without political risk of civil disunity and social chaos?

With tragic foresight, Edwin Sandys (1516–88), Archbishop of York under Queen Elizabeth, saw dangers in separating political and religious authority. He argued vigorously that there were limits to religious liberty because diversity of religion was 'dangerous to the commonwealth' and imperilled its national life. He pronounced: 'One God, one King, one faith, one profession, is fit for one monarchy and commonwealth. Let conformity and unity in religion be provided for; and it shall be as a wall of defence unto this realm.' But Sandys was too late. His hopes for a harmonious and effective merger of church and state were, in any event, unrealistic. The 'Elizabethan Settlement' did not bring an end to theological debates within the Church of England or found a community of faith whose beliefs and customs were fixed for all time. Indeed, there was still much unfinished business, with continuing debate and greater discussion about the essence of Christian faith and how doctrine would be reflected in the Church's life, and in interactions between Christians and the world. Regrettably, the Queen and those advising her believed that conscience could be commanded and compliance could be coerced. The doctrines contained in the Prayer Book and the Articles were imposed by law. This made dissent a subversive activity and illegal. Persuasion rather than legislation would have been the better way to proceed. The marriage of church and state made this an unnecessary option in the minds of some. In the same way that national loyalty could be secured, religious adherence could be achieved. It was a policy that was bound to fail.

Continuing conversation and conflict

It is, of course, a mistake to think there was a halcyon period in ancient history when Christians were united in common belief and the Church was untroubled by organic division. It is similarly wrong to imply that the intricacies of Anglican doctrine were completely settled within the reign of Elizabeth I or that Anglicans were of one heart and mind in the way they worshipped publicly, simply because their rites were authorised by the English Parliament and everyone was obliged to embrace them. No such period of unanimity has ever existed in Christian history, nor has such uniformity ever prevailed among Anglicans or any English-speaking people. It is clear from the New Testament that the apostles vigorously debated critical points of doctrine touching on salvation, while the early Church was occasionally fractured by disagreement on questions of order and discipline as well as doctrine. There were continuing discussions about the nature of the Trinity, the person and work of Christ, the ordering of ministry and sacramental practice, and the means of discerning and preserving divine truth. It is also apparent from a careful study of Reformation history that in the sixteenth century there were no universally held positions on the character of church–state relations, the transmission of authority within the Christian community or the character of God's sovereign action in the world. The English Reformers were far from convinced that they had settled every theological debate, nor had they sought to close off the possibility that outward forms of worship might change.

The church was internally divided between the high churchmen, who were Catholic but not Roman, the low churchmen who were Reformed but not Puritan, and the broad churchmen (exemplified by the Cambridge Platonists, who were active between 1633 and 1688) who were neither but relished mystery without being Unitarian. These factions demonstrate the early existence of diversity of belief and custom within the Church of England. But not all was in a state of flux. Some things remain unchanged. Anglicanism had declared its faithfulness to the apostolic witness and its corporate submission to the authority of Holy Scripture. The Articles of Religion, the *Book of Common Prayer* and the three historic creeds (Apostles', Nicene and Athanasian) were definitive of Anglican belief and normative of Anglican custom. And in the same way that the early Church was commanded to reflect the entirety of the apostolic witness and the complete revelation of Scripture (Article XX states: 'the Church must not so expound one place of Scripture, that it be repugnant to another'), the Church resisted the temptation to go beyond the intention of its formularies to require assent to mere opinions 'thought requisite or necessary to salvation' (Article VI). Nor did the Church exalt or exclude any aspect of its diverse inheritance in claiming that one approach to worship or witness constituted a more genuine or fulsome Anglican expression of belief and custom than another, when 'it is not necessary that traditions and ceremonies be in all places one, and utterly alike' (Article XXXIV). Debate continues in the Church about core doctrines and key beliefs.

Reading the Articles today

In her very carefully argued book *The Language of the Book of Common Prayer*, Stella Brook observes that 'the prose of the Rubrics, Prefaces and Articles of Religion, unlike the prose of the Prayers and Orders of Service and of the Psalter, is intended to be read, rather than to be spoken and heard'. She notes that these documents are 'free from the stylistic requirements which govern the liturgical parts of the *Book of Common Prayer*'. The Articles were originally drafted in Latin. When readers encounter the Articles in the Prayer Book, they are, Brook explains, 'confronted with a translation rather than the original, but not necessarily with a close translation.' She notes that 'the relationship between the English and Latin versions of the Articles can show a different approach to translation from that illustrated by some of the liturgical parts of the *Book of Common Prayer* founded on Latin originals'. She points out that some of the Latin phrases which were intended to be rhythmic or melodic were translated into English with a concern only to convey and confirm meaning. The many aural dimensions of the Latin text were lost. In some places the English translation follows Latin grammatical structure while in other places it does not, preferring English idiom 'achieved partly by expansion, partly by rearrangement and partly by a substitution of other parts of speech than those used in Latin'.

For instance, the Latin adjectives *divina* and *humana* in Article II are translated 'Godhead' and 'Manhood'. In several places the translator has actually inserted words that do not appear in the Latin text to make the meaning clearer to the English reader. Again drawing on Article II which talks about the nature of Christ, the words 'that is to say' in the phrase 'so that the two whole and perfect natures, *that is to say*, the Godhead and Manhood, were joined together in one person' do not appear in the Latin text while the Latin words *inseparabiliter conjunctae* have been loosely translated 'never to be divided'. She also notes that some of the words used in the Articles mean very different things today from what they did in 1571. For instance, the word 'fond' used in Article XXII 'the Romish doctrine concerning Purgatory ... is a fond thing vainly invented' meant this doctrine was considered either 'foolish' or 'silly' in the sixteenth century whereas modern readers will understand it to mean 'affection'. Not unlike the need for careful handling of texts of Scripture which were written in Hebrew and Greek and translated into English with varying levels of precision and sometimes with undisclosed theological intent, the Thirty-Nine Articles also need to be read and understood with an eye and an ear to the original text and context.

What, then, do the Articles say and why were they so warmly received by the Church of England in the sixteenth century? The next chapter addresses all thirty-nine articles in turn, expands on their meanings and comments on the relevance of each today.

2 The Articles and Anglican belief

SECTION ONE Articles I–VIII

Article I: Of Faith in the Holy Trinity

> *There is but one living and true God, everlasting, without body, parts, or passions; of infinite power, wisdom, and goodness; the Maker, and Preserver of all things both visible and invisible. And in unity of this Godhead there be three Persons, of one substance, power, and eternity; the Father, the Son, and the Holy Ghost.*

It is easy to forget the claim that there is only one God is far from obvious. In the West, we have become used to the alternative of either one God, or no God. The one-ness of God (if it is not to be God's 'none-ness') has become rather an abstract piece of data. But the existence or non-existence of God has not been the principal choice in most of human history. Surely in the vast universe, with all its diversity and array, and all its flux and change, there is room for a variety of gods? In fact, why should we believe that the tumult and struggle we encounter do not correspond to a divine tumult and cosmic struggle: that there is not a chaos of gods with their special interests and foibles? According to Scripture – and to a great deal of human experience, too – there are other spiritual beings. But none of them is 'divine': which means none of them is equal to God in the things that make God the measure of all things.

God's one-ness is a declaration of divine supremacy over all other contenders for deity. And the corollary for human beings is that there is none other worthy of worship. This is to say, no other being ought to be in competition for our allegiance and our devotion. The word 'ought' appears as a deliberate decision. There is a natural imperative that springs from the one-ness of God. If God is one, then there is none other to whom we ought to respond with everything in our being. There is not an alternative ultimate for us to be directed towards.

Christianity, and hence Anglicanism, is a monotheistic faith. But it is a very curious form of monotheism. The orthodox Christian creeds testify that within this unity is a triplicity. The unity of God is not simple, but complex; it is not a unity of sameness, but a unity of difference. This is the doctrine of the Trinity. At the time of the Reformation, there were those on the more extreme end of the Protestant side who had denied the Trinity. The English Reformers were adamant that this was not their teaching.

The Trinity *identifies* the Christian deity – it helps us to name God and to know God, to speak to God and about God. In a world which presents us with a smorgasbord of gods, the Trinity specifies who it is the Christians worship. It is the God 'who raised Jesus from the dead' by the power of the Spirit (Romans 8:11). The first article emphasises the sheer transcendence of this deity and his freedom, matched by the three-fold cord of the classic attributes of power, wisdom and goodness. But some negatives need to be put, too: God is 'without body, parts, or passions.'

That God is declared to be 'without passions' is liable to create controversy among contemporary readers, perhaps implying that God is impassive or lifeless. But what this term is meant to convey is that God is not prey to emotions or whims. God is not irascible or moody, a victim of God's own nature. The overwhelming consensus in twentieth century theology was that divine impassability had become an untenable doctrine. In the wake of the horrors of Auschwitz and Hiroshima, it seemed impossible to believe in a God who is not sensitive, emotional and compassionate.

Although the tradition has fairly consistently taught impassibility of one form or another for 1900 years, there are good biblical grounds for at least questioning it. And, to be fair, the doctrine of God *has* on occasion been presented in such abstractions that the deity described resembles a de-personalised force – a 'God of the philosophers', who is more theoretical concept than reality. While rejecting impassability might reflect the contemporary *zeitgeist*, its wholesale rejection cannot in any way be said to reflect orthodox Christian teaching. The English theologian Oliver O'Donovan writes: 'if anyone finds comfort in asserting "God is near"... this comfort is found upon its being *God* of whom these things are said.' That is: if it is to be said, as Christian teaching does say, that the personal God loves human beings, and indeed acts out of this love for them to save, then it should also be remembered that it is a *divine* person who so loves and acts.

Article II: Of the Word or Son of God, which was made very Man

> *The Son, which is the Word of the Father, begotten from everlasting of the Father, the very and eternal God, and of one substance with the Father, took Man's nature in the womb of the blessed Virgin, of her substance: so that two whole and perfect Natures, that is to say, the Godhead and Manhood, were joined together in one Person, never to be divided, whereof is one Christ, very God, and very Man; who truly suffered, was crucified, dead, and buried, to reconcile His Father to us, and to be a sacrifice, not only for original guilt, but also for all actual sins of men.*

There is nothing too radical, it seems at first blush, in this account of the person and work of Christ. In fact, that seems to confirm that Anglicans uphold the doctrines affirmed at the Councils of Nicaea in 325 and Chalcedon in 451. The point of difference with the Church of Rome is not here, but in the doctrines of salvation and the church. Anglican heritage is continuous with that of the development of orthodoxy. The great Creeds continue to be a part of the liturgy. Perhaps, a Roman Catholic response might be to say that you can't have the orthodox definitions of Christology while not being a part of Christ's true body on earth. But Anglicans have not made that close identification.

Like Chalcedon and the Creeds, this definition of Christology is highly abstract. It seems to begin a long way from the Jesus we encounter in the Gospels. We could complain that there is nothing in the article of Jesus in his teaching ministry or as a great healer and miracle worker. We do not learn of his life of obedience to the Father. But the great conceptual engines of third and fourth century Christological thinking are gathered up and pointed in a very significant direction. Just as Athanasius' great piece *On the Incarnation of the Word* is a soteriological tract because it is a Christological tract, so here the great statements about the two natures of Christ joined together in one person, the one who shares a substance with the Father and with the blessed Virgin, 'true God and true human' (*vere deus et vere homo*) are framed so because they are necessary to his mediatory work. The reconciler can only be divine; but must also be human.

There are two significant points being made at the end of the article. First, note who is being reconciled to whom here: Christ reconciles the Father to us. Today we would be more likely to state it the other way around: sin has separated us from God, we need to be reconciled to him. But reconciliation actually cuts both ways – there is our enmity towards God, but also the divine wrath at our sin. The sacrifice of the cross must deal with both. Second, the article is quite careful to say that Christ's sacrifice was not merely for original guilt but for 'all actual sins of men'. There is here indeed a slight against those theologies which would say that Christ's death atones for *original sin,* but that there needs to be some further penance or sacramental act to deal with the guilt accruing from individual sinful acts. That is not the Anglican theology of the sacrifice of Christ. The liturgy reminds us of the completeness of Christ's sacrifice as 'his one oblation of himself once offered a full, perfect, and sufficient sacrifice, oblation, and satisfaction, for the sins of the whole world.'

Article III: Of the going down of Christ into Hell

> *As Christ died for us, and was buried, so also is it to be believed, that he went down into Hell.*

It certainly seems odd, from a twenty-first century perspective at least, that this statement was thought to deserve an article on its own. A rhythm is apparent: Article II has the death, Article IV has the resurrection. Article III covers the intervening period, namely, Holy Saturday.

This doctrine has a venerable tradition. The article echoes a statement found in the Apostles' Creed which likewise devotes a line to what became known as 'the harrowing of hell'. In 1 Peter two references are given to the proclamation of the gospel in the underworld (3:19–20 and 4:6). In Ephesians 4:8–10 Paul rather elliptically refers to the descent of Jesus to the lower, earthly regions. These are not unproblematic passages and commentators differ markedly in their interpretations. It is reasonable to infer that what happened on the cross was not merely of human significance, but that it had ramifications for the whole cosmos, including whatever mysterious beings exist in realms of which we know so very little. The gospels themselves read Jesus in this way – think of the 'strong man' teaching in Mark's Gospel for example, and the temptation narratives in the Gospels of Matthew and Luke, which seem to pre-empt Jesus' conquest of Satan on the cross. Christ's work was a victory over the whole of evil and not just the human parts of it. He was victorious over whatever suprahuman powers were ranged against him and the Father. As always with the New Testament, we do not get a full cosmology. Rather, we are handed a teaching which refers to cosmological elements.

But the Swiss reformer John Calvin thought something more ought to be understood by this doctrine. He asserted that the full consequence of evil and sin was borne by Jesus on the cross. The extent of his suffering was not merely a physical death (and his death would not be particularly remarkable if it was); in fact, his suffering for us included bearing the brunt of God's judgement on sin. As Calvin put it in his *Institutes of the Christian Religion*:

> If Christ had died only a bodily death, it would have been ineffectual. No – it was expedient at the same time for him to undergo the severity of God's vengeance, to appease his wrath and satisfy his just judgment. For this reason, he must also grapple hand to hand with the armies of hell and the dread of everlasting death ... the Creed sets forth what Christ suffered in the sight of men, and then appositely speaks of that invisible and incomprehensible judgment which he underwent in the sight of God in order that we might know not only that Christ's body was given as the price of our redemption, but that he paid a greater and more excellent price in suffering in his soul the terrible torments of a condemned and forsaken man. (*Institutes*, II.xvi.10)

The atonement concepts of victory and the sin-bearing sacrifice flow together rather than being competing alternatives as some modern theologians have seen them. Christ's death was a victory over evil insofar as he bore its full effects – and the wrath of God it attracts – 'in his body on the tree' (1 Peter 2:24). There is, however, some sleight-of-hand in Calvin's account. He wants to say that the descent to hell or hades occurred on the cross itself and not after Jesus' burial. As in the article here, the Creed puts the descent of Jesus *after* the burial and this seems the plainest reading of the biblical texts upon which this article is based.

Article IV: Of the Resurrection of Christ

Christ did truly rise again from death, and took again his body, with flesh, bones, and all things appertaining to the perfection of Man's nature; wherewith he ascended into Heaven, and there sitteth, until he return to judge all Men at the last day.

Did the fact of the resurrection really need to be reasserted in the sixteenth Century? Was it being denied? One suspects not in the way that it is today among some theologians and church leaders. Providentially it seems, the drafters of the Articles felt the need to make a strong statement about the physicality of the resurrection. The fourth article goes to some lengths, beyond the Creeds indeed, to assert the comprehensiveness of Jesus' resurrection from the dead: 'flesh, bones, and all things appertaining to the perfection of Man's nature'. The Risen Christ is not an apparition, a ghost or a formless presence. The resurrected Jesus is the one into whose side Thomas was invited to place his hands; the one who ate fish in the presence of his disciples. But, he is also the one who appeared and disappeared, even in a locked room. The biblical accounts of the first Easter and what followed are not to be understood as collected nostalgic memories of Jesus or the warming of the disciples' grieving hearts with a spiritual experience they named 'resurrection'.

The Scriptures are clear: it was not the Son of God now denuded of his ugly and ungodly physicality that ascended into heaven; rather, it was the full man resurrected and glorified. Just as the Son of God, in his entire divinity essentially 'pitched his tent among us' (John 1), so, in his full humanity, Jesus Christ entered into the heavenly realm to sit at the right of God. The apostles announce that a transformed human being reigns over the world from the heavenly throne. The Jesus known in the temporal realm does not become someone else in the heavenly realm. The resurrection of Jesus indicates that redemption is of the whole human person *as a human person*. Redemption indicates the liberation of human beings from their bondage and corruption, and from their destiny of death and judgement.

When redemption is seen in terms of resurrection, what comes into view is the restoration of humans in their entirety, including the emancipation of their bodies. Flesh and blood, after all, cannot inherit the Kingdom of God. The empty tomb is a sign that Christ, as a complete and integrated human person, died and rose again. We also understand that he came to redeem human beings as complete and integrated people, body *and* soul. The resurrection of Jesus, too, speaks the definitive word from God about the goodness of his creation in all its physicality. Moreover, Jesus will return to judge the world. It was this aspect of resurrection faith that particularly energised the early preaching of the apostles, giving it urgency. We observe this fervour in the ministry of Paul at Athens when he explained that God 'has set a day when he will judge the world with justice by the man he has appointed. He has given proof of this to all people by raising him from the dead' (Acts 17:31). The resurrection stands as a terrifying truth as well as a glorious one. The world faces a day of just judgement.

Article V: Of the Holy Ghost

The Holy Ghost, proceeding from the Father and the Son, is of one substance, majesty, and glory, with the Father and the Son, very and eternal God.

This seems a rather thin statement about the Holy Ghost's (Spirit's) person. Is it, once again, a case of the 'forgotten person of the Trinity', as some have complained? In the Nicene Creed, the statement of belief in the person of the Holy Spirit forms a heading which encompasses the *work* of the Spirit – the application of salvation to human beings, and the foundation of the church; ('the communion of saints, the forgiveness of sins …'), so that the creed is unified by its trinitarian form, all the parts of it ordered to one person of the Trinity or another.

But here, in the Thirty-Nine Articles, the Spirit is not placed in such a strategic position.

The Holy Spirit, the article claims, proceeds from both Father *and* Son. The drafters of the Articles did not think that the old controversy about the 'filioque' clause (the Latin word *filioque* means 'and the Son') in the Nicene creed – 'We believe ... in the Holy Spirit, the Lord, the giver of life, who proceeds from the Father *and the Son*' – which had split the church into its Eastern and Western parts was worth revisiting. Nor is there any assertion that the Anglican Reformation is orthodox as far as the West goes and Augustinian in its understanding of this important business.

What, then, is at stake? The West affirms that the Spirit is the Spirit *of Christ* as well as the Spirit of God. The Spirit is not just a third entity of the Godhead, a second parallel emanation from the Father, but is ordered to Christ, and is tasked with testifying to Christ. The Spirit does not draw people into the life of God outside of Christ, or by an alternative route. There is some exegetical support for this view: John's Gospel presents Jesus as the giver of the Spirit, breathing on to the disciples in a pre-Pentecost moment of inspiration. It is worth remembering, however, that it is the Spirit who designates Jesus as the Christ – being present at his baptism and so on. If the Spirit is the Spirit of Christ, it is also fair to say that the Christ is the Christ of the Spirit – the one designated and anointed by him as the Messiah, and declared to be Son of God with power by being raised from the dead (see Romans 1:1–5).

More significant is the article's insistence that the Holy Spirit is fully divine. It was the goal of the greatest treatise on the Spirit in the whole of earthly church history, by the Cappadocian theologian Basil of Caesarea (330–79), to establish this crucial point. The Spirit shares in all the substance and essence of divinity. The Spirit is not secondarily divine. The implications of this conclusion are not drawn out in the article, but this means that an encounter with the Spirit is an encounter with the very and eternal God. Being filled with the Spirit, as Christians are said to be, is not being bound into the life of a lesser being. Those things filled with the Spirit ought to be treated with reverence and awe because they are divinely filled. Appealing for sexual purity, Paul reminds the Corinthians that their bodies are 'temples of the Holy Spirit'. God is mediated to us by the Holy Spirit, but it is an immediate mediation, because it is involvement in the very life of the Godhead.

Article VI: Of the Sufficiency of the Holy Scriptures for Salvation

Holy Scripture containeth all things necessary to salvation: so that whatsoever is not read therein, nor may be proved thereby, is not to be required of any man, that it should be believed as an Article of the Faith, or be thought requisite or necessary to salvation. In the name of the Holy Scripture we do understand those canonical Books of the Old and New Testament, of whose authority was never any doubt in the Church.

Of the Names and Number of the Canonical Books.

Genesis
Exodus
Leviticus
Numbers
Deuteronomy
Joshua
Judges
Ruth
The First Book of Samuel
The Second Book of Samuel
The First Book of Kings
The Second Book of Kings
The First Book of Chronicles
The Second Book of Chronicles
The First Book of Esdras
The Second Book of Esdras
The Book of Esther
The Book of Job
The Psalms
The Proverbs
Ecclesiastes or Preacher
Cantica, or Songs of Solomon
Four Prophets the greater
Twelve Prophets the less

> *And the other Books (as Hierome saith) the Church doth read for example of life and instruction of manners; but yet doth it not apply them to establish any doctrine; such are these following:*
>
> *The Third Book of Esdras*
> *The Fourth Book of Esdras*
> *The Book of Tobias*
> *The Book of Judith*
> *The rest of the Book of Esther*
> *The Book of Wisdom*
> *Jesus the Son of Sirach*
> *Baruch the Prophet*
> *The Song of the Three Children*
> *The Story of Susanna*
> *Of Bel and the Dragon*
> *The Prayer of Manasses*
> *The First Book of Maccabees*
> *The Second Book of Maccabees*
>
> *All the Books of the New Testament, as they are commonly received, we do receive, and account them Canonical.*

This might have been the first Anglican article. The 1646 Westminster Confession, for instance, starts with a statement about Scripture before it moves to God and the divine attributes. But in the Thirty-Nine Articles there is a conscious choice to put Scripture *after* God in the list. We can justly infer that Scripture is a function of the doctrine of God and not the other way around. Significantly, it is the soteriological adequacy of Scripture – its sufficiency for salvation – and not its authority that is emphasised here although the important issue of scriptural authority is addressed in later articles. The Scriptures were given for a purpose and they are good for that purpose. Indeed, they are guaranteed by God. There is no particular view of inspiration or inerrancy disclosed in this article because its main interest is elsewhere. For salvation, Scripture tells us what we need to know. To have an understanding of this article we need to remember the polemical context in which it was drafted. There is a definite desire to take issue with the Roman Catholic Church and its tendency to accord significance to extra-scriptural tradition, including its claim to be a source of saving knowledge of God apart from, and in addition to, the witness of Scripture.

The Anglican response was not to deny the usefulness of other writings and sources. It was rather to put them in their proper place. The radical Protestant response to Rome had been to make the Scriptures an exclusive rather than a sufficient collection of edificatory writings. The English Reformers did not share this view as they explain in this article in relation to the Apocrypha. This body of writing has much to teach, and has a good deal that is worthy and beneficial. But the Apocrypha is not to be regarded as a source of saving doctrine in the same way as the canonical books of the Old Testament and New Testament are deemed authoritative and trustworthy. The Reformers could look to the great translator Jerome (c.347–420), mentioned in the Articles as 'Hierome', as a source of authority on this point. 'Manners' and 'example of life' could be learned from the Apocrypha. Determining 'doctrine' was not among its purposes. This was not a minor debating point in the sixteenth century. In confirming the extra books as canonical, the Council of Trent declared in 1546 that 'he is also to be anathema who does not receive these entire books, with all their parts, as they have been accustomed to be read in the Catholic Church, and are found in the ancient editions of the Latin Vulgate, as sacred and canonical.' With their high view of Scripture's authority, the Reformers were loath to admit to the list of inspired writings those with a rather blighted past. They also know that some beliefs had gained currency through them, principally prayers for the dead in purgatory (from 2 Maccabees 12:43–45).

It might seem an insignificant matter to non-Roman Catholics but purgatory was crucial to sixteenth century Roman Catholic theology and devotion. The massive industry that were the endowed chantry houses in which there was daily intercession for the souls of the dead was testimony to its power and pervasiveness. By way of example, Oxford University was built in and around institutions whose principal task was to pray for the liberation of departed souls. As acts of piety, the laity was encouraged to make arrangements to have masses said for departed loved ones in the hope of reducing the duration of their relatives' torment in purgatory.

Retention of the long-standing list of canonical texts had, then, a very obvious theological outcome. The Reformation was a direct challenge not just to the theology of purgatory but the assertion that it even existed. With the closing of the chantries, the effect of this challenge was experienced in the everyday lives of the English people.

Article VII: Of the Old Testament

> *The Old Testament is not contrary to the New: for both in the Old and New Testament everlasting life is offered to Mankind by Christ, who is the only Mediator between God and Man, being both God and Man. Wherefore they are not to be heard, which feign that the old Fathers did look only for transitory promises. Although the Law given from God by Moses as touching Ceremonies and Rites, do not bind Christian men, nor the Civil precepts thereof ought of necessity to be received in any commonwealth; yet notwithstanding, no Christian man whatsoever is free from the obedience of the Commandments which are called Moral.*

Some of the earliest descriptions we have of the Christian community refer to their meeting together to pour over the Scriptures in the light of the gospel of Christ. And yet, again and again, there have been those who have sought to pit the Old Testament against the New, as if they were two opposing and contrary dispensations. Others have alleged discontinuity between the two, claiming that the Old Testament deity was a rather nasty character in contradiction to the gentle New Testament God of love. This was the Marcionite heresy; and it led to the affirmation by the church that the Christian Bible most definitely included, and indeed was incomprehensible without, the Hebrew Scriptures. This was not an unproblematic decision. The Old Testament was, the early Christians discovered, a difficult body of writing to digest in places. The challenges of interpretation (not to mention the linguistic difficulties) seemed all but insurmountable. And yet, determined as they were to consider the whole Scripture *as* Holy Scripture, the fathers of the Church concocted allegorical ways in which they could read the Old Testament. Unfortunately, the way in which the New Testament modeled reception of the Old Testament was rather neglected.

In the Reformation, it could have been argued that the spirit of Marcion lived again. Luther's polemic against law was read by his accusers as a very negative depiction of the Old Testament indeed, and led him to defend himself from the charge of antinomianism at great length (see his *Large Catechism* of 1529). He had set up the grace/law antinomy with such vigour that the charge had some weight. Other Reformation thinkers of the period were less dialetical, less polemical and less inclined to equate the Hebrew religion with the practices of the Roman Church.

The key to understanding this article is the place of Christ in holding together both Testaments. The Old Testament is Christian because it testifies to Christ. The history that the Bible narrates is a continuous one, driven forward by the promises and covenants of God with Israel, and consummated in the coming of Jesus and the inauguration of his Church. And so, the Old Testament is not merely a book of antiquarian interest whose promises and ordinances have in some way lapsed. But there is a question to be answered: what is the Christian to do with the Old Testament law, with its combination of local ceremonial customs and universal truths? The threefold division of the law was the hermeneutical solution. Ceremonial and civic laws as given in the Old Testament were particular to the time and place and related entirely to the stage of salvation history whence they were given. This is not an unreasonable suggestion, because of the effort that the New Testament writers spend in saying that the Old Testament rituals and sacrifices are fulfilled in Christ and that the inclusion of the Gentiles in the people of God meant the end of the necessity for a civic law (see the whole of the Letter to the Hebrews, for example). The moral law is not in the same way abrogated. It is, if anything, intensified by the teaching of Jesus (Matthew 5:17).

The weakness of the scheme is that the division of the law is not found in the text of the Old Testament itself although it could be inferred from it. What is more, the neat division into the three types of law is not so easy. Is looking after widows, for example, a moral or a civic law? Is the principle of respect for animal life now no longer demanded of Christian people? On close reading, the division seems somewhat artificial.

Article VIII: Of the Three Creeds

Three Creeds, Nicene Creed, Athanasius' Creed, and that which is commonly called the Apostles' Creed, ought thoroughly to be received and believed; for they may be proved by most certain warrants of Holy Scripture.

The faith of the Church of England is creedal, insofar as the Creeds teach doctrine that can be reconciled with the Scriptures. Once more, the drafters of the Articles wanted to position the reformed English Church as one possessing a Catholic and Orthodox outlook, rightly sharing in the continuous tradition of Christian belief. In this statement, it would seem that the Creeds are to function as confessions in summary form of the ancient faith. As such, they may certainly be used as guide to the reading of Scripture. But the Creeds in themselves have a secondary place and this is probably the point being made rather gently. The Creeds are not authoritative in and of themselves, nor does their special standing derive from their having been determined and declared by a significant council of the early Church. They function as summaries of the teaching of Scripture.

Anglicanism is, then, creedal because Christianity is creedal. It has always been the case in the life of the Christian church that matters of doctrine and practice have been asserted, contested, decided and codified. The New Testament itself records this process. See, for example, the Council of Jerusalem in Acts 15. Truth matters. The concern is not just the *process* of coming to the truth but the actual truth of doctrinal propositions themselves. The English theologian Frances Young in her book *The Making of the Creeds* shows that a notion of orthodoxy came to shape Christian identity in a way similar to the function of national boundaries and practices in Judaism. And the creedal statements that emerged served not only as baptismal confessions and catechetical aids but also as instruments of exclusion. With the help of the Creeds, false teaching could be distinguished from the true and the good deposit properly guarded. This is not, of course, to deny that doctrinal squabbles can be petty, intractable and divisive. But the English Reformers here, in deciding to uphold a creedal faith, declared that the idea of orthodoxy was something they could not do without and still be Christian.

That all three Creeds are here asserted, however, has been contested. The so-called Athanasian Creed (it was certainly not written by Athanasias of Alexandria, c. 293–373) has been left out in some later versions of the Articles. The English theologian FD Maurice campaigned against the inclusion of this Creed on conscientious grounds. There is no doubt that the Athanasian Creed seems to go too far in stating that only by believing its content in full can a person be saved, thereby making a person's belief and not Christ's death the crucial factor. There appears to be grounds for revising this article on the basis of a revision of the scriptural authenticity of this creed, which has, in any event, fallen almost entirely out of use in modern Anglican worship.

SECTION TWO Articles IX–XVIII

Article IX: Of Original or Birth-Sin

> *Original sin standeth not in the following of Adam, (as the Pelagians do vainly talk;) but it is the fault and corruption of the Nature of every man, that naturally is engendered of the offspring of Adam; whereby man is very far gone from original righteousness, and is of his own nature inclined to evil, so that the flesh lusteth always contrary to the Spirit; and therefore in every person born into this world, it deserveth God's wrath and damnation. And this infection of nature doth remain, yea in them that are regenerated; whereby the lust of the flesh, called in Greek, phronema sarkos, which some do expound the wisdom, some sensuality, some the affection, some the desire, of the flesh, is not subject to the Law of God. And although there is no condemnation for them that believe and are baptized; yet the Apostle doth confess, that concupiscence and lust hath of itself the nature of sin.*

Article IX introduces a sequence of articles (IX – XVIII) concerning the life of faith (the first eight having asserted the trinitarian faith and its sources). The background to and impetus for the Reformation doctrine of justification by faith alone is the utter helplessness of humankind under the power of original sin. The alternative explanation is that offered by the 'Pelagians': that original sin is an imitative and not 'genetic' problem. They held that it comes from each human being's copying the evil acts he or she observes in other humans being rather than being the overwhelming spiritual state into which we are born. If that is the case, then the solution is for Christ – the second Adam – to be offered as a better model to follow, and for human beings to act on the power that resides within them to behave morally and so please God.

We should not underestimate the power and appeal of this alternative. It was, and remains enticing because it is morally serious; it does not allow for human beings to be complacent or to despair. It asks them to embrace maturity and to be morally responsible in the world. It asks human beings to live up to their potential. Even though the thoroughgoing Pelagian option was rejected by the Church at the Council of Orange in 529, it is a measure of the cogency of this teaching that it continued, albeit in modified form. The theological account of humankind given in this article paints a very different picture. Original sin is not something we fall into by nurture. It is a fact of our nature. And the infection runs very deep. If Augustine made rather too much of the sexual transmission of original sin, it was only because he recognised from his personal experience and his reading of Scripture that sin is very deeply embedded in the human being to the point of sin being intertwined with our weak flesh, our desires and our intentions. 'The spirit is willing, but the flesh is weak'. There is a division even within the human person between our knowledge of what constitutes the good and our failure to desire it unerringly.

A propensity to sin is a universal human experience. It exists prior to our decision to indulge in sinful action. As Paul stresses in Romans 3, *all* have sinned and fall short of the glory of God. There is no exception other than the second Adam – Jesus Christ. Our inclinations always and everywhere will inevitably lead us to opposition to God and rebellion against his law. As WH Griffith Thomas (1861–1924) put it, 'it is the presence of a moral disturbance in our nature, and concerns the dispositions and tendencies before the will begins to act'. The doctrine of original sin makes sense of our own mysteriousness even to ourselves. Paul's account of the human condition is profound in its discernment of the way we really are and in its utter tragedy. Terrifyingly, original sin is deserving of the wrath and condemnation of God. Humankind does not stand anywhere except where Adam and Eve, as representatives of all humanity, stood figuratively after the fall – under sentence of death.

It is important to note that the article stresses that although the Christian may become free from judgement of sin, original sin is not erased by regeneration. The Christian is, as Luther said, 'at the same time just and a sinner', (*simul iustus et peccator*). The tendency to evil – the 'concupiscence which is of its nature sin' – is not yet removed, although the regenerate sinner need no longer fear the consequences of sin. The *Book of Common Prayer* keeps reminding us of the reality of our fallen state in a profoundly personal way, stressing as it does the need for confession – even for those who are Christian:

> We do not presume to come to this thy Table, O merciful Lord, trusting in our own righteousness, but in thy manifold and great mercies. We are not worthy so much as to gather up the crumbs under thy table. But thou art the same Lord, whose property is always to have mercy; Grant us therefore, gracious Lord, so to eat the flesh of thy dear Son Jesus Christ, and to drink his blood, that our sinful bodies may be made clean by his body, and our souls washed through his most precious blood, and that we may evermore ever dwell in him, and he in us. Amen

Article X: Of Free-Will

> *The condition of Man after the fall of Adam is such, that he cannot turn and prepare himself, by his own natural strength and good works, to faith, and calling upon God: Wherefore we have no power to do good works pleasant and acceptable to God, without the grace of God by Christ preventing us, that we may have a good will, and working with us, when we have that good will.*

The title of this article is somewhat misleading. It is actually not about 'free will' at all but 'bound will'. As with Article IX, Article X paves the way for the doctrine of justification that is presented in the next few articles. Human will, the article asserts, is *not* free after the fall of Adam. As Paul puts it in Romans 7:18–19: 'For I have the desire to do what is good, but I cannot carry it out. For what I do is not the good

I want to do; no, the evil I do not want to do—this I keep on doing.' Augustine explained the human predicament this way: 'We have no power to do good works without God working that we may have a good will, and co-operating when we have that good will.'

These words clearly provided the basis of the second part of this article. The human will is, to borrow the title of a book published in 2000 by the English theologian Alistair McFadyen, *bound to sin*. If it was in its created pre-fall state properly described as a 'free' will, then there is no way in which it could be accurately described as such now. Even the turning to God is not something that lies within the capacity or inclination of human beings. The human person is not able to prepare him or herself for the embrace of faith. It is not even the case that, as Duns Scotus (1265–1308) taught in the early fourteenth century, the sincere *effort* of human beings to do good, however meagre the results, was to be met with a 'congruous grace'. This conviction was where Reformation ideas differed sharply not only with much medieval theology (though notably not with Aquinas) but also with the new learning that was taking hold in Europe in the sixteenth century. The famous dispute between Luther and Erasmus was not so much a dispute between the old theology and the new, but between two new alternatives with much in common – although of course both had ancient origins. Erasmus' optimism was noble and urbane, but ultimately, as Luther showed, a dangerous fantasy and a fatal delusion. The soul is curved in on itself, therefore it will always tend to serve its own ends.

The article's teaching about the human will has contemporary significance in the context of contemporary secular liberal humanism, which asserts the eventual triumph of the human will and sacralises individual autonomous choice. It is by the sheer act of willing things that we exert control and assert our identities. Yet, the biblical diagnosis is that our actions, following our intentions, run along very familiar and predictable lines. But the picture is not all bleak. The human person, with the help of God who 'prevents' us (note the archaic use of 'prevent' which meant 'going ahead of') may indeed do good works, may indeed be in the possession of a good will and may even co-operate with God in the accomplishment of good works in abundance. The continual co-operation of the Spirit of God with us in doing the works that are pleasing to God is a significant point against those who pictured God 'getting the ball rolling' in the Christian life and leaving us to get on with it from there. The converse is true. We are aided and abetted in doing the things that please God in every step.

Article XI: Of the Justification of Man

We are accounted righteous before God, only for the merit of our Lord and Saviour Jesus Christ by Faith, and not for our own works or deservings: Wherefore, that we are justified by Faith only is a most wholesome Doctrine, and very full of comfort, as more largely is expressed in the Homily of Justification.

In this article we reach a series of statements that effectually serve as the centre of gravity for the entire document. Given the prevailing religious and political controversies this is not surprising. Furthermore, given the statements about the pervasiveness and seriousness of sin that have just preceded it, justification by faith can really be the only answer. In this doctrine, we find at once God's self-vindication and God's mercy. God is not only the just judge, but is also the one who justifies the ungodly. Jesus in his person and work is the indispensible link, because his righteousness is the basis of our being declared right with God. Although the word 'imputed' is not used here, it is certainly a concept taught by the article. Human beings are being counted righteous entirely because of Jesus being counted righteous by God. The accusation that the doctrine of imputed righteousness is a legal fiction has been alleged against the words of the article. This would only be fair if the notion of imputation is taken out of the context of the other doctrines which support it, such as the work of the Spirit and union with Christ. Imputation is not the whole story but it is certainly part of the story.

Confusion has also been generated since the Reformation on account of the word 'faith'. To be 'justified by faith' is a slogan in shorthand. More accurately, we are justified by grace through faith. Faith is not a replacement work. It is not a merit-claiming thing we possess or a virtue we may exercise which God must honour. Neither is it belief in doctrines: one is not justified by right belief, although orthodox belief is a corollary of justification. To believe otherwise would be to infer that in some way we were deserving of justification. Clearly this is not what the Reformers took the Bible's teaching to mean. Faith in itself 'not your own ... the gift of God' (Ephesians 2:9) is unremarkable. It is a matter of receiving the Word of God and, in response, clinging to that Word in the power of the Holy Spirit. It is not the ground of our justification but the means. As the 'Homily on Salvation' (incorrectly named here as the 'Homily on Justification') puts it:

> Faith putteth us from itself, and remitteth or appointeth us unto Christ for to have only Him remission of our sins or justification. So that our faith in Christ (as it were) saith unto us thus: It is not I that take away your sins, but it is Christ only, and to Him only I send you for that purpose, forsaking therein all your good virtues, words, thoughts and works, and only putting your trust in Christ.

This doctrine may indeed be promoted as a 'very full comfort'. It would be of no comfort at all if we had to count on our own merits or on some quality within us. There would be nothing but fear if that were the case.

Postscript

Readers should be aware that a controversy has arisen in recent times concerning justification and its understanding in the light of the 'New Perspective on Paul' as a theologian and preacher. It would be impossible to do justice to the issues in a brief comment. It is sufficient to say, however, that the helpful contribution from recent New Testament studies has been the way in which salvation-history has become the guiding paradigm used to understand Paul rather than justification being an abstract concept treated in isolation from his other writing and ministry. It is a mistake to see the two as mutually exclusive; nor would we see the Reformation debates about human nature and the grace of God as now eclipsed by this new emphasis of scholarship. Quite the opposite is true: how does God justify the ungodly? How does God include the Gentiles in his people? These questions are both pertinent to and 'resolved' in the propitiatory sacrifice of atonement Jesus made on the cross.

Article XII: Of Good Works

Albeit that Good Works, which are the fruits of Faith, and follow after Justification, cannot put away our sins, and endure the severity of God's judgment; yet are they pleasing and acceptable to God in Christ, and do spring out necessarily of a true and lively Faith; insomuch that by them a lively Faith may be as evidently known as a tree discerned by the fruit.

The English Reformers were attacked, of course, for the moral licence that seemed to be permitted by promoting the doctrine of justification by faith. Were they not antinomians of the worst kind? Was not the teaching about grace a teaching that allowed for laxity? Was it not in fact the fear of hell that kept society in check? To avoid underestimating the seriousness of the charge, we ought to consider the Lutheran Copenhagen of Søren Kierkegaard's time (1813–55), when he inveighed against the deadening nominalism of his fellow church-goers. Was this the outcome to which justification by faith inevitably leads? The answer was 'no' if the doctrine was understood as its early teachers taught it. Good works, they asserted, do not emit the power of forgiveness and justification. Even after the fact of justification (understood here as the beginning of the Christian life, though of course Paul uses this language at times to speak of its end), Good works do not acquire the power to ameliorate our sins or help us in the day of our trial. They have another function. They are rather the natural outgrowths of a life imbued with the Holy Spirit of God in Jesus Christ himself. They are found in the changed nature and quality of the tree and the fruit it bears.

Certain works are pleasing and acceptable to God. 'Offer your bodies as living sacrifices, holy and pleasing to God—this is your spiritual act of worship' says Paul in Romans 12:1. There is a proper and pleasing worship, a right and good and pleasing sacrifice to offer, that *we* ourselves may offer in Christ. This is not meant as a salvific pleasure. It is the outcome and result of God's own work in the sinner to make them holy, and to draw them into a relationship of righteousness with God. God takes real pleasure in the good we do, not unlike a parent who delights in their child's faltering steps, their early attempts at drawing, or their readiness to share things with others. Our very purpose as 'new' creatures is to do the good works we were made to do and which were prepared for us. But the ground of our salvation is not these works. It is 'grace through faith'. The relationship of faith and works is famously expressed in Ephesians 2:8–10:

> For it is by grace you have been saved, through faith—and this not from yourselves, it is the gift of God—not by works, so that no one can boast. For we are God's workmanship, created in Christ Jesus to do good works, which God prepared in advance for us to do.

And the faith which produces a good crop of good works is indeed a *lively* faith – a faith which enlivens, and is evidence of abundant life, present and to come. Faith without good works is indeed dead, as the Apostle James says.

Article XIII: Of Works before Justification

> *Works done before the grace of Christ, and the Inspiration of his Spirit, are not pleasant to God, forasmuch as they spring not of faith in Jesus Christ, neither do they make men meet to receive grace, or (as the School-authors say) deserve grace of congruity: yea rather, for that they are not done as God hath willed and commanded them to be done, we doubt not but they have the nature of sin.*

Article XIII is the mirror-image of Article XII. If good works following faith are pleasing to God, then works preceding faith, though they may have the appearance of righteousness, are in fact *not so*. There is no sense in which 'doing things', which in fact do meet the requirements of some part of the divine law and which serve the interests of others, might merit a gracious response. The problem being addressed in the article is the context and manner of the good deed if it is outside Christ's command. It is still impacted by sin and still ultimately motivated by a desire that is not oriented to God, however much contrary claims are made. Christ is the only avenue by which human beings may please God; a righteous relationship with God is necessary to enable the proper orientation and intent and consequence of acts such that they may really be called 'good'. Furthermore, so-called good works may be a great distraction to the person who does them and extract pride from them. Pride, in the Augustinian tradition, is the essence of sin; the person who self-justifies is in grave spiritual danger. Just like the Pharisee in the temple (Luke 18:9–14), such a person will make claims and demands on God based on their own inherent goodness. To the English Reformers, here was the problem with the teaching of the 'School-men', that God meets our good works with a congruous grace that makes good our deficiencies in response.

This sounds very harsh. Surely, one might argue, it is better that the right thing is done than that people are told that even the good they do is actually sinful by nature? It would certainly better to encourage uprightness than to discourage it, whatever the motive. The article is, it must be said, an arrow targeted against the assertion that these works have a salvific power: that they are a labour to which God will grant a proper wage. Still, it is a feature of the modern outlook to count belief of very secondary importance and to elevate right action. WH Griffith Thomas cites the lines of the English poet Alexander Pope (1688–1744):

> For creeds and forms let senseless bigots fight,
> His can't be wrong whose life is in the right.

What the theology embedded in this article diagnoses is the tendency of the human heart to corrupt even the most noble acts by self-interest or self-righteousness. Heaven is not a middle class suburb inhabited by the good.

Article XIV: Of Works of Supererogation

> *Voluntary Works besides, over and above, God's Commandments, which they call Works of Supererogation, cannot be taught without arrogancy and impiety: for by them men do declare, that they do not only render unto God as much as they are bound to do, but that they do more for his sake, than of bounden duty is required: whereas Christ saith plainly When ye have done all that are commanded to you, say, We are unprofitable servants.*

This article springs directly out of the context of the Reformation, and serves as a further riposte to the religious practices of which the Reformation doctrine of justification was a critique. The idea of supererogatory works is an ancient one, originating in the Decian persecution of the third century. In that period, there were examples of great spiritual heroism and endurance, and also instances of lapses and compromises. This is a problem of community that most people don't face in the contemporary West. But it must have caused a great deal of pain and shame for the early Church. Who could blame those who, faced with the terrifying prospect of torture and death, fled persecution or abandoned their faith? The hope of those who lapsed and later repented was that they could by some means gain from prospective martyrs – those waiting in prison for their deaths – something of their undoubted credit, and thereby be restored to the Church's fellowship and the company of the saved.

With the spread of monasticism in the fourth and fifth centuries with its emphasis on virginity and other ascetic practices, there was a further emphasis on spiritual heroism, and the hope that ordinary people could benefit vicariously from the merits of those who subjected themselves to extreme discipline. By the medieval period, this idea of the saintly excess of transferrable good works (it has been called 'a kind of spiritual *iTunes* voucher') became linked especially to the practices of selling and granting what were known as 'Indulgences'. We can see here developing an exchange economy trading in spiritual and moral merits. Admiration for the saints and their courage and devotion is benign. Reflecting on God's grace in their lives can even be beneficial. Such reflection continues as a feature of Anglican liturgical prayers. But once reflection becomes attached to a view of justification based on the accumulation of merits and rewards that God must honour, it becomes a terrible distortion of the gospel of grace.

Article XV: Of Christ alone without Sin

> *Christ in the truth of our nature was made like unto us in all things, sin only except, from which he was clearly void, both in his flesh, and in his spirit. He came to be the Lamb without spot, who, by sacrifice of himself once made, should take away the sins of the world, and sin, as Saint John saith, was not in him. But all we the rest, although baptized and born again in Christ, yet offend in many things; and if we say we have no sin, we deceive ourselves, and the truth is not in us.*

The fifteenth article puts Christ forward as unique among the human race in living a sinless life. Article XIV has already contended that a Christian is powerless, even with heroic effort, to exceed in doing what God requires from human beings and so be in a position to distribute their excess merit to others. Article XV makes an important Christological point which has an anthropological consequence: Christ's supreme obedience and sinlessness stand in contrast to the inevitable and continuing sinfulness of the rest of humanity. The danger and vanity of teaching that a saintly life might gain merit enough to please God is terribly grave. Although the Church encourages its members to do the things that God wants done, there is no accrued benefit to the doer of the works in terms of removing the stain of sin or the finality of death.

Sin is self-deceptive and especially so in the Christian. In his first letter to a hard-pressed Church in Greece, the apostle John writes not only to the non-Christian who might be unaware of the extent of his or her sinfulness, but also to the Christian who might be in danger of self-deception. His words are familiar to anyone acquainted with Cranmer's liturgies: 'If we say we have no sin, we deceive ourselves, and the truth is not in us' (I John 1:8). Being baptised and born anew in Christ looses us from the power of sin and the sentence on sin but it does not remove our terrible recidivism evidenced by a refusal to live the righteous life.

This article seems very pessimistic and glib, and readers might protest that the Holy Spirit is the Christian's aid in doing righteous things and trying to please God. Do not the Articles themselves, following Scripture, speak of pleasing God in righteous works? That is indeed so, but in the teaching of the English Reformers, these works are not pleasing in a justifying or salvific sense. They please God as responses to God's work for us in Christ.

Article XVI: Of Sin after Baptism

> *Not every deadly sin willingly committed after Baptism is sin against the Holy Ghost, and unpardonable. Wherefore the grant of repentance is not to be denied to such as fall into sin after Baptism. After we have received the Holy Ghost, we may depart from grace given, and fall into sin, and by the grace of God we may arise again, and amend our lives. And therefore they are to be condemned, which say, they can no more sin as long as they live here, or deny the place of forgiveness to such as truly repent.*

If previous articles had seemed stern and uncompromising, this article reveals the truly merciful heartbeat of the gospel and the pastoral concern which lies at the forefront of Anglican doctrine. Even serious sin is not an obstacle to the extension of forgiveness to the Christian and their standing before God as redeemed sinners. There are two common distortions in view here. One is that baptism and receiving the Holy Spirit is a guarantee of a future sinless state of life. This is a recipe for spiritual arrogance. The other is that sin after baptism is utterly unforgiveable. This is a counsel of unremitting despair. The article carefully avoids both errors. The Christian will certainly continue to sin as the old nature is not yet conquered. But the grace of God revealed in the gospel of Christ is unrelenting. Even the worst of sins does not necessarily put the Christian beyond the reach of grace. If the murderer repents, then the declaration of the free forgiveness is available to them. This is the judgement of God and is revealed on the cross of Jesus Christ. Could a church deny this, then, in its practice?

Believers must deal with the uncomfortable reality that all Christians, including those with whom we share Christian fellowship, may be people who have done truly despicable things that have led to trauma and enduring suffering. Modern secular societies have deep trouble accepting that people can really be forgiven. Western popular culture never lets the guilty forget what they have done even if they are changed profoundly and no longer have demonstrated the capacity for criminal behaviour. But the Church hasn't this option if it is to be true to its own message. It cannot underestimate the power of the cross as the sign and seal of forgiveness.

Article XVII: Of Predestination and Election

> *Predestination to Life is the everlasting purpose of God, whereby (before the foundations of the world were laid) he hath constantly decreed by his counsel secret to us, to deliver from curse and damnation those whom he hath chosen in Christ out of mankind, and to bring them by Christ to everlasting salvation, as vessels made to honour. Wherefore, they which be endued with so excellent a benefit of God be called according to God's purpose by his Spirit working in due season: they through Grace obey the calling: they be justified freely: they be made sons of God by adoption: they be made like the image of his only-begotten Son Jesus Christ: they walk religiously in*

good works, and at length, by God's mercy, they attain to everlasting felicity.

As the godly consideration of Predestination, and our Election in Christ, is full of sweet, pleasant, and unspeakable comfort to godly persons, and such as feel in themselves the working of the Spirit of Christ, mortifying the works of the flesh, and their earthly members, and drawing up their mind to high and heavenly things, as well because it doth greatly establish and confirm their faith of eternal Salvation to be enjoyed through Christ, as because it doth fervently kindle their love towards God: So, for curious and carnal persons, lacking the Spirit of Christ, to have continually before their eyes the sentence of God's Predestination, is a most dangerous downfall, whereby the Devil doth thrust them either into desperation, or into wretchlessness of most unclean living, no less perilous than desperation.

Furthermore, we must receive God's promises in such wise, as they be generally set forth to us in Holy Scripture: and, in our doings, that Will of God is to be followed, which we have expressly declared unto us in the Word of God.

It is no accident that this article is by far the longest. To say that it is a thorny issue in Christian history is to acknowledge the heated controversies and divisions it has engendered. The thought that somehow God chose some people and not others long ago, even 'before the foundation of the world' (Ephesians 1:4), is an idea that many people have found distinctly *un*comfortable. It seems to pit God's sovereignty against God's love. It vexed those living in the sixteenth century as well. For them the question was more existential: if I am one of God's chosen people, then what are the signs confirming that status? How can I know that I am one of the elect? What if my name is not written in the Book of Life? This became a significant pastoral problem as well as a matter of theological dispute. The article itself issues a warning about the 'curious and carnal persons' who misuse this doctrine and end up in the grip of a kind of fatalism – that produces either psychological desperation or moral licence.

Yet the article does not treat this teaching as an ethical embarrassment nor as an academic puzzle. It is when rightly considered ('godly consideration'), a 'sweet, pleasant and unspeakable comfort'. It is actually of great pastoral help because it gives the Christian great security *in God*. This flows directly from the teaching on original sin and justification previously expounded in the Articles. Salvation is entirely a divine work from origin to outcome, and inspiration to achievement. This truth was operative at the beginning of all things, when the salvation of God's people was decreed by God. It runs through the whole gamut of the Christian life from the call of the Christian, to their adoption into God's household, the Christian's life of obedience to God and finally to obtaining 'everlasting felicity'. There is no greater stability or assurance than to be found in knowing this doctrine. How can this be so? The article does not tease us by inviting speculation on what the Bible doesn't address and what we cannot know. Instead, it asks us to contemplate what we *do* know. The gospel of Jesus Christ is our assurance that 'if God is for us, who can be against us?' (Romans 8:31).

Predestination, or election, is a scriptural teaching through and through. Those opposing predestination oppose a strong witness from Scripture itself. The article draws on the thoughts of Paul in Ephesians 1:1–12. He writes: 'In him we were also chosen, having been predestined according to the plan of him who works out everything in conformity with the purpose of his will, in order that we, who were the first to hope in Christ, might be for the praise of his glory.' Christ is the focus of the passage, because the revelation of the purposes of God is supremely found in him. Despite this being the longest of the Articles, it refuses to comment on anything other than the Biblical insistence that those who are saved are chosen by God for life. Of the apparently logical corollary – that those who are not chosen for life are thereby chosen for damnation – it does not speak. This is not a kind of theological opportunism. Indeed, it is far from it. It is, rather, a wise reticence, a refusal to go beyond the teaching of the Bible however inviting it might be to do so.

Article XVIII: Of obtaining eternal Salvation only by the Name of Christ

> *They also are to be had accursed that presume to say, That every man shall be saved by the Law or Sect which he professeth, so that he be diligent to frame his life according to that Law, and the light*

> *of Nature. For Holy Scripture doth set out unto us only the Name of Jesus Christ, whereby men must be saved.*

The sequence of articles on the subject of individual salvation that began with Article XI ends with this very strong statement against the view that, in the religious life, it is sincerity and diligence in belief that matter more than the content of belief. The sentiment is still heard: that it is how a person holds to their belief, not what they actually believe, that counts. It suits our anti-doctrinal culture well to place the emphasis on whatever might be deemed to be right *practice* over any claims to right *teaching* (as if those are opposites). Fear of stoking theological controversy – whose sparks, we well know as the Reformers did, could flare up with destructive force into sectarian violence – makes us wary of dogmatic particularities. We would rather hold with the Enlightenment philosopher John Locke that 'every man is orthodox unto himself (and others heretical).'

There is, however, a confusion of alternatives here. One could insist that there are better and worse ways to construe and to practise the Christian faith without also insisting that salvation itself is exclusive to that way of thinking about it and living it out. And so the article does not respond to the attempt to downplay the differences between the various 'Laws' or 'Sects' of Christianity with its own denominational triumphalism, as if to say, 'the Church of England, and its doctrine and ceremonies, are the only means by which any person may be saved'. This is not the intent of the article. One can be saved *in* a law or sect but not *by* it. Throughout, the Articles have told a story of the priority of God's grace over human initiative. That grace is displayed uniquely and supremely in Jesus Christ. It is in keeping with this story that the article teaches that there is 'no other name in heaven or on earth by which human beings may be saved' (Acts 4:12). It is not simply a matter of faithful observance, whatever its direction, but of faith in a powerful object – Jesus Christ, the Son of the living God.

There is not a particular reference here to the 'other' religions of the world or any speculation about those who have never heard the name of Christ. The words 'law or sect' seem to indicate a sphere of reference that is intra-Christian. However, the ramifications for all humankind seem obvious: 'there is no other name'. If any are saved, then Christ must be the saviour. Thus the article comes out very strongly against the notion that the truth about Christ is a matter of indifference. To teach otherwise is a grave distortion of the gospel of grace. It is also very likely to become a Christianity without Christ.

SECTION THREE   Articles XIX–XXIV

Article XIX: Of the Church

The visible Church of Christ is a congregation of faithful men, in the which the pure Word of God is preached, and the Sacraments be duly ministered according to Christ's ordinance in all those things that of necessity are requisite to the same.

As the Church of Jerusalem, Alexandria, and Antioch have erred: so also the Church of Rome hath erred, not only in their living and manner of Ceremonies, but also in matters of Faith.

Where on earth – what on earth – is the Church? A key Reformation insight concerned the nature and character of what was commonly called 'the Church'. The Reformers argued that the institution bearing that name and observable in history is not the equivalent of the Church as it will be at the end of all things. The transformed and resurrected church that gathers around the heavenly throne – for that is what a church is, a gathering, from the Greek *ekklesia* – is certainly an overlapping set with the Church in history. But strict equivalence between the two is not to be found. There are, no doubt, members of the institutional/historical Church who are not to be found members of the true Church. This is because membership in Christ – the Head of the Church – is spiritual, and vital; and membership of the earthly manifestation of this Church may or may not equate to that vitality.

Why was this important? Because the Church of Rome asserted that it was coterminous with the final Church. It consequently overemphasised its perfections and became blind to its own imperfections. The Reformers thus distinguished between the *visible* and *invisible* aspects of the Church. Perhaps spuriously, Luther used Jesus' parable of the 'Wheat and the Tares' (Matthew 13:24–30) to illustrate the point: the Church on earth is a mixed gathering. In some sense the true membership of the Church is concealed from view, for that is a spiritual matter. But church membership is expressed visibly in the gathering of believers in the here and now. Members of the visible Church may not be members of the invisible Church; but members of the invisible Church will express their union with Christ in membership of the visible Church. For its part, Rome had made visibility the cause rather than the consequence of membership in the invisible Church.

The visible Church, then, is 'a congregation of the faithful.' That is, it is a group of people gathered or located in time and space. It is a community, we might say: it has an observable togetherness in its membership whose common characteristic is its faithfulness to Jesus Christ. Two activities feature in its gathering and serve as its standard. They are preaching the pure Word of God, and the administration of the Sacraments 'duly'. These have traditionally been called the 'marks of the church' or, in Latin, the *notae ecclesiae*.

That preaching is to be 'pure' in relation to the Word of God and the Sacraments administered 'duly' implies that there are qualitative standards in both of these activities. It is possible to fail in these areas. Indeed failure is a grave matter. It is possible to *look* like a church in outward appearance, and yet not *be* a church, in inward reality. What these standards are, and how they are to be measured, is not specified in this article. However, it is safe to say that the teaching of the rest of the articles gives a good indication of what was meant in both instances. Notice that the ordained ministry is not mentioned in this context as a visible sign of the Church. It is not the identity or nature of particular kinds of ministers that makes the Church, though the activities of those ministers certainly have that effect.

Rather definitely, the article points to the witness of history which implies that the Eastern Church wandered into error as the basis of the article's central claim that the Church of Rome has also erred. Several subsequent articles will specifically identify particular ways in which this is claimed to be the case concerning matters of ceremony and ritual. Several of the previous articles argued that serious errors are apparent in core matters of faith and belief. The simple theological point being made in the article is that the visible Church will always fall short of perfection this side of the last things. The Church of

England must include itself in this too. Thus, we have the rather odd situation in which the Church of England declares its own fallibility in its own statement of faith.

Article XX: Of the Authority of the Church

> *The Church hath power to decree Rites or Ceremonies, and authority in Controversies of Faith: And yet it is not lawful for the Church to ordain anything contrary to God's Word written, neither may it so expound one place of Scripture, that it be repugnant to another. Wherefore, although the Church be a witness and a keeper of Holy Writ, yet, as it ought not to decree any thing against the same, so besides the same ought it not to enforce any thing to be believed for necessity of Salvation.*

The Church is charged with the responsibility of living out the Christian faith in history, with all that means. This responsibility includes regulating its life. It has to give expression to its faith in all its corporate activities. Furthermore, in controversial matters, it has to decide as far as possible what is to be accorded the status of truth. And so it ought to be understood that it has the authority to do so. How ought authority to be exercised in the Church? Nothing is said in the article about synodical government, episcopal authority, apostolic succession, or the papacy. The means by which a church may be governed is left, according to circumstance and custom, an open question. Power and authority can be distributed and exercised variously. It is not the shape of the institutions or standing of the offices in the Church that equate to authority in the Church. The bishop or the council may exercise due authority over the Church's life – but only in a derivative sense.

The one clear source of authority in the Church is the written Word of God. Whatever the Church does it must do without contradicting Scripture or setting one part of Scripture against another. The Church cannot be selective about the parts that suit its own conviction or convenience. If it finds itself setting a portion of Scripture against another, then it has to ask whether it is really practising the authority of Scripture or whether human reason or experience is effectually overshadowing the text. So much of the Reformation's rationale is found in the principle set out in this article. The Church has authority, yes, and ought to be respected by the individual Christian. However, the Church ought not to think that it can contradict its own source of authority, and deny its own role as a 'witness and a keeper of holy Writ'. If it fails in this duty, we are entitled to doubt that the 'pure Word of God' is being preached. The Reformers felt that the medieval Church of Rome had denied its own essence in erroneous teaching about the papacy, indulgences and purgatory. It had added to Scriptural teaching on salvation its own declarations and customs.

This article uses Scripture, however, as the minimum, and not the maximum, of what the Church may do. That is, it endorses the 'normative' rather than the 'regulative' principle of Scripture. Richard Hooker is probably the most famous exponent of the normative principle. He concluded that the Church has freedom in matters of worship and ceremony to decide what it thinks is most apt, so long as Scripture is not contradicted. The regulative principle, on the other hand, restricts church practices to only those that can be found in Scripture. By the end of the Elizabethan period, it was clear that the Church of England would not head down this path, believing it to be a wrong application of Scripture.

Article XXI: Of the Authority of General Councils

General Councils may not be gathered together without the commandment and will of Princes. And when they be gathered together, (forasmuch as they be an assembly of men, whereof all be not governed with the Spirit and Word of God,) they may err, and sometimes have erred, even in things pertaining unto God. Wherefore things ordained by them as necessary to salvation have neither strength nor authority, unless it may be declared that they be taken out of Holy Scripture.

How may the Church, or a church, express its authority, given the principles set out in Article XX? In Christian history, the role of a 'General' Council has appeared to meet the need at the heart of this very question. During the Reformation the possibility of summoning such a Council to resolve a number of theological disputes was debated. In the end, Pope Paul III called the Council of Trent in 1545 but decided against inviting the Reformers.

The word 'General' in this context means 'universal'. The vocabulary which is sometimes used is 'ecumenical'. This means that if a council is properly a 'General' Council and wants to accrue to itself the authority that this name implies, the *whole* Church is to be represented. The biblical model for this kind of gathering is found in Acts 15. The Council of Jerusalem was called by the apostles to discuss the existence of any special conditions associated with the acceptance of the Gentiles into the new faith. Notably, the Council met to clarify and respond to a new state of affairs – the conversion of the Gentiles – rather than to create such a state. There was vigorous discussion and eventually a resolution was reached that was essentially a compromise. Those councils referred to as 'General' or 'Ecumenical' were convened much later in Christian history. The number of councils which may rightly hold this title and bear this authority varies between the different Christian traditions. There is, however, broad consensus about the first six: Nicaea (325), Constantinople I (381), Ephesus (431), Chalcedon (451), Constantinople II (553), and Constantinople III (680). At these meetings the great statements and creeds of Christian doctrine were hammered out, and the great heresies, such as Arianism and Nestorianism, were repelled.

The article insists that only secular princes can summon a General Council. In the context of the Reformation, it is possible to see why this was thought a necessary statement to append to the article as a way of limiting papal authority, and of ensuring adequate lay involvement. But it is hard to see how this principle can be justified theologically. Certainly, this was the pattern of the six Ecumenical Councils, all of which were called by Emperors. In any case, the article is suspicious of appeals to the authority of General Councils as an absolute foundation for theological understanding. Like no church, no council could ever claim inerrant status. Though the article is thin on particulars, it is confident that even these great Councils of the Church have not produced infallible rulings. Some words from Gregory of Nazianzen (c. 329 – 390) were included in a statement that Archbishop Cranmer himself signed in 1536:

> If I must write the truth, I am disposed to avoid every assembly of bishops; for of no synod have I seen a profitable end; rather an addition to, than a diminution of, evils; for the

love of strife and the thirst for superiority are beyond the power of words to express.

It is quite clear from the history of the Councils that, despite their substantial and significant achievements, they were often bitter power struggles conducted with threats of force and the exploitation of process. Council members were plainly not 'governed with the Spirit and Word of God'. But it is not merely the particulars of history that matter here. The article is in principle pointing to the fact that even the rulings of General Councils are themselves only authoritative insofar as they are subject to Holy Scripture. Their rulings have no independent authority. Neither does their authority consist in the status of the participants, whether popes, bishops or princes. Although the clarifications and articulations of the Councils may indeed gain status as authoritative expressions of the Church's reading of Scripture, it is only in a derivative sense that they are deemed authoritative.

It would indeed be an extraordinary thing if a new Ecumenical Council were to be called today. But even then, the article asserts, its decisions would not be infallible and would be subject to Scripture rather than to a simple show of hands. Truth is not decided by majorities.

Article XXII: Of Purgatory

> *The Romish Doctrine concerning Purgatory, Pardons, Worshipping, and Adoration as well of Images as of Reliques, and also invocation of Saints, is a fond thing vainly invented, and grounded upon no warranty of Scripture, but rather repugnant to the Word of God.*

The view that there is a process of purification for the Christian *post mortem* (after death) has an ancient heritage within Christianity, but an uncertain Scriptural provenance, if at all. The appeal to 1 Corinthians 3:15, which speaks of being saved 'through flames', certainly amounts to a very weak basis in Scripture for the doctrine of purgatory. To this day, purgatory remains the official teaching of the Roman Catholic Church. According to the *Compendium of the Catechism of the Catholic Church* (2005) there is a third state, in addition to heaven and hell, where souls which are not yet purged of their sin endure a suffering discipline. These souls may be helped by the faithful still on earth. As the Catechism explains: 'the faithful who are still pilgrims on earth are able to help the souls in purgatory by offering prayers in suffrage for them, especially the Eucharistic sacrifice. They also help them by almsgiving, indulgences, and works of penance.'

As we have already noted, during the Reformation the notion of purgatory had become one of the most visible aspects of European Christianity with numerous chantry houses founded to offer prayers for the souls of those who were in purgatory. It served a commercial and a religious interest. The critique of the Reformers may have led to a reform of its worst abuses but it also prompted a firm statement from the Council of Trent that this indeed *was* the official teaching of the Roman Church. In the nineteeth and final in the series of 'Tracts of the Times' published in 1841, the Reverend John Henry Newman famously tried to argue that this article was not intended to deny the doctrine of purgatory *per se*, but only the Romish version of the doctrine. He read the word 'Romish' in the article as determinative rather than as a simple adjective. It was a clever piece of reading, if not ingenious. It was, however, a failure. It is quite clear from the theology of the Articles taken as a whole that a doctrine of purgatory – whatever the pedigree – could not occupy any coherent place within Biblically-based Christianity.

There were two main objections to purgatory. First, the teaching that salvation is effected by the grace of God, through faith alone, does not admit of degrees of being saved. The Reformed theology had no place for a system of meritorious works that involved the purging of sin and the earning of merit, either pre- or post mortem. The Articles declare the uniqueness and complete sufficiency of Christ's death as an atonement for sin. Christ's death was (in the words used in the Holy Communion service) a 'one oblation of himself once offered, a full, perfect, and sufficient sacrifice, oblation, and satisfaction, for the sins of the whole world.' If the suffering and death of Christ is effective in taking away sin, there is no need for some further atoning for sin to be made. Second, Article XXII gives an example of the kind of teaching that sits counter to the principle of authority laid out earlier in the articles – namely, the authority of Scripture. The notion of purgatory is a church teaching which not only lacks a sure Scriptural warrant, it actually runs counter to the witness of the Scriptures concerning the means by which men and women attain eternal life. It also illustrates the Reformers' claim that the Church may indeed err and thus find itself in need of correction.

The notion of purgatory is undoubtedly appealing to those who are grieving for loved ones. Why wouldn't a person want to feel that they could help lost loved ones on their journey towards heaven? Why wouldn't a sincere Christian want assurance that their prayers were actually doing some lasting good? The Reformers held that purgatory was a notion that threatened and contradicted what was found in Scripture. That is why the language used is so polemically strong. For the same two reasons, the article decries the adoration of sacred relics and the practice of offering prayers to the saints.

Article XXIII: Of Ministering in the Congregation

It is not lawful for any man to take upon him the office of publick preaching, or ministering the Sacraments in the Congregation, before he be lawfully called, and sent to execute the same. And those we ought to judge lawfully called and sent, which be chosen and called to this work by men who have publick authority given unto them in the Congregation, to call and send Ministers into the Lord's vineyard.

One of the underlying tensions in the Articles and indeed, in the English Reformation as a whole, was that which existed between personal faith and social order. While the Reformation was the discovery of an 'inward' form of Christianity, with an emphasis on individual faith as a work of the Holy Spirit, the need to maintain some sense of centralised control of the popular practise of religion in the realm was never stronger. Sixteenth century monarchs were well aware of the potentially subversive implications of the Reformed faith and it was advisable for theologians and church officials to show that they could contain religious passions. The bloodshed of the Peasant's Rebellion in Germany during 1525 was a salutary reminder of the cost of losing civic control and the destructiveness of religious extremism.

It is a matter of dispute among historians as to whether the Reformation was imposed on the English people from above or arose as a more popular movement. Whatever view one takes, it was certainly the intention of the Reformers to centralise and to administer carefully the propagation of the Reformed faith on English soil. The *Book of Common Prayer* became the chief instrument in securing this conformity. Ordering of the Church's ministry was to be another. So the article introduces the language of law. The Scriptures themselves, most prominently in the Pastoral epistles, speak of an authorisation and designation of ministry. In Titus 1, Titus is authorised to 'appoint elders in every town' on the island of Crete. But the Articles institutionalise this authorisation of ministry for the national Church – the word 'Congregation' here indicates not a local parish but the whole Church in England. The vitality of the ministry, Cranmer and others realised, was essential to the vitality of the national Church. This made careful oversight of its development imperative.

Article XXIV: Of speaking in the Congregation in such a tongue as the people understandeth

It is a thing plainly repugnant to the Word of God, and the custom of the Primitive Church, to have publick Prayer in the Church, or to minister the Sacraments in a tongue not understood of the people.

One of the great achievements of Reformation was promoting the use of vernacular languages. Faith, as the Reformers described it, was not merely giving assent to propositions but *trust*. It was trust *in the Word of God*. For faith to be instilled, the Word of God was something that needed to be heard and understood by the people. It is no surprise that so much energy was given to translating the Bible. The vision of the great translator William Tyndale (1494–1536) was of the ploughboy reading Scripture and understanding it for himself. This was a cause for which he was prepared to give his life. Likewise, liturgies were to be in the language 'understanded of the people'. Understanding is the essential principle in the article. It is not merely that the language employed is to be the language of the people who were gathered – it had to be used in an intelligible way. The Prayer Book itself reminds ministers to speak 'in a loud voice' and to 'turn to the people' so that their words may be clearly heard. Inaudible muttering is not acceptable for the corporate worship of God's people.

Paul had pressed this point on the Corinthian Church (1 Corinthians 12–14). Christian meetings should, above all, be edifying to those who participate in them. As the drafters of the Articles realised, how could this be so if the greater number present could not understand a word being said? Paul condemns the use of speaking in other tongues if they are not translated for the benefit of all others present. Hence this article speaks strongly about the use of foreign tongues in the service. Such a practice is 'plainly repugnant to the Word of God'. Not only this, the practice of the 'Primitive Church' likewise told against the continued use of an incomprehensible language in the worship of the Christian community.

In the first version of this particular article, which was drafted in 1553, the Reformers had rendered this point in a positive vein. The Council of Trent declared anathema those who pleaded for the Mass to be said in the vernacular in 1562. The article, as we now have it, came into its final form in 1571 and most likely reflects a more deliberate response to the resolution of Trent. It is worth pointing out that since the Second Vatican Council held during the 1960s, the Roman Catholic Church itself has adopted the practice of having its Bible translated and its services in the vernacular.

SECTION FOUR   Articles XXV–XXXI

Article XXV: Of the Sacraments

Sacraments ordained of Christ be not only badges or tokens of Christian men's profession, but rather they be certain sure witnesses, and effectual signs of grace, and God's good will towards us, by the which he doth work invisibly in us, and doth not only quicken, but also strengthen and confirm our Faith in him.

There are two Sacraments ordained of Christ our Lord in the Gospel, that is to say, Baptism, and the Supper of the Lord. Those five commonly called Sacraments, that is to say, Confirmation, Penance, Orders, Matrimony, and extreme Unction, are not to be counted for Sacraments of the Gospel, being such as have grown partly of the corrupt following of the Apostles, partly are states of life allowed in the Scriptures; but yet have not like nature of Sacraments with Baptism, and the Lord's Supper, for that they have not any visible sign or ceremony ordained of God.

> *The Sacraments were not ordained of Christ to be gazed upon, or to be carried about, but that we should duly use them. And in such only as worthily receive the same have they a wholesome effect or operation: but they that receive them unworthily purchase to themselves damnation, as Saint Paul saith.*

Debates about the Sacraments – and they were passionate – occupied a central place in the Reformation disputes over doctrine and custom. The Reformers themselves, having rejected the Roman view of the Sacraments, could not agree on how to interpret them. They did agree, however, that the Sacraments were never to be thought of as entities independent of the Word of God. The Sacraments were understood to be an enacted form of the Word itself. It is not surprising, therefore, that the Articles contain a series of statements about the Sacraments, at once upholding their vital importance for church life and fellowship and at the same time clarifying what the Reformers felt were medieval distortions of the New Testament teaching about them – including their number, purpose and meaning.

The definition of the 'Sacraments' given in the article is critical. They are indeed 'badges or tokens' of the faith – but they are 'not only' this. They are also 'sure witnesses of grace'. That is, they testify not only to our faith but to the gospel itself – to the work of God in Jesus Christ. And these signs work. They are *effectual*. This is not to confuse the sign with the thing itself, which was what the Reformers sought to oppose and refute. The Sacraments are still *signs* but more than mere tokens.

How should we understand this? It all goes back to what the Reformers taught about grace and salvation. The article links 'grace' with 'God's good will towards us'. This is a vital development from the medieval conception of grace as a 'substance'. Grace is an attitude of God towards men and women, rather than a thing that was transferred to them by means of the Sacrament. They are effectual signs because they do deliver that divine disposition to us. They do speak of God's mercy in such a way that our faith can be extraordinarily strengthened. They convey what they promise. The great Anglican divine Richard Hooker wrote:

> Grace is a consequent of Sacraments, a thing which accompanieth them at their end, a benefit which they have received

from God Himself, the Author of Sacraments, and not from any natural or supernatural quality in them.

We could also put it this way: the Reformers' view was that Sacraments were effective as actions accompanied by grace rather than as specially sanctified objects. The purpose of the Sacraments is not to increase our merit but, by the work of God occurring invisibly within us, to increase our faith. They are verbs rather than nouns.

Why were there only two specific Sacraments? The criterion that the Reformers used in restricting the number to two was that Baptism and the Holy Communion were 'ordained by Christ in the gospel'. In one sense, this choice of criterion is not particularly convincing. After all, as Oliver O'Donovan asks: 'Why should the Lord's command be more weighty than his practice or the practice of the apostles?' As the article itself suggests, the Reformers were pursuing a policy of caution regarding the Sacraments which, in their view, had sprouted numerous abuses and caused much confusion.

Article XXVI: Of the Unworthiness of the Ministers, which hinders not the effect of the Sacrament

Although in the visible Church the evil be ever mingled with the good, and sometimes the evil have chief authority in the Ministration of the Word and Sacraments, yet forasmuch as they do not the same in their own name, but in Christ's, and do minister by his commission and authority, we may use their Ministry, both in hearing the Word of God, and in receiving of the Sacraments. Neither is the effect of Christ's ordinance taken away by their wickedness, nor the grace of God's gifts diminished from such as by faith and rightly do receive the Sacraments ministered unto them; which be effectual, because of Christ's institution and promise, although they be ministered by evil men.

Nevertheless it appertaineth to the discipline of the Church, that inquiry be made of evil Ministers, and that they be accused by those that have knowledge of their offences; and finally being found guilty, by just judgement be deposed.

Ideally, a centralised and institutionalised Church authority could guarantee the education and virtue of its ministers throughout a defined ecclesiastical jurisdiction. The reality of things, then as now, was that some genuinely ill-suited people are admitted to Christian ministry. What assurances could be offered to those who feared they might be receiving Word and Sacrament from such a person? The situation was no doubt exacerbated at the time of the Reformation by the dearth of well-educated and thoroughly-trained clergy and the system of patronage by which various livings were distributed. The Reformers' claim was that the old system had fostered a largely corrupt and not particularly spiritual clerical class, notorious for laxity in morals and greedy for material gain. There was certainly an element of propaganda in this. But there was also more than a grain of truth in their allegations.

Something of the answer provided by this article is found in Paul's reassurance of the Philippians that even those who preach Christ out of selfish ambition may indeed still truly preach Christ without their proclamation in any way endorsing their sinful behaviour or excusing their corrupt motives. As Paul says: 'But what does it matter? The important thing is that in every way, whether from false motives or true, Christ is preached' (Philippians 1:18). This article is another extension of the earlier emphasis on the primacy of the divine action in the Sacraments expressed in Article XXV. God's grace is not hindered by any lack of holiness in the human beings through whom God chooses to work. The effectiveness of Word and Sacrament resides in their source – namely, Christ himself – and not in whatever conduit through which they pass, however poor and unworthy they turn out to be.

This is not, of course, to deny the seriousness of the general call to holiness among those who serve in the Church. This is the balance the article is seeking to strike. There *ought* to be a reckoning and some accountability for 'evil Ministers'. The offices of the Church are not so indelibly stamped on the person concerned that they ought to see in this article a lack of concern for their manner of life. With great sorrow the churches have been forced to concede woeful laxity in this area. The expulsions from ministry envisaged by this article have perhaps been too infrequent.

Article XXVII: Of Baptism

Baptism is not only a sign of profession, and mark of difference, whereby Christian men are discerned from others that be not christened, but is also a sign of Regeneration or new Birth, whereby, as by an instrument, they that receive Baptism rightly are grafted into the Church; the promises of forgiveness of sin, and of our adoption to be sons of God by the Holy Ghost, are visibly signed and sealed; Faith is confirmed, and Grace increased by virtue of prayer unto God. The Baptism of young Children is in any wise to be retained in the Church, as most agreeable with the institution of Christ.

Article XXVII attempts to apply the general sacramental theology expressed in Articles XXV and XXVI to the particular Sacrament of Baptism. Quite clearly, baptism had enormous significance in New Testament times. The Gospels record Jesus himself receiving baptism in the Jordan River, from John the Baptiser. Matthew's Gospel ends with Jesus' command to the disciples to 'make disciples of all nations, baptising them in the name of the Father and of the Son and of the Holy Spirit' (Matthew 28:19). In the New Testament we see a steady transformation of the theory and practice of baptism, with John announcing the way in which Christ would offer 'baptism in the Holy Spirit'. Clearly, there was a deeper spiritual reality prefigured by baptism in water. Baptism became the Christian rite of entry into the people of God, signifying membership of that group. Since this is a group with a common profession of faith, it became customary to declare this faith at one's baptism. If the candidate was an infant the faith would be declared on their behalf.

The article makes the point very clearly that it is the inward, spiritual reality which baptism signifies that is the essence of the Sacrament. It is a 'sign of Regeneration or new Birth', which echoes the theology of conversion that is found in both John 3 and Romans 6. Baptism is not, then, primarily about the actions or responses of human beings. It is principally about the activity of God the Holy Spirit in the lives of believers. The primacy of divine action over human action distinguishes the view of the Articles from the Anabaptist position which emphasises the act of profession.

Quite carefully, the article distinguishes itself from the suggestion that baptised children are automatically regenerated by being so baptised. What, then, are we then to make of the way in which the *Book of Common Prayer* baptismal rite proclaims that 'this child is regenerate'? Is it the case that all baptised children are to be considered 'born again'? If this is the case, it would seem that baptism operates in a mechanistic or automatic way, something which the Reformers would have been quick to repudiate. As Bishop John Charles Ryle of Liverpool (1816–1900) explains, the principle of the 'charitable supposition' needs to be understood as having sway here. We need to recall that the article itself describes the need for baptism to be 'rightly' received as the counterpart to the inward spiritual reality. As Ryle writes in his 1885 explanatory work *Knots Untied*:

> The men who drew up our Baptismal Service, held that there was a connection between baptism and spiritual Regeneration and they were right. They knew that there was nothing too high in the way of blessing to expect for the child of a believer. They knew that God might of His sovereign mercy give grace to any children before, or in, or at, or by the act of baptism. At all events they dared not undertake the responsibility of denying it in the case of any particular infant, and they therefore took the safer course, to express a *charitable hope of all*.

Understanding the operation of this charitable principle allows for a consistency between the *Book of Common Prayer* and the Articles.

The baptism of infants was, thus, not repudiated by the Church of England. What we have in the Articles is an enthusiastic endorsement of the practice without it being a vigorous or definitive command. Certainly, baptism services for those who are 'of riper years' found their way in to successive editions of the Prayer Book. But because baptism is not primarily a sign of the human response to God but rather a sign of God's grace in forgiveness, infant baptism was retained without any suggestion that the act of water baptism itself results in the regeneration of the child.

Article XXVIII: Of the Lord's Supper

> *The Supper of the Lord is not only a sign of the love that Christians ought to have among themselves one to another; but rather it is a Sacrament of our Redemption by Christ's death: insomuch that to such as rightly, worthily, and with faith, receive the same, the Bread*

which we break is a partaking of the Body of Christ; and likewise the Cup of Blessing is a partaking of the Blood of Christ.

Transubstantiation (or the change of the substance of Bread and Wine) in the Supper of the Lord, cannot be proved by Holy Writ; but is repugnant to the plain words of Scripture, overthroweth the nature of a Sacrament, and hath given occasion to many superstitions.

The Body of Christ is given, taken, and eaten, in the Supper, only after an heavenly and spiritual manner. And the mean whereby the Body of Christ is received and eaten in the Supper is Faith.

The Sacrament of the Lord's Supper was not by Christ's ordinance reserved, carried about, lifted up, or worshipped.

In Article XXVIII we see a strong repudiation of medieval sacramental theology in an appeal to the authority asserted within the Articles – the teaching of Scripture. It is not merely a case of providing a different, equally valued interpretation of the Lord's Supper. Transubstantiation, the teaching that the elements of the Communion *become* in substance the Body and Blood of Christ, is a doctrine that the drafters of the Articles understood to be 'repugnant to the plain words of Scripture'.

As we have seen, the English Reformers were prepared to countenance practices, teachings and interpretations that were not explicitly taught in Scripture if they were in harmony with Scripture. But they were unequivocal about transubstantiation. It was not a doctrine in this category. Given that the Council of Trent had recently reaffirmed this teaching, the reference to transubstantiation in the article is particularly pointed. In fact, in focusing so much speculative attention on the metaphysics of the Eucharist, the true 'nature of a Sacrament' had been much obscured by this kind of teaching. What might this mean? The notion of transubstantiation collapses the sign (the bread/wine) into the thing it signifies (the body/blood of Jesus). In so closely identifying them with each other, the bread and wine cease to be Sacraments – that is, they are no longer *signs*. The article, by contrast, upholds the distinction between the sign and the thing signified by refusing any explanation of *how* Christ is present in the Holy Communion and 'overthroweth the nature of a Sacrament'. It is for this reason that the Articles insist that the Sacramental elements are not to be 'reserved, carried about, lifted up or worshipped'. These activities involve mistaking the sign for the thing itself. This distorts our understanding of the way God works in the world by attaching his operation to objects.

Like baptism, the Lord's Supper has to do with the Church and its relationships. Just as baptism was partly a sign of membership in the fellowship of Christ's people, so also the Lord's Supper is an effectual sign of Christian love. This meaning is quite clear from the discussion of the Lord's Supper in Paul's first Corinthian letter, where we read that Christians are one body *because* we all partake of the one bread (1 Corinthians 10:17). But this bond between Christians – as the Sacrament of the body and blood shows – is itself dependent on the redemption that flows from Christ's death. Therefore it is natural that the article moves beyond mere table fellowship in its explanation of Holy Communion. If there is a union and fellowship between Christians expressed in the Lord's Supper, it is because of the death of Christ and the way the benefits of that death are intensified in shared partaking in the meal. If it is received 'rightly, worthily and with faith', there is full expectation that this will be a true sharing in the body and blood of Christ.

Faith is crucial. The language of 'given, taken and eaten only after an heavenly and spiritual manner', for example, is strongly reminiscent of the language of the Genevan Reformer John Calvin. The Zürich Reformer Ulrich Zwingli (1484–1531) had argued that Holy Communion is effective only in the sense that it is a memorial meal. For Calvin, whose thought is reflected in the article, this was not enough. He explained that the sharing of the believers in the body and blood of Christ is certainly *actual*. The believer participates in, and is nourished by, this holy meal by faith and not because of some substantial change in the elements themselves. It is more akin to believing in the promises of God which attach to the signs that Christ himself provided for his church.

Article XXIX: Of the Wicked which eat not the Body of Christ in the use of the Lord's Supper

> *The Wicked, and such as be void of a lively faith, although they do carnally and visibly press with their teeth (as Saint Augustine saith) the Sacrament of the Body and Blood of Christ, yet in no wise are they partakers of Christ: but rather, to their condemnation, do eat and drink the sign or Sacrament of so great a thing.*

By making faith a vital component in the right administration of the Lord's Supper, the Reformers risked making the Sacrament into something almost subjective by making the effectiveness of the Sacrament dependent in some undisclosed way on the spiritual state of the person receiving it.

In Article XXIX, an implication of the non-substantial view of the Lord's Supper is spelt out: without faith, the Sacrament does not enable a partaking in Christ. The taking of the Sacrament cannot operate where a true and lively justifying faith crucial to uniting a person to Christ is absent. The Word, ever the necessary companion of the Sacraments, calls for faith. Where faith is absent, the mere action of taking and sharing of the bread and wine cannot replace it. But this is not to say that without faith the Lord's Supper is inconsequential. On the contrary, Paul uses stern words in 1 Corinthians 10–11. The Anglican Holy Communion liturgy includes Paul's warning in 11:27: 'Therefore, whoever eats the bread or drinks the cup of the Lord in an unworthy manner will be guilty of sinning against the body and blood of the Lord.' The article announces that the 'Wicked' and unbelieving eat the Sacrament to their own condemnation. The sign of redemption and sharing in Christ by his death is effective whether one believes in it or not – it is just effective in a different way. The emphasis, as ever, is on *God's* action, albeit this time in judging rather than in confirming and in strengthening.

Article XXX: Of both kinds

> *The Cup of the Lord is not to be denied to the Lay-people: for both the parts of the Lord's Sacrament, by Christ's ordinance and commandment, ought to be ministered to all Christian men alike.*

It was the widespread practice of the medieval church to withhold the common cup from the laity and only distribute the bread to them, despite the well-documented practice of the early Church. In 1 Corinthians 11:28 it is certainly the case that both bread and wine are being shared by all the members of the community. When he inaugurated the Lord's Supper, Jesus said to the disciples 'Drink from it, all of you;' (Matthew 26:27).

The reasons for the development of the practice of distributing communion in one kind are obscure. Attempts to defend it in terms of hygiene or reverence are unconvincing. The critique of the Reformers was that the practice increased the impression that the Church was hierarchical in essence and that the clergy were a spiritually-privileged group. The Eucharistic elements were to be kept as far from human contamination as possible. Even the bread was placed on the tongue of the recipient rather than handled. The Hussites of Bohemia had attempted to vary this in the fifteenth century and this had led to a firm denunciation from the Council of Constance in 1415. In the 1560s, the Council of Trent determined that:

> ... although the usage of Communion under two kinds was not infrequent in the early ages of the Christian religion, yet, the custom in this respect having changed almost universally in the course of time, holy mother the Church, mindful of her authority in the administration of the Sacraments, and influenced by weighty and just reasons, has approved the custom of communicating under one kind, and decreed it to have the force of a law, which may not be set aside or changed but by the Church's own authority.

In one sense, the debate is trivial. But, to insist on the laity receiving communion in both kinds was consistent with the Reformers' conviction about *the priesthood of all believers*. They were convinced that the lay-clerical distinction was not sustainable on the terms proposed and maintained by medieval theology. Withholding the cup from the laity only served to contradict (in symbolic terms) the essential equality of each member's access to grace. It is worth noting that the practice of receiving in both kinds is now commonplace in Roman Catholic churches today – especially in English-speaking countries.

Article XXXI: Of the one Oblation of Christ finished upon the Cross

The Offering of Christ once made is that perfect redemption, propitiation, and satisfaction, for all the sins of the whole world, both original and actual; and there is none other satisfaction for sin, but that alone. Wherefore the sacrifices of Masses, in the which it was commonly said, that the Priest did offer Christ for the quick and the dead, to have remission of pain or guilt, were blasphemous fables, and dangerous deceits.

The brace of Articles about the Sacraments which began with Article XXV ends with this statement of plain theological principle. The cascade of terms employed – 'redemption, propitiation, satisfaction' – may strike us as synonyms and excessive. It may imply a struggle to bring clarity to a theology of the atonement. In fact, each term had a distinct and powerful resonance in the Tudor mind.

Redemption and *propitiation* are biblical terms. The former term is a market concept with an added allusion to the Exodus of Israel from Egypt. The death of Christ was a liberation of the people achieved at the cost of Jesus' own life. The latter term – used in 1 John 2:2 and alongside 'redemption' in Romans 3:24–5 – is a temple concept, relating to the sacrifices made there. A *propitiatory* sacrifice not only obliterates sin and cleanses the sinner; it also appeases the wrath of God against sin. Christ's death was, as the New Testament describes it, such that it turned aside God's wrath against sin.

Satisfaction, on the other hand, is a term that comes from the history of theology and from the pen of Anselm in his famous work *Cur Deus Homo* (translated: 'Why did God Become Man?') completed in 1099. It describes how the wounded honour of a feudal overlord might be restored. Despite its lack of direct biblical provenance, Reformers like Cranmer and Calvin evidently thought it was a term that, in combination with the others, offered them another angle from which to describe the work of Christ upon the cross. Christ was, they explained, the unique substitute for sin who stood in the place of fallen humankind. Not only was his qualification to be such a substitute unique by dint of his perfect life of obedience to the Father, the power of the sacrifice he made upon the cross was sufficient to atone for 'all the sins of the whole world, both original and actual'. There is a finality and completeness to Christ's death – no supplementary offering is required. The letter to the Hebrews underscores the way in which the sacrifice of Christ's own body made redundant all other forms of sacrifice for sin. Not only were these now unnecessary, continuing to offer them would be to misread badly the significance of the cross itself.

It is for these reasons that the statement about the atonement in this article is put with polemical force against a statement about the sacrifice of the Mass. If medieval theology presented the Mass as a complementary form of satisfaction for sin *in addition to that offered on the cross*, such a theology was fatally flawed. In effect the human action in the present trumps the divine, once-for-all, historic act, thus calling the finality of Christ's sacrifice into question.

SECTION FIVE   ARTICLES XXXII–XXXIX

Article XXXII: Of the Marriage of Priests

Bishops, Priests, and Deacons, are not commanded by God's Law, either to vow the estate of single life, or to abstain from marriage: therefore it is lawful for them, as for all other Christian men, to marry at their own discretion, as they shall judge the same to serve better to godliness.

The marriage of clergy remains to this day an obvious point of difference between the Roman Catholic and non-Roman Catholic churches. In one sense, it is a trivial difference – a mere matter of ecclesiastical order. It goes without saying, however, that matters of sex and sexuality are rarely trivial in effect. The same was just as true in the sixteenth century. Furthermore, the marriage of clergy was one in a number of crucial steps which illustrated adherence to a deeper principle. Archbishop Cranmer was married to the niece of the Reformer Andreas Osiander in 1532. This was another sign that he was becoming more convinced in his own person of Reformed ideas. He subsequently kept the marriage concealed from the more conservative King Henry VIII who, in any event, was preoccupied with his own marital difficulties. While the 'Six Articles' of 1539 re-affirmed clerical celibacy, it was during the reign of King Edward VI that clerical marriage was legalised and accepted by church and state.

Since the Scriptures do not expressly prohibit the members of various orders of ministry from becoming married – indeed, the pastoral epistles speak explicitly of members of all three offices *being* married (I Timothy 3:2,12 and Titus 1:6) – the Reformers felt they were being true to their own enunciated principles of ecclesiastical authority in allowing clergy to marry. Reference to the Apostle Peter's mother-in-law (Mark 1:30) indicates that he too must have been married. The tradition of compulsory clerical celibacy was one of those traditions that the English Reformers felt they were quite justified in overturning, since it was evident that many clergy found it an intolerable burden. Though Paul himself had praised those called to a life of celibacy, he had not commanded it. In fact, he insisted that godliness of life was the priority, writing 'it is better to marry than to burn with passion' (1 Corinthians 7:9).

Forbidding clerical marriages was an implicit judgement against the holiness of sexual union, even between husband and wife. Occasionally the idea of even marital intercourse being a form of spiritual pollution was made explicit. The corollary of this view was the spiritual superiority of the clerical life which was set apart from the concerns of the daily world of labour and domestic life. The Reformation represented an affirmation of the spiritual vitality of the ordinary life in all its aspects, including the marriage bed. If this was true it hardly needed to be said that the Church laws forbidding clerical marriage were redundant. Marriage was not, then, to be prohibited among the clergy of England's national Church. The article allows them to exercise their discretion in the cause of godly living.

Article XXXIII: Of Excommunicate Persons, how they are to be avoided

> *That person which by open denunciation of the Church is rightly cut off from the unity of the Church, and excommunicated, ought to be taken of the whole multitude of the faithful, as an Heathen and Publican, until he be openly reconciled by penance, and received into the Church by a Judge that hath authority thereunto.*

What can it possibly mean to treat someone as a 'Heathen and Publican'? This unfamiliar language, taken from Tyndale's 1534 translation of Matthew 18:17, reveals the nature of church discipline envisaged by the Reformers as much as their attempts to ground discipline in New Testament principles. The excommunicated person is to be avoided and treated as a pagan unbeliever and a disreputable person until such time as reconciled to the Church. The charitable assumption afforded the baptismal candidate has been overturned.

Compared to the rigorous system of church discipline operating in Calvin's Geneva, this article may be seen as fairly vague and embodying a lenient attitude to the management of the Church's affairs. No judicial violence or imprisonment is allowed as an instrument of ecclesiastical punishment. Neither is there a list of offences that might result in excommunication. The teaching of the article arises from New Testament teaching about church discipline found in passages such as Matthew 18 and 1 Corinthians 5. A church without some kind of system of church discipline would scarcely have a right to call itself a New Testament church. Ironically, of course, to hear Jesus talk of treating someone like a 'heathen or a publican' (or, in the *New International Version*, a 'pagan or a tax collector') means to act with their salvation very much in mind.

The resumption of fellowship for the excluded person is *via* an act of penance and reception by an authorised judicial officer. The article is not specific about the details – the nature of the penance and the identity and status of the proposed adjudicator and the source of his or her 'authority' may vary. It is intriguing that penance – which the Reformers spoke against in a soteriological context – has a place in this ecclesiological context. To their way of thinking, the public and symbolic nature of an act of penance is 'open'. It effectively serves a public purpose in showing to all the nature of an individual's sorrow for sin and willingness to be restored to fellowship, lest there be any doubt in the community that the person has been restored. This is not a statement about the spiritual reality of the person concerned. If they are forgiven by God, it is not on account of some penitential act. These public acts are necessary and beneficial for the welfare of the Church visible on earth.

Article XXXIV: Of the Traditions of the Church

> *It is not necessary that Traditions and Ceremonies be in all places one, and utterly like; for at all times they have been divers, and may be changed according to the diversities of countries, times, and men's manners, so that nothing be ordained against God's Word. Whosoever through his private judgement, willingly and purposely, doth openly break the traditions and ceremonies of the Church, which be not repugnant to the Word of God, and be ordained and approved by common authority, ought to be rebuked openly, (that others may fear to do the like,) as he that offendeth against the common order of the Church, and hurteth the authority of the Magistrate, and woundeth the consciences of the weak brethren.*
>
> *Every particular or national Church hath authority to ordain, change, and abolish, ceremonies or rites of the Church ordained only by man's authority, so that all things be done to edifying.*

This article goes together with the principles of biblical interpretation and reception outlined in Article XX. Article XX, as the leading Cranmer scholar Ashley Null pointed out, 'established the definitive Anglican principles for biblical interpretation'. The Church of England refused to countenance the possibility of producing a replacement Magisterium and confined itself to the role of 'witness and keeper of Holy Writ'. Article XXXIV articulates what this means in relation to church order and practice.

This article is an expression of a remarkable liturgical flexibility. Modifications can and should be made for local customs of the place. Christians do not meet according to a rigidly fixed pattern, nor must they replicate the historical dress and practices of previous decades or centuries. But the principle here is normative, not regulative. Freedom is allowed only so far as it is constrained by God's Word. There are no universal or timeless dictates. But the middle section of the article expresses quite a strong disapproval of anyone who would take this as a licence for the unfettered reign of individual judgement or personal style. That is, even though there is a freedom for individual national churches to change the tenor (for want of a better word) of their services – and indeed they ought to do so – it is also most definitely *not* a matter of 'private judgement'. Local clergy are not entitled to vary the practices of their congregation without authorisation and/or consultation. Why? Out of deference to the weak consciences of the faithful and because authority so set up is undermined or usurped by the practice.

While there is nothing in the article to suggest that the agreed liturgical practice is soteriologically significant or that it cannot be varied or even radically changed, there is no attempt here to diminish the importance of maintaining church order. In casual discussions about church practices, regard for order is sometimes neglected or overlooked. Church order is the way in which each church or fellowship of churches puts into practice the kind of teaching received from Paul in 1 Corinthians 8–14. Church order is not a substitute for that teaching. It is, in fact, an expression of it because 'God is not a God of disorder but of peace' (1 Corinthians 14:33). The Church's observance of ordered corporate worship is a reflection of the divine character. (Ordered doesn't mean 'formal'. It simply means that things are done a manner that is consistent with the purpose of mutual edification).

Note, too, that the ministry of the Sacraments is certainly not optional as far as the articles are concerned – because these were rites not instituted by human authority, but by the divine initiative (see Articles XXV-XXXI). It is difficult to see how anyone could possibly argue that the Sacraments themselves are optional or merely 'helpful' and remain a conscientious Anglican in any meaningful sense. But *how* the Sacraments might be ministered may indeed be varied on the condition that this is not a matter of private judgement – because this kind of troubling disorder reflects badly on the God whose name Christians seek to honour.

To summarise: It is possible to have an agreed church order and to take that order seriously without suggesting that observance of that order is somehow a matter of salvation or a work that allegedly accrues some kind of salvific merit for us. Conversely, a person shouldn't break from church order merely on the grounds that it suits them. Every Christian is to have a proper regard for the fellowship of churches into which they are called. At the same time, churches should be innovative in allowing for variations in the way that that ecclesiastical order can be expressed.

Article XXXV: Of Homilies

The second Book of Homilies, the several titles whereof we have joined under this Article, doth contain a godly and wholesome Doctrine, and necessary for these times, as doth the former Book of Homilies, which were set forth in the time of Edward the Sixth; and therefore we judge them to be read in Churches by the Ministers, diligently and distinctly, that they may be understood of the people.

Of the Names of the Homilies

1. *Of the right Use of the Church.*
2. *Against peril of Idolatry.*
3. *Of the repairing and keeping clean of Churches.*
4. *Of good Works: first of Fasting.*
5. *Against Gluttony and Drunkenness.*
6. *Against Excess of Apparel.*
7. *Of Prayer.*
8. *Of the Place and Time of Prayer.*
9. *That Common Prayers and Sacraments ought to be ministered in a known tongue.*
10. *Of the reverent estimation of God's Word.*
11. *Of Alms-doing.*
12. *Of the Nativity of Christ.*
13. *Of the Passion of Christ.*
14. *Of the Resurrection of Christ.*
15. *Of the worthy receiving of the Sacrament of the Body and Blood of Christ.*
16. *Of the Gifts of the Holy Ghost.*
17. *For the Rogation-days.*
18. *Of the State of Matrimony.*
19. *Of Repentance.*
20. *Against Idleness.*
21. *Against Rebellion.*

This version of the article, dating from 1571, added and then listed the *Second Book of the Homilies* to the First as a source of authorised teaching in the Church. In Article XI, we have observed a reference to the 'Homily on Salvation' which is held up as an authoritative extension of the theology that the drafters of the Articles wished to express. In this article the other Homilies are introduced and commended.

In keeping with their insistence on the priority of the Word in both turning people to God and in ordering the Church, the Reformers emphasised preaching as the means by which the churches would be nurtured and taught. An educated or even competent ministry was not always in evidence, however. Nor could the leading Reformers guarantee the uniformity or consistency of the theological convictions held by the clergy. The Homilies were provided, therefore, in order to meet the need for lucid theological and biblical instruction in the new teaching. The *First Book of Homilies* was published during the reign of Edward VI although it was probably in preparation for many years. It is likely that Archbishop Cranmer was the chief author of the homilies as they reflect his literary style. The *Second Book of Homilies* was published in 1562, shortly after the reign of Elizabeth I began. The fear that the Homilies would not be received with interest and enthusiasm in all places is revealed in the directive that they be read 'diligently and distinctly'. A reluctant minister might be otherwise tempted to mumble the words quietly and beyond the hearing of the people.

It is in general rather than in particular that subscription to this article equates to subscription to the teaching of the Homilies. That the Homilies 'contain' wholesome doctrine allows some latitude when it comes to individual statements found in the Homilies themselves. The article also speaks of the relevance of the Homilies 'for these times'. At five centuries distance we are rightly invited by this phrase to consider the ways in which the teaching of the Articles might be applied to *these* times. What we certainly can learn from them is the wisdom in having practical as well as theological instruction for the people of God. The topic headings in each of the Homilies disclose some down-to-earth concerns with no issue deemed too trivial, as the homily entitled 'Against Excess of Apparel' testifies.

It is a fair question to ask whether the Homilies add anything to the Articles or differ significantly from them in any way. The Homilies are far more vigorous and polemical than the Articles in accusing the Church of Rome of idolatry, for example. Most commentators tend to agree in the end that subscription to the article does not demand agreeing with the Homilies at every point.

Article XXXVI: Of Consecration of Bishops and Ministers

The Book of Consecration of Archbishops and Bishops, and Ordering of Priests and Deacons, lately set forth in the time of Edward the Sixth, and confirmed at the same time by authority of Parliament, doth contain all things necessary to such Consecration and Ordering: neither hath it any thing, that of itself is superstitious or ungodly. And therefore whosoever are consecrated and ordered according to the Rites of that Book, since the second year of the forenamed King Edward unto this time, or hereafter shall be consecrated or ordered according to the same Rites; we decree all such to be rightly, orderly, and lawfully consecrated and ordered.

This article does not seem to be saying very much at all about the issue it describes; other than directing attention to another text, namely, the Ordinal. The Ordinal is described by the article as sufficient, Biblical and legitimate to achieve its stated purpose which is the ordination of ministers for Christ's Church. The article is responding to the charge that the Ordinal does not contain 'all things necessary' for the true consecration and ordering of the various ministers of the Church. The validity of Church of England ministerial orders without the authorisation of Rome was hotly contested in sixteenth century Europe. Even to this day, ordination according to Anglican rites is not recognised as valid by the Vatican.

But it is not merely a matter of institutional connection with Rome that is involved in asserting its adequacy. Ordination, as set out in the Ordinal of the Church of England, has a different significance altogether. It is telling that the Roman Catholic argument against the Anglican view of the ministry is that the Ordinal does not set out the ministry in sufficiently priestly terms. In the Roman view, the Ordinal does not confer on the ordinand the power to offer the sacrifice associated with the Mass. The Reformers knew this and were deliberate in their intention to avoid any suggestion that such a power was conferred upon or conveyed to the ordinand.

Plainly, the two churches have a rather different view of the ministry at least as far as this is represented in the Ordinal. The emphasis in the Anglican Ordinal is on the minister's obligation to be a 'faithful dispenser of the Word of God and of His holy Sacraments'. It is consistent with the emphasis of the Articles on the authority and priority of Scripture to envisage a ministry dedicated to the teaching and preaching of the Word and the administration of the Sacraments, without the sense that they are serving as indispensible mediators between God and the Christian.

Article XXXVII: Of the Civil Magistrates

> *The King's Majesty hath the chief power in this Realm of England, and other his Dominions, unto whom the chief Government of all Estates of this Realm, whether they be Ecclesiastical or Civil, in all causes doth appertain, and is not, nor ought to be, subject to any foreign Jurisdiction.*
>
> *Where we attribute to the King's Majesty the chief government, by which Titles we understand the minds of some slanderous folks to be offended; we give not to our Princes the ministering either of God's Word, or of the Sacraments, the which thing the Injunctions also lately set forth by* [the monarch ruling] *doth most plainly testify; but that only prerogative, which we see to have been given always to all godly Princes in Holy Scriptures by God himself; that is, that they should rule all estates and degrees committed to their charge by God, whether they be Ecclesiastical or Temporal, and restrain with the civil sword the stubborn and evildoers.*
>
> *The Bishop of Rome hath no jurisdiction in this Realm of England.*
>
> *The Laws of the Realm may punish Christian men with death, for heinous and grievous offences.*
>
> *It is lawful for Christian men, at the commandment of the Magistrate, to bear weapons, and serve in the wars.*

The Reformation was certainly not the first time that the English monarchy had wrestled with the Roman Papacy. This article, dating in its present form from the Elizabethan period, marks the decisive victory of the Queen in the assertion of temporal authority. The monarch is given authority to rule whatever God has given to his or her charge, whether ecclesiastical or secular – without being subject to foreign interference.

The article is clear, however, that the Prince is not given 'the ministering either of God's Word, or of the Sacraments'. The sovereign is not made a kind of deacon, priest or bishop in the Church nor given any prerogative to serve as its chief theological director. The argument being presented is that Scripture has assigned to the ruler a twofold task: to 'rule all estates and degrees' and to 'restrain with the civil sword the stubborn and evildoers.' The latter phrase reflects the contents of Romans 13 which is a classic text for Christian political theology. Of course, the New Testament was written before Christians ever dreamed that they might one day be in a situation where they were living under a Christian governor. Its advice is not directly to emperors and kings but rather to those who are subject to them. In Romans 13, Paul assigns to the ruler – even the pagan one – a God-given authority for pursuing justice in his domain. It is not, then, for the Christian to hinder the ruler in this task – indeed he or she is entitled to prayer and honour within that scope.

The Old Testament, on the other hand, which chiefly has to do with the life of the kingdom of Israel, has many examples of a theocratic leader. King David is the supreme exemplar not merely of a ruler charged with administering justice in the terms set out by Paul in Romans 13, but a 'man after God's own heart' – a messianic ruler of God's own people. During the Reformation period the Old Testament kings were commonly set up as models for the political arrangements of the day. The sermon preached by Thomas Cranmer at Edward VI's accession to the throne, for example, was an exposition of the life of Josiah, the young king of Israel, who rediscovered the forgotten Law. The use of Old Testament precedents as models for a Christian ruler is extremely theologically problematic given the New Testament designation of Christ, the descendent of David, as the King of the people of God.

The article applies its vision of church–state relations into two highly controversial examples: military service and capital punishment. It goes without saying that the drafters of the Articles felt they had biblical warrant for both of these policies. In general, these examples assert that the individual Christian is not removed from the responsibilities of citizenship; neither is membership of the Church, or even of the clergy, protection from the King's justice. An alternative vision for Christian citizenship could be found among the various Anabaptist sects who preached rigorous pacifism.

While this article is arguably a fair response to centuries of political and ecclesiastical turmoil, and indeed to international politics as it had been played out over several centuries, the article has bequeathed to the English Church many confusions and ambiguities. Changing political circumstances (the transition to constitutional monarchy and the rise of Westminster-style parliamentary democracy) have meant that church–state relations have been a perennial source of dispute. How should the church relate to the state in contemporary secular Australia? How would this relationship vary, for instance, in Nigeria or Myanmar?

Article XXXVIII: Of Christian men's Goods, which are not common

> *The Riches and Goods of Christians are not common, as touching the right, title, and possession of the same, as certain Anabaptists do falsely boast. Notwithstanding, every man ought, of such things as he possesseth, liberally to give alms to the poor, according to his ability.*

It is important to remember that when we are speaking about 'Anabaptists' the term is not analogous to the 'Roman Catholics' or 'the Anglicans.' These are complex institutional bodies with variegated membership with multi-layered loyalties. The term 'Anabaptist' was applied to a variety of smaller church groups with a diversity of beliefs.

In the sixteenth century, the claim was frequently made that Christians ought to hold their earthly goods in common, and injunction derived from the custom of the early Christians in Acts 2:44 and 4:32. The rest of the New Testament seems to indicate, however, that this was a voluntary practice and that it was not universally encouraged even among the earliest churches. The command to the rich in 1 Timothy 6:17 is not that they should divest themselves of all their wealth but that they should not put their hope in temporal riches. An insistence on giving to the poor is, however, a fundamental duty and obligation. The urging of the New Testament to generosity towards those who lack is both prevalent and forthright. In Hebrews 13:16, for example, the Christian is commanded to 'share with others'.

There is no invocation in the article of the Old Testament principle of tithing which was a rule for giving a specified proportion of one's earnings. The word 'liberally' acknowledges the principles of free, cheerful and generous giving that Paul lays down in 2 Corinthians 8–9. Christian generosity is founded on the gracious self-giving of

God himself in the gospel, not on the establishment of a law of giving which effectively denies the giver any scope for generosity.

Article XXXIX: Of a Christian man's Oath

As we confess that vain and rash Swearing is forbidden Christian men by our Lord Jesus Christ, and James his Apostle, so we judge, that Christian Religion doth not prohibit, but that a man may swear when the Magistrate requireth, in a cause of faith and charity, so it be done according to the Prophet's teaching, in justice, judgement, and truth.

The final of the three 'political' or 'civil' articles again takes aim at yet another Anabaptist teaching. The intent is to underscore the positive relationship that the Church of England envisages itself having with the state and its instrumentalities. The Christian is always a citizen or a subject, as well as being a member of the Church.

Some Anabaptists declared that oath-taking was wrong for Christians in all circumstances. They based this judgement on Christ's strongly-worded injunction in Matthew 5:33–37: 'simply let your 'Yes' be 'Yes', and your 'No', 'No'; anything beyond this comes from the evil one.' (See also James 5:12). The article agrees that the 'vain and rash' making of oaths is a profane and disgraceful practice that has no place in the Christian life. Such action is an attempt to forestall providence – to secure for a human being what it is not appropriate for any but a divine person to secure. But the article also gives permission for oath-taking in the sense of 'making a solemn and public affirmation of some truth'. Paul the apostle does something like this when he writes to the Galatians: 'I assure you before God that what I am writing you is no lie' (Galatians 1:20). In appropriate circumstances, then, invoking God's presence 'in a cause of faith and charity', as the article puts it, is amply justified.

The final part of the article outlines the manner by which an oath ought to be sworn 'according to the Prophet's teaching'. The reference is to Jeremiah 4:2 where the Word of the Lord encourages the practice of swearing 'in a truthful, just and righteous way'. It is the Magistrate who may rightly ask for an oath. The context of having to administer justice in an imperfect society disfigured by human sin affirms that the guarantees provided by oaths have their usefulness. The article does not exempt the Christian from aiding the cause of justice in this way.

3 The Articles in Anglican life and witness

Every community organisation requires its leaders and representatives to profess certain beliefs, share specific commitments, exhibit particular behaviours and promote prescribed objectives. The Christian Church is no different in this respect. From the moment that Jesus imparted beliefs that undergirded genuine spiritual maturity and displayed the manner of living that disclosed the coming Kingdom of God, the Christian community has assumed that those called to positions of responsible leadership will uphold the Christian faith in their actions and attitudes. The earliest commissioning of deacons and presbyters either followed or was accompanied by an examination of the candidate's beliefs so that the whole people of God could be assured that those they proposed to admit to positions of authority held to the teaching of Jesus and were prepared to promise that they would not depart from that teaching in their duties.

After the tumultuous events that marked the period between the rejection of papal authority in 1534 and the Pope's excommunication of Queen Elizabeth in 1570, it was to be expected that the clergy of the Church of England were obliged to give their formal assent to a doctrinal statement that identified where and why the Reformed Catholic faith of England differed from the religion of Rome and Geneva. Before then, only the members of Convocation were required to subscribe to the Articles. In what was considered a largely uncontroversial matter at the time, the English Parliament made subscription to the Thirty-Nine Articles mandatory for all ordination candidates, for clergy before being licensed for any new ministry and, in some instances, for judges serving in the courts and undergraduates studying at the universities. It also required anyone ordained using a form of service other than those authorised in the reign of Edward VI or Elizabeth herself to subscribe 'to all Articles of Religion, which only concern the confession of the true Christian faith and the doctrine of the Sacraments'. This requirement ensured a common profession of belief among all clergy, including those ordained during Mary's reign. The inclusion of the word 'only' in the Act was intended to assist the Puritans who were willing to subscribe to the doctrinal articles but not the disciplinary ones. But after the Articles were revised, Convocation required subscription to all the Articles. There were four principal reasons for this requirement. The first was to ensure the Church of England could claim to be 'a true and Apostolical Church, teaching and maintaining the doctrine of the Apostles'. The second was a desire to ensure that clergy were men of sound faith who would not lead astray the laity. The third reflected a desire to promote Christian unity by 'the establishing of consent touching true religion'. And fourth, there was an attempt to set some Biblically sanctioned limits to diversity of belief and comprehensiveness of opinion.

Although no words of subscription were formally prescribed in 1571, Archbishop John Whitgift drafted a form of words that appeared in the 'Three Articles' of 1583. Clergy were obliged to subscribe to this document as well. It required acknowledgement of, and submission to, the 'Royal Supremacy' in matters temporal and spiritual. It required affirmation of the consistency of the entire Prayer Book with Scripture and a pledge to use only its forms in public worship. And it required assent to the statement: 'That I allow the Book of Articles of Religion agreed upon by the Archbishops and Bishops of both provinces and the whole Clergy in Convocation holden at London in the year of our Lord God 1562 and set forth by Her Majesty's authority and do believe all the Articles therein contained to be agreeable to the Word of God'. With the latter declaration, it was possible for the Church and State to enforce the Articles and prosecute those who departed from its doctrine in their teaching and preaching. The 'Three Articles' were authorised by Convocation in 1604 and with slight adjustment included in the Canons of 1604 which were promulgated after the Hampton Court Conference of that year. The subscription declaration now read: 'I do willingly and *ex animo* [translated: from my heart] subscribe to the Thirty-Nine Articles of Religion of the United Church of England and Ireland, and to the three Articles in the thirtieth Canon, and to all things therein contained'. This declaration raised the stringency of the Articles and the scope of subscription. More than 200 clergy, mostly those of Puritan sentiment, objected to the Canons and refused to subscribe, preferring to leave the Church and their livings rather than submit their conscience to matters they could not profess. The laity were not required to subscribe to the Articles but the fifth Canon of 1604 required that, at the very least, they not attack them publicly.

Despite the controversy caused by the strengthened subscription requirements, a formal statement preceded the Articles in the pages of prayer books printed after 1628 in the reign of Charles I (1625–49). The statement, instigated by William Laud (1573–1645), the Archbishop of Canterbury, and shaped by a conference of bishops, demanded that:

> no man shall hereafter either print, or preach, to draw the Article aside any way, but shall submit to it in the plain and full meaning thereof; and shall not put his own sense or comment to be the meaning of the Article, but shall take it in the literal and grammatical sense.

Conscious of resistance to both the content of the Articles and the stringent requirement to subscribe to them, John Bramhall (1594–1663), Archbishop of Armagh, offered the following explanation of the force and effect of the Articles in the Church's life: 'we do not hold our Thirty-Nine Articles to be such necessary truths 'without which there is no salvation'; nor enjoin ecclesiastical persons to swear unto them, but only to subscribe them, as theological truths, for the preservation of unity among us'. Notably, he distinguished between statements in the Articles which were similar to those 'contained in the Creed; some others of them are practical truths, which come not within the proper list of points or articles to be believed; lastly, some of them are pious opinions or inferior truths which are proposed by the Church of England as not to be opposed, not as essentials of

Faith necessary to be believed'.[1] This view was echoed by George Bull (1634–1710), Bishop of St David's in Wales, one of the finest thinkers of his day, who explained that:

> the Church of England professeth not to deliver all her Articles as essentials of faith, without the benefit whereof no man can be saved; but only propounds them as a body of safe and pious principles, for the preservation of peace to be subscribed, and not openly contradicted by her sons. And, therefore, she requires subscription to them only from the clergy, and not from the laity.

But the Articles needed to be understood in their original context to discern their intent and to grasp their meaning. This important point was made forcefully by the theologian Daniel Waterland (1683–1740), the Master of Magdalene College at Cambridge, in his famous essay, *The Case Against Arian Subscription*, which he published in 1721. A fervent defender of trinitarian theology, Waterland spoke against the right of Arians and Unitarians to make a minimal assent to the Articles. He rejected the view that the Articles 'may conscientiously be subscribed in any sense in which [men] themselves, by their own interpretation, could reconcile them to Scripture, without regard to the meaning and intention either of the persons who first compiled them or who now imposed them'. In effect, the Articles could not be interpreted according to one's own preferences or prejudices. Any interpretation had to be faithful to circumstances and decisions of the sixteenth century.

By 1750 the anti-subscription movement gathered momentum. Leadership of the movement was assumed by Francis Blackburne (1705–87), the Archdeacon of Cleveland, when he came to the defence of the Reverend John Jones, the Vicar of Alconbury, who was vigorously denounced after publishing his *Free and Candid Disquisitions Relating to the Church of England* in 1749. Jones had called for a revision of the *Book of Common Prayer*. Blackburne produced an *Apology* to announce his solidarity with Jones in 1750. Blackburne also supported Robert Clayton, the Bishop of Clogher in Ireland, who published 'An Essay on Spirit' in which he called for excision of the Athanasian Creed from the Church's formularies, a thorough review of liturgy and the abolition of subscription to the Articles.

Blackburne threw his weight behind Clayton's demands in a letter to Thomas Secker, the Archbishop of Canterbury, in 1754. He told the Archbishop that removing all subscription tests was the only way to bring an end to the gross immorality of the times in which he was writing. Despite pressure to resign, Blackburne resolved to remain in the Church of England after his son-in-law, Theophilus Lindsey, resigned his parish and opened the first Unitarian chapel in London. Blackburne was persuaded by certain theologians that the Articles could be interpreted in a manner that squared with his own convictions. But this contentment did not last long. Writing of himself in the third person, Blackburne explained that 'when, upon another prospect of advancement in the church, he began to consider the subject more intensely and found reason to think that the authorities on which he had depended, were not of sufficient weight or force to over-rule his own scruples, from that time he settled with himself never to subscribe again.'[2]

His treatise on the need for liberal-minded reform was published anonymously in 1766 with the title, *The Confessional,* and the sub-title, 'A full and free inquiry into the right, utility and success of establishing confessions of faith and doctrine in Protestant churches'. By now a well-known devotee of the writings of the Enlightenment philosopher John Locke, Blackburne set out his objection to any church claiming it was entitled to impose any statement of faith or articles of belief on its members. He believed that Christians had a right to search the Scriptures for themselves before coming to a clear mind as to their meaning. He argued that every confessional document that had come to his notice contained at least one statement with which he could reasonably dissent. He decried any 'attempt to settle religion once for all in an uncontrollable form'. Those who knew the book's author encouraged Blackburne to go further.

The now notorious archdeacon and his friends met at the Feathers' Tavern in the Strand at London in 1771 and drafted a 'Petition' calling on Parliament to repeal legislation requiring clerical subscription to both the Articles and the Prayer Book. It carried the title 'Proposals for an Application to Parliament, for relief in the matter of Subscription to the Liturgy and Thirty-Nine Articles of the Established Church of England, humbly submitted to the consideration of the learned and conscientious clergy of the said Church'. Blackburne claimed that 'the original protestant principle reserves to every man his right of private judgement ... Archbishop Cranmer was no more infallible than Pope Leo X ... We have indeed been told, that the Church of England does not propose all her articles to be subscribed as points necessary to salvation. But one would be glad to know where she draws the line, or makes any distinctions to this effect.'[3] Blackburne and the 250 signatories to the petition demanded liberty to interpret the Bible in their own way, free of the constraints imposed by the Creeds and the Articles. The signatories included Arians and Deists as well as orthodox clergy, such as the famous natural theologian and Christian apologist, Archdeacon William Paley. The petitioners claimed 'a natural right ... to judge in searching the Scriptures what may or may not be proved thereby'. Requiring subscription to the Articles deprived them of that right. They hoped that Parliament may relieve them 'of such an imposition upon their judgements and be restored to their undoubted rights as Protestants of interpreting the Scriptures for themselves, without being bound by any human explications thereof, or required to acknowledge by subscription or declaration the truth of any formulary whatsoever beside Holy Scripture itself'. When the Petition was presented to Parliament, Blackburne's controversial campaign was denounced by the conservative philosopher Edmund Burke. He poured scorn on Blackburne and his supporters.

> They want to be preferred clergyman of the Church of England as by law established, but their consciences will not allow them to conform to the doctrines and practices of that Church, that is, they want to be teachers in a church to which they do not belong, and to receive the emoluments appropriate for teaching one set of doctrines while they want to teach another. This is an odd sort of hardship.[4]

The Blackburne campaign came to nothing. A small number of clergy defected to the Unitarians; the majority remained in the Church of England and kept their doubts, scruples and objections to themselves. The growth in the eighteenth century of liberal sentiment, usually referred to as 'Latitudinarianism', was resisted by High and Low Churchmen who were wary of any movement that might lead to spiritual anarchy or promote doctrinal incoherence. Such were fears for the place and privileges of the Church of England that a *Bill*

Chapter 3   The Articles in Anglican life and witness

for the Relief of Protestant Dissenters was finally passed in 1779 after being rejected by Parliament six years earlier. The 'emancipation' of Roman Catholics was still another fifty years away. The launch of the French Revolution in 1789 heightened fear of liberal sentiment and institutional reform. The Church of England with the aid of the State would protect its traditions and resist all calls for change. At a time of political turmoil and naval threat, the Church promoted itself as a bulwark against barbarism. Change was not only unwise, it was dangerous.

Although many English Christians still objected to the Articles and to the notion of a legally Established Church which claimed a monopoly on Christian mission and ministry, the Articles remained a firm fixture in English life until the mid-nineteenth century when a number of intellectual movements, scientific and spiritual, drew attention to alleged deficiencies and apparent ambiguities in the Articles while arguing for the recognition of sincere and conscientious dissent in relation to complex theological questions. The publication of *Essays and Reviews* in March 1860 by a group of Anglican theologians, that were described by one reviewer as 'Seven against Christ', brought acute doctrinal disagreement into the open. [5] The book was a religious response to the publication of two controversial works the previous year: Charles Darwin's *On the Origin of Species* in 1859, which offered a naturalistic account of the origins and forms of all living things, and John Stuart Mill's political treatise *On Liberty*, which was an attempt to set strict limits on the state's prerogatives and powers. Mill had stressed the supreme standing of the individual, rejected state paternalism and elevated personal liberty to the highest of all social goods. This collection was intended, in part, to show that Christianity was not necessarily antithetical to Darwin's new book or essentially hostile to Mill's ideas. The approach of the essayists was to ask critical questions of the Biblical texts in a spirit of free and unfettered inquiry. Charles Wycliffe Goodwin (1817–78), the only laymen to contribute to the collection, submitted a chapter entitled 'The Mosaic Cosmogony'. He asserted that the creation story was a Hebrew myth adapted to the needs of its first audience. Goodwin, a lawyer and an Egyptologist, resigned his Cambridge fellowship after being unable to take holy orders. The only essay to include mention of Darwin's name was written by the Reverend Robert Baden Powell (1796–1860), Savilian Professor of Geometry at Oxford.

In an essay entitled 'On the Study of the Evidences of Christianity' Baden Powell contended that Christianity no longer depended for its verification on external evidences, especially miracles, but on the appeal to moral and spiritual experience. He argued that there was no conflict between science and religion as long as the practitioners of both disciplines observed the proper Baconian separation. He praised *Origin* as a 'masterly volume' because it offered a workable theory based on the principle that the self-governing powers of nature revealed the means by which God worked. Baden Powell and others had sought evidence to support the literal interpretation and chronology of Genesis despite frequent charges that the search for evidence implied the narratives were not true and persistent claims that this kind of questioning theology would lead to atheism.

But the Church's theological travails were not yet over. The Bishop of Natal in South Africa, John William Colenso (1814–83), published the first part of *The Pentateuch and Book of Joshua Critically Examined* in 1862. Colenso also questioned the literal truth of Genesis and its Mosaic authorship, and challenged traditional approaches to Biblical interpretation.[6] He was charged with heresy, found guilty and ejected from his diocese. The resulting controversy led to the first international controversy within the Anglican world over doctrinal differences and prompted the first Lambeth Conference of Bishops which was held in 1867. Colenso was not invited to attend. To add colour to the dispute, the self-declared agnostic biologist Thomas Henry Huxley (1825–95) led a public campaign to defend Colenso and was supported by a range of leading public figures including the popular novelist Anthony Trollope (1815–82).

The ordained contributors to *Essays and Reviews* were accused of violating their ordination vows and teaching doctrines contrary to the Thirty-Nine Articles. In 1864, they were formally condemned for heterodoxy by the Church, a ruling that was later overturned. There was even greater outrage that Colenso, as a bishop, was undermining the authority of Scripture by propounding radical views and dividing the Church with teaching that was contrary to the doctrine laid down in the Articles. He was subsequently excommunicated by Robert Gray, the Bishop of Cape Town. Controversies over divergent belief were not new. They had steadily escalated in number and seriousness after the 'Anglo-Catholic Revival' gained momentum in the second half of the 1830s. The *Church Discipline Act* of 1840 instituted legal tests of orthodoxy and made it an offence to teach doctrine that was inconsistent with the Articles and to use forms of service not found in the Prayer Book. The Act did not make the Church of England any more unified; it merely led to more acts of defiance and eventual prosecutions.

By 1864, parliamentarians noted that if there was such diversity in the beliefs of Anglican scholars and even bishops, was subscription to the Articles still possible let alone appropriate? Should the Articles be revised or the requirement for subscription be weakened or removed? When the ordained contributors to *Essays and Reviews* appealed their conviction, the Privy Council's Judicial Committee ruling made it plain that legal limits to individual interpretations of the Thirty-Nine Articles were much broader than previously imagined and many bishops liked. Indeed, the judgement implied that subscription to the Articles was located within the realm of individual conscience and its honest and sincere exercise. In effect, the person subscribing to the Articles was entitled to their own interpretation of what they meant and that such interpretation was valid if undertaken honestly and sincerely. The ruling acknowledged that the requirement for honesty might work against the desire for precision in doctrine. But there was an unwillingness to meet the cost of precision at the expense of conscience.

A Royal Commission into clerical subscription to the Articles held in 1865 made a number of recommendations including freeing university graduates from the need to subscribe to the Articles and altering the words of subscription to those which would take the form of a declaration rather than an oath. The *Clerical Subscription Act* (1865) contained a declaration that was incorporated into a revision of Canon Law that was ratified by the Crown in 1866. The new form of subscription required clergy to 'assent to the Thirty-Nine Articles of Religion ... [and] I believe the doctrine ... therein set forth, to be agreeable to the Word of God'. Whereas previously clergy were obliged to 'acknowledge all and every [Article] to be agreeable to the Word of God', some commentators thought the new declaration required only a general subscription to the Articles. What legislators intended or implied by the word 'assent' was not altogether clear. It soon became the focus of disagreement. The leading interpreters of the day thought it implied 'complete legal acceptance' of the doctrine contained in the Articles although what this actually meant in the context of religious faith and the exercise of pastoral ministry was not further developed or defined. Some ecclesiastical authorities argued that it meant no more than agreeing not to contradict the Articles in public while others felt it obliged a wholehearted inward commitment to every phrase.

In his major study of the Articles, EJ Bicknell claimed that the 1865 alteration 'was made of set purpose to afford relief to scrupulous consciences' by requiring not agreement to the proposition that 'the Articles are all agreeable to the Word of God, but that the doctrine of the Church of England as set forth in the Articles is agreeable to the Word of God. That is, [the clergy] are not called to assent to every phrase or detail of the Articles but only to their general sense'.[7] The English priest MJM Paton contended that the mode and form of subscription was modified:

> to relieve the consciences of those who felt unable to subscribe fully and sincerely to all the precise details of a document which bears so painfully the marks of the controversies among which it was composed. The assent now required is somewhat general, and can be given in good faith by anyone who accepts fully the Apostles', Nicene and Athanasian Creeds.[8]

But the apparent shift from conscientious belief to general assent did not satisfy everyone. There were some who wanted all forms of subscription to the Articles abolished.

Thomas Hughes (1822–96), a British Liberal parliamentarian, author of *Tom Brown's Schooldays*, Broad Churchman and supporter of the continued union between church and state, advocated the abolition of subscription. In a book entitled *The Old Church: What Shall We Do With It?* published in 1878, Hughes claimed the 'definitions and formulas of three hundred years ago' were incompatible with 'the national faith of today'. He alleged that 'in the face of the wider and larger knowledge which science and biblical criticism have opened to our generation, it is hopeless to expect that men of cultivation and ability can solemnly pledge themselves, even in the general form now required, to the propositions contained in the Thirty-Nine Articles.'[9] While they may have served the best interests of the Church and the community in the sixteenth century, to persist with them as tests of belief was 'to put a wholly unnecessary impediment in the way of candidates for holy orders, and to encourage dishonesty, and self-deception, in the very places where, before all others, there should be truthfulness and clearness of sight.'[10]

Although Hughes regarded the eminent Victorian theologian Frederick Denison 'FD' Maurice as a 'prophet', Maurice supported subscription and had earlier contended with Liberals like Hughes who wanted to discard the Articles and dispense with subscription. Maurice, who left the Unitarians as a young man to join the Church of England in 1830, consciously refused all party labels. He demanded to know what would be put in their place and how commonality of belief would be secured. He asked:

> what if those Articles have kept us from sinking into a particular theological system, and have compelled us to feel that there were two sides to truth, neither of which could be asserted to the exclusion of the other? What if the abandonment ... [of the Articles], or the reduction of them to our present standards of thought, should bring the Church into the most flat and hopeless monotony, should so level her to the superstitions of the nineteenth century, so divorce her from the past and the future that all expansion would forever be impossible?[11]

In subscribing to the Articles when he was instituted to the incumbency of St Peter's Church on Vere Street at London, Maurice told the congregation that he had declared his 'unfeigned assent and consent to the Articles' because they did not 'put themselves in the place of Christ; because I hold that they protect the faith of the simple Christian from a number of theological subtleties and technicalities which have threatened it and threaten it still.'[12] Maurice was particularly impressed by Article II and its placement of redemption before the fall, and its location of righteousness before sin because it meant Anglican theology was constructed on God's action rather than human deeds. It was the quality of the theology rather than on legal sanction that prompted Maurice to endorse subscription until he saw that they were being used as a test of orthodoxy and reluctantly concluded that subscription did more harm than good.[13] He commented: 'if we use the Articles to find out the errors of other men, and not to help us out of our own, I do not think we shall ever know what they mean, or in any real sense believe in them.'[14] In 1870 he remarked:

> The Liberals were clearly right in saying that the Articles did not mean to those who signed them at the universities or on taking orders what I supposed them to mean, and I was wrong. They were right in saying that subscription did mean to most the renunciation of a right to think, and, since none could renounce that right, it involved dishonesty. All this I have been compelled by the evidence of facts sorrowfully to confess. I accept the humiliation. I give the Liberals the triumph they deserve. But they feel and I feel that we are not a step nearer to each other in 1870 than we were in 1835. They have acquired a new name. They are called Broad Churchmen now, and delight to be called so. But their breadth seems to me to be narrowness. They include all kinds of opinions. But what message have they for the people who do not live upon opinions or care for opinions?[15]

By this time, the Liberals succeeded in gaining greater ground for diversity of interpretation.

It was not until the period after World War I that the place of the Articles in Anglican polity was again considered seriously. A new desire for a shift in emphasis became apparent. The Doctrine Commission appointed in 1922 by the Archbishops of Canterbury and York finally reported in 1938. The Commission's report did not focus much attention on the Articles. Indeed, the drafters stated:

> There is much ignorance and much confusion of mind about the Articles. They have not, at any rate from the early seventeenth century onwards, taken in our system the place occupied in the Lutheran system by the Augsberg Confession. They are, indeed, too short for such a purpose. They are not a complete confession of faith, but a declaration of the position adopted by the Church of England at a critical moment in relation to the chief controversies of that moment.[16]

The report claimed that the Catechism and the Prayer Book were more suitable for doctrinal instruction than the Articles, especially since the Articles were 'largely concerned with questions no longer foremost in our minds'. The Commission members decided against using the Articles and the Prayer Book to resolve 'the questions that chiefly divide Anglicans', preferring to 'handle these questions as best we could in the light of reason, of modern knowledge, and that universal Christian tradition to which our Reformers themselves appealed'.[17]

But the Commission did note that the historic 'Anglican formularies', which included the Articles (although they were ranked least among them), represented 'the doctrinal and historical position of Anglicanism in relation to the rest of Western Christendom in the sixteenth century' and confirmed that 'the position of the Church of England in relation to other Christian bodies is still defined by the retention of those formularies'.[18] It explained that these formularies 'should not be held to prejudge questions which have arisen since their formulation or problems which have been modified by fresh knowledge or fresh conceptions'. In situations in which 'an Anglican theologian thinks a particular formulary not wholly adequate, he has a special obligation to preserve whatever truth that formulary was trying to secure, and to see to it that any statement he puts forward as more adequate does in fact secure this'.[19] The Commission, whose members paid scant attention to the Articles, then offered seven resolutions on the matter of 'On Assent'. After explaining that assent to 'authoritative formularies, doctrinal and liturgical' could 'reasonably be expected from members of the Church', the Commission explained that 'assent to formularies ... should be understood as signifying such general acceptance without implying detailed assent to every phrase or proposition thus employed'. This being so, 'a member of the Church should not be held to be involved in dishonesty merely on the ground that, in spite of some divergence from the tradition of the Church, he has assented to formularies'. In the case of 'authorised teachers', the Church nonetheless 'has a right to satisfy itself that those who teach in its name adequately represent and express its mind'. Indeed, those authorised to teach have an 'obligation not to teach, as the doctrine of the Church, doctrine which is not in accordance with the Church's mind'. The Commission hoped that in the exercise of ecclesiastical discipline in relation to the teaching office, 'great regard should be paid to the need for securing a free consensus, as distinct from an enforced uniformity.'[20]

After World War II when the English Church was obliged to review and overhaul Canon Law and the emerging ecumenical movement obliged Anglicans to consider impediments to organic unity, it was obvious that many within the Anglican Communion felt only antipathy towards the Articles and hostility towards formal subscription. Bishop Arthur Michael Hollis, the first Bishop of Madras (1942–47) and the first Moderator of the Church of South India (1947–54), thought the Articles' existence and the subscription requirement was part of an odious legalism infecting contemporary Anglicanism. After complaining about the myriad rules and regulations applying to the conduct of Anglican worship, he deplored the Church's 'clinging to more or less obsolete formulae of belief'. While noting that every denomination struggled with 'traditional confessions' of belief, he was disturbed that 'too many Anglicans are apparently not willing officially to recognise the absolute necessity of explicitly allowing a reasonable liberty of interpretation to those who are called on to assent to any such statement of belief.'[21] He argued that every church ought regularly 'to re-examine its requirements to see whether it is not possible to avoid misunderstandings and to ease the strain upon sensitive minds and consciences'. In his view, the Reformation period 'produced far too many and too detailed Confessions'. He was disappointed that Anglicans have persisted with subscription to the Articles although their content had not been altered in four centuries. The leading Anglo-Catholic bishop, William Wand, claimed the Articles are 'not intended to have the same binding force on the conscience' as the Creeds. He thought that subscription 'does not mean that clergy must accept them as a sufficient statement of Christian doctrine. It means that they agree to accept them as a basis of teaching and not to teach anything contrary to them.'[22]

After the Church of England was disturbed by the publication in 1963 of *Honest to God* by the Bishop of Woolwich, John Robinson, and unsettled by leading clergy publicly questioning the validity and expression of core Christian beliefs, the Archbishops of Canterbury and York appointed a Doctrine Commission in March 1967 to 'consider the place of the Thirty-Nine Articles in the Anglican tradition and the question of Subscription and Assent to them'. The

Commission presented its report in July 1968. The Commission noted that the Articles were:

> evidently not meant as, nor were they ever claimed to be, a complete systematic statement of Christian truth; they had the more limited aim of determining questions – some of them, certainly, very important questions – which disturbed the peace of the Church in the mid-sixteenth century. They were thus intended to set boundaries within which the stream of Anglican theology was thenceforth to run.[23]

The Report explained that the Articles needed to be understood first in their historical context before any attempt was made to project their meaning into the present. However, the interpretation of the Articles from an historical perspective is not without its complications. These complications would seem to preclude confident assertions about what the drafters intended to define or conclude in the Articles. The Articles also needed to be interpreted in the context of the *Book of Common Prayer* and the Ordinal for which subscription was also required. There is no clear guidance on whether the Articles are to be interpreted in the light of the other formularies or the reverse. The stronger argument appears to favour interpreting the Articles through the Prayer Book and the Ordinal because, the Report noted, the 'liturgical formularies are taken as representing the continuing tradition of the Church's teaching as expressed in sacrament and common prayer.'[24]

The Commission was even more concerned about 'what kind of commitment the Church actually requires, and is morally entitled to require, of subscribers' and 'what normative force the Articles may have held to have' when 'many of [the Articles'] presuppositions are allowed to be disputable.'[25] Do the Articles 'tyrannise the conscience in a way that destroys intellectual integrity?' In claiming that the Articles could be proved by appeals to Scripture, the Commission noted that some of the Biblical interpretations were narrow and excluded alternative viewpoints that could also be reconciled to Scripture. In effect, the Articles opted for one doctrinal prescription when others were permissible and were, in some instances, possibly nearer to the intentions of the Biblical writers.

What, then, ought to be the future of the Articles? One solution was the abolition of subscription and the treatment of the Articles 'as a document of merely historical interest, perhaps no longer even printed with the Prayer Book'. Those supporting such action claimed the Articles are 'distressingly irrelevant to the twentieth-century Anglican, who believes and works within a different climate of thought and faces different practical and theological problems.' The arguments directed against 'the contemporary Roman Catholic Church as it was understood by the Reformers, and against Anabaptists, is unsuited to present theological needs in the light of the ecumenical hopes of the Anglican Communion'. Those advocating abolition of subscription noted that 'assent to the Articles is not a part of the Lambeth Quadrilateral and is not a necessary distinguishing mark of other parts of the Anglican Communion' and contended that because few other Churches 'bind their Reformation confession of faith in with their liturgical book', the Articles do not belong in the Prayer Book and should no longer be included in future printings. Those wanting to retain subscription saw the Articles as 'an "identity card" for the Church of England in the twentieth no less than in the sixteenth century – or at least as the "title deeds" of a particular tradition within Anglicanism.' Removing the Articles from the Church's formularies might be seen as a 'public rejection of the Church's commitment to the biblical faith as they understand it' and give the impression that the 'Church no longer regarded doctrinal belief as important'. Furthermore, it appeared that 'the Articles as they stand are accepted without difficulty and positively cherished by a substantial number of the clergy and ordinands' and retaining them in the pages of the Prayer Book gave them a standing and an authority that would be lost if they were deleted.

The Commission considered all the evidence and arguments but was 'not prepared to recommend either that the Articles be no longer printed with the Prayer Book or that mention of them be omitted from formulae of doctrinal subscription within the Church of England'. The Commission did, however, suggest that a standard preface be read before assent was declared. This preface began with a statement of the Church's identity and its witness to Christian truth in the 'historic formularies – the Thirty-Nine Articles of Religion, and the Book of

Common Prayer, and the Ordering of Bishops, Priests and Deacons'. It also recommended a new form of assent.

In the closing moments of the 1968 Lambeth Conference, the bishops voted strongly in favour of a motion (Resolution 43) that accepted the main recommendations of the 1968 report on subscription and suggested that:

> each Church of our communion consider whether the Articles need be bound up with its Prayer Book ... assent to the Thirty-Nine Articles be no longer required of ordinands ... when subscription is required to the Articles or other elements in the Anglican tradition, it should be required, and given, only in the context of a statement which gives the full range of our inheritance of faith and sets the Articles in their historic context.

After the revised Canon C 15 came into force in 1975, clergy in the Church of England have been required to 'affirm, and accordingly declare my belief in the faith which is revealed in the Holy Scriptures and set forth in the catholic creeds and to which the historic formularies of the Church of England bear witness; and in public prayer and administration of the sacraments, I will use only the forms of service which are authorized or allowed by Canon.' Clergy were also freed from the requirement to read the Articles to the congregation in which they were licensed before commencing their ministry.

An echo of the Articles was heard at Sydney Cove when the Australian continent was first settled by Europeans. Captain Arthur Phillip RN, the Governor of the penal colony of New South Wales, was required to read a decidedly Reformed theological declaration on taking office: 'I, Arthur Phillip, do declare that I do believe there is not any transubstantiation in the sacrament of the Lord's Supper or in the elements of bread and wine at or after the consecration thereof by any person whatsoever.' His chaplain, the Reverend Richard Johnson, had subscribed to the Thirty-Nine Articles and from all accounts appeared to believe them wholeheartedly. Those who followed Johnson were similarly obliged to declare their assent to the Articles using the form of words provided in English Canon Law.

Following the formation of a Federal Commonwealth in 1901 and the gradual assumption of all the responsibilities of independent nationhood, the place of the Articles became a key issue in the long and protracted negotiations that led to the achievement of a constitution for the Australian Church in 1962. When serious attention was given to the Australian Church's need for a Constitution, representatives of the Diocese of Sydney were keen to ascertain the place of the historic formularies in any proposed arrangements. As committees met and a consolidated draft was produced in 1932 for general consideration, the Queensland provincial synod requested that any document circulated for comment make plain that the Thirty-Nine Articles were not given 'the same authority in the Church as the Bible, the Nicene Creed, the Sacraments of Baptism and Holy Communion and the Order of the Episcopate'.[26] This request, encouraged by the newly installed Archbishop of Brisbane, William Wand, revealed the attitude of Anglo-Catholics to the Articles in particular and ecclesiastical authority in general. Ernest Burgmann, the liberal-leaning Bishop of Goulburn, had other objections to a prominent place for the Articles. He told Francis Batty, the Bishop of Newcastle: 'the Thirty-Nine Articles interpreted as a legal document by Sydney or even Brisbane sends a shiver down my back. At present it is an old document. If we fresh it up and give it new authority the angels will have to work overtime to save Anglicanism in Australia.'[27] Speaking on behalf of Sydney, Archdeacon TC Hammond said the existing obligations on clergy to assent to the historic formularies needed to be retained because he could not accept 'that foundation truths of this character should be subject to the decision of a majority of the General Synod of the Church of Australia'. This was because, he said, 'the Christian faith is not subject to the changing circumstances of time'. In order to secure Sydney's support, the Articles were included in the final document eventually circulated to each diocese for approval in the late 1950s.

The place and function of the Articles in the polity of the Anglican Church of Australia is set out in the 'fundamental declarations' that form the first part of the Constitution that came into operation on 1 January 1962. As 'part of the One Holy Catholic and Apostolic Church of Christ', the Anglican Church of Australia 'holds the Christian Faith as professed by the Church of Christ from primitive times and in particular as set forth in the creeds known as the Nicene Creed and the Apostles' Creed'. As an off-spring of the Church of England, the

Australian Church retains 'the doctrine and principles of the Church of England embodied in the *Book of Common Prayer* together with the Form and Manner of Making Ordaining and Consecrating of Bishops, Priests and Deacons and in the Articles of Religion sometimes called the 'Thirty-Nine Articles' with the *Book of Common Prayer* and the Thirty-Nine Articles' which were to serve as 'the authorised standard of worship and doctrine in this Church'. The Constitution stated that 'no alteration in or permitted variations from the services or Articles therein contained shall contravene any principle of doctrine or worship laid down in such standard'.

When clergy are required to declare their assent to the doctrine and formularies of the Church, they swear that they 'firmly and sincerely believe the Catholic Faith' and give their assent to 'the doctrine of The Anglican Church of Australia as expressed in the *Book of Common Prayer* and the Ordering of Bishops, Priests and Deacons and the Articles of Religion, as acknowledged in section 4 of the Constitution'. They are obliged to state their belief that this doctrine is 'agreeable to the word of God'. There is no requirement for the laity in Australia (other than deaconesses, lay ministers and catechists licensed in the Diocese of Sydney) to give their assent to the Articles.[28] The Articles are not mentioned in the Ordinal for deacons and priests although candidates must sign them before they are ordained. Reference is made to them in the liturgy for consecrating bishops although it is common for a statement to be read that the necessary declarations and assents have been taken. Where the declarations are included in the liturgy, the archbishop repeats the text of the fundamental declarations from the Constitution and asks the bishop-elect to 'make your Declaration and Assent to this faith'. The bishop-elect replies: 'I believe that doctrine to be agreeable to the Word of God'. It is notable that the emphasis is on faith and doctrine rather than on the text of the Articles. In *A Prayer Book for Australia* which was authorised for use in 1995, the Articles appear in a section headed 'Supplementary Material'. After an outline order of Holy Communion and a Catechism and some explanatory notes about changes to traditional wording in liturgy, the Articles appear in their original form without explanation or commentary.

The place of the Articles in Australian Anglican polity has rarely been challenged. In more recent times this is perhaps because their place and function is poorly understood. During the protracted negotiations from 1920 to 1960 that led to agreement on a Constitution for the Australian Church, it was assumed that the *Book of Common Prayer* and the Articles would be retained as the Church's standard of belief and custom. For some, retention of the Articles would ensure the survival of its Reformation heritage; for others it would guarantee the Australian Church's organic relationship with the English Church. When the Church turned its mind to liturgical revision in the 1960s, there was a concern that introducing a new Prayer Book was tantamount to doctrinal change. Given that most Anglicans imbibed their theology through the liturgies of the prayer book, this concern was not unreasonable. It proved to be well founded.

In contrast to the experience in Australia, the Articles have been retained, revised, replaced or removed from the Church's polity in other Anglican provinces around the world. The Lambeth Conference held in 1888 resolved that 'newly constituted Churches, especially in non-Christian lands ... should not necessarily be bound to accept' the Articles in their entirety. Whereas the Church in New Zealand has slightly revised the Articles, the Australian Church retains them in their 1571 format. The American Church has dispensed altogether with assent to the Articles while the Australian Church has only abolished the requirement for verbal assent (written assent being retained).

What, then, is the Church trying to achieve by retaining the Articles? What is the Church seeking when it asks ordinands to put their names to them? Does the Church require general assent that the Articles reflect the essence of the Christian faith when considered as a unity (allowing disagreement on several specific points) or detailed assent that every Article and each phrase reflect the essence of the Christian faith (precluding any disagreement on any aspect of the Articles)? And does the Church expect clergy who have assented to the Articles to base their teaching and preaching upon them?

Regardless of a person's attitude towards the content of the Articles or subscribing to them, it is doubtful whether even the most ardent devotee and most sincere subscriber to the Articles would see them as constituting a teaching syllabus. Indeed, the authors have never known the Articles to be used in any pedagogical or didactic way in parish or chaplaincy settings. From our perspectives, the Church needs to clarify what is meant by assent and why assent is important. Might the Church then deal more effectively with any suggestion that a candidate for ordination was being either insincere or evasive when they did declare their assent to the Articles ahead of being made deacon or priest? The most common caveat – that ordination candidates assent that this was what the Church believed in the sixteenth century – is theological sophistry. Plainly, there needs to be clearer and more concentrated study of their meaning and their place in ordained life. In this respect, the Articles do not usually attract the attention they deserve. This, we believe, needs to change.

Notes

1. John Bramhall, *Works*, vol. II, 1655, pp. 201, 476.
2. *The Works of Francis Blackburne*, seven vols, Cambridge, 1804; vol. I, p. 28 quoted.
3. Blackburne, *Works*, vol. VII, p. 4.
4. Burke's speech was published in *Works of the Right Honourable Edmund Burke*, vol. V, *Miscellaneous*, Rivington, London, 1812, p. 328.
5. See Ieuan Ellis, *Seven Against Christ: A Study of 'Essays and Reviews'*, Studies in the History of Christian Thought, no. 23, Leiden, 1980.
6. See Jeff Guy, *The Heretic: A Study of the Life of John William Colenso 1814–1883*, Raven Press, Johannesburg, 1983 and John Rogerson, *Old Testament Criticism in the Nineteenth Century: England and Germany*, Fortress Press, Philadelphia, 1984, pp. 220–37.
7. Bicknell, *The Thirty-Nine Articles*, p. 21.
8. MJM Paton, 'Can we ignore the Establishment?' in David Paton (ed.), *Essays in Anglican Self-Criticism*, SCM Press, London, 1958, p. 136.
9. Thomas Hughes, *The Old Church: What Shall We do With It?*, Macmillan, London, 1878, p. 160.
10. Hughes, *The Old Church*, p. 161.
11. FD Maurice, *The Kingdom of Christ*, vol. II, p.323. Maurice's first published work, *Subscription No Bondage*, which appeared in 1835 dealt with subscription to the Articles at the universities. It was not primarily directed at clerical subscription although Maurice was at pains to show that the Articles warned students against superstition and contained theology that would ensure all subjects studied at the university were considered in a profound way.

12. FD Maurice, *Faith of the Liturgy*, p. 23 and *Lincoln's Inn Sermons*, vol. I, p. 25.
13. See *The Life of FD Maurice*, vol. II, p. 491, 506.
14. FD Maurice, *The Prayer Book and the Lord's Prayer*, p. 13.
15. F Maurice (ed.), *The Life of FD Maurice*, vol. I, Macmillan, London, 1884, p. 183.
16. *Doctrine in the Church of England*, The Report of the Commission on Christian Doctrine Appointed by the Archbishops of Canterbury and York in 1922, SPCK, London, 1938, p. 9.
17. *Doctrine in the Church of England*, p. 9.
18. *Doctrine in the Church of England*, p. 36.
19. *Doctrine in the Church of England*, p. 37.
20. *Doctrine in the Church of England*, p. 39.
21. AM Hollis, 'Anglicanism and Unity', in Paton (ed.), *Essays in Anglican Self-Criticism*, pp. 212–13.
22. William Wand, *What the Church of England Stands For*, Mowbray, London, 1951, p. 64.
23. *Subscription and Assent to the Thirty-Nine Articles: a Report of the Archbishops' Commission on Christian Doctrine*, SPCK, London, 1968, para. 3, p. 10.
24. *Subscription and Assent to the Thirty-Nine Articles*, para. 14, p. 15.
25. *Subscription and Assent to the Thirty-Nine Articles*, para. 17, p. 15.
26. John Davis, *Anglicans and their Constitution*, Acorn Press, Melbourne, 1993, p. 88.
27. Davis, *Anglicans and their Constitution*, p. 93.
28. Regulation 2d to the *Deaconesses, Readers and Other Lay Persons Ordinance 1981*, Acts & Ordinances of the Diocese of Sydney, *www.sds.asn.au/Site/102031.asp?ph=y*

4 Assertions, arguments and articles

Setting forth Anglican belief

In the sixteenth century the Church of England resolved that its beliefs and customs would be set forth publicly in a number of formularies that are usually listed as the *Book of Common Prayer*, the Homilies, the Ordinal and the Articles of Religion. Much can be gleaned from these historic sources about what Anglicans believe and practise because these have a continuing role in the life of the Church. But what, if anything, is really distinctive about 'Anglicanism'? Does it consist more of customs than convictions, or of laws than liturgies? Does it exist more in symbols than substance? Are there characteristic Anglican beliefs or quintessential practices? Is it a theological method or a spiritual mood? Can Anglicanism take similar outward forms to Lutheranism or Calvinism?

These questions have been the subject of almost continuous debate, especially among Anglicans. More than four centuries ago, Richard Hooker delineated a uniquely Anglican understanding of the Reformation and Christianity in defending distinctly English practices against the complaints and objections of Papalists and Puritans. In more recent times, this understanding has resonated in the works of Bishop Stephen Neill (1900–84), who remarked that there is no Anglican faith but rather an Anglican attitude, and in the writings of Archbishop Michael Ramsey (1904–88), who spoke of an Anglican atmosphere with its own temperament linking liturgy to belief. Professor Alec Vidler (1899–1991) and Bishop Stephen Sykes (1939–) have both pointed to the *Book of Common Prayer* and public worship as being normative of Anglicanism. There have also been attempts at locating a unifying centre. Poet and theologian Samuel Taylor Coleridge (1772–1834) argued for the 'directionality of love'. The existence of several approaches to defining or describing what is essentially or uniquely Anglican reflects both the complexity and subtlety of historic and contemporary Anglicanism, and marks the extent to which its formularies have been variously interpreted and inconsistently applied.

Part of the difficulty associated with defining central Anglican beliefs and discerning core Anglican commitments lies in the intention and approach of those who drafted the Articles of Religion in the sixteenth century. Notably, the Church of England resolved to call its statement of beliefs and commitments a set of Articles rather than a 'declaration'. This was a deliberate decision with far-reaching consequences. Although the Articles were set within the context of contemporary sixteenth century disputes about doctrine and reflect the tensions of that time, they also attempted to clarify and confirm elements of Christian belief that were timeless and unchanging. In his attempt to penetrate the mindset of the early English Reformers, the English Evangelical theologian Oliver O'Donovan thought the Articles were best understood as 'a church document intended to exercise a normative role as a standard of belief in its community'.[1] He considered that as a formal statement intended to outline a range of theological positions:

> it is brief. It invites elaboration, providing a skeletal structure which its readers may cover with the flesh and blood of their own argumentation. It purports to speak for a whole community, and to say only that which the community can and must say together.'

O'Donovan pointed out that when 'we engage with the Articles we engage with a whole community, and not with an individual genius'. What, then, have the three main traditions comprising modern Anglicanism – Evangelicalism, Anglo-Catholicism and Liberalism – made of the Articles and their place in Christian witness and discipleship?

Evangelicals and the Articles

Anglican Evangelicals claim to have inherited the spirit of the sixteenth century Reformation and jealously guard its legacy. While claiming a lineage that works its way to Cranmer, Ridley and Latimer, they also point to the stirrings of a consciously Evangelical movement that gathered momentum in England from the 1740s. It was marked by a return to a scriptural understanding of sanctification and a renewed sense of urgency in the conduct of mission and in the provision of spiritual care. The Movement's leaders were prompted by disgust at the worldliness and nominalism evident among the clergy of the time, and by their despair at the general disinterest of the laity in pursuing personal holiness. There were frequent complaints in the 1700s that Anglican worship was cold, austere and cerebral. Few of England's burgeoning working classes ever attended divine service. They neither felt welcomed by the clergy nor adequately prepared for participation in the liturgy. The Christian message needed, the Evangelicals insisted, to speak to the heart as well as renew the mind. They emphasised the teaching and preaching office of the clergy, focussed on proclamation of the Word of God. The renowned Evangelical leaders of this period were Charles Simeon (1759–1836) and Henry Venn (1796–1873) who proclaimed a strong message of repentance and salvation, while laymen such as William Wilberforce (1759–1833) and Lord (Anthony Ashley Cooper) Shaftesbury (1801–85), provoked by pastoral concern, were determined to tackle pressing social problems. The Church Missionary Society, founded in 1799, gave the Evangelical Movement an international focus, and the Simeon Trustees (instituted by Charles Simeon) and the Church Pastoral Aid Society, established in 1836, supported and extended evangelical ministry in England.

A liberal faction subsequently emerged within the Evangelical Movement. One of the dividing issues was the manner of Holy Scripture's inspiration, with conservatives in a later period being unfairly and inaccurately labelled 'fundamentalists' by their opponents. The twentieth century label 'fundamentalist' originated in the work of a group of American theologians who produced a series of studies on Christian 'fundamentals' between 1910 and 1915 and circulated them to English-speaking clergy throughout the world. Differing attitudes to Scripture became an acute issue for most Anglicans when biblical 'higher criticism' and 'scientific inquiry' challenged the authoritative character of Scripture and reduced the confidence individual believers could place upon biblical teaching. Other dividing issues were the character of the Church's engagement in social reform movements, and the primacy of mission and evangelism over other religious activities.

One of the most influential works for Evangelicals in the twentieth century was *The Catholic Faith: A Manual of Instruction for Members of the Church of England* by WH Griffith Thomas.[2] This book was designed for use in relation to pastoral ministry, catechesis and ordinand training. The Thirty-Nine Articles are dealt with as one of the 'standards of doctrine' in the Church of England alongside the Creeds and the Homilies. Thomas explained that:

> all the Reformed Communions stated their position [with respect to Rome] in the form of Articles or Confessions or Faith. Our Articles are therefore analogous to the documents of the Continental Reformed Churches, and not only analogous to them, but clearly influenced by them ... The Articles are thus never to be separated from their historical root in relation to the Church of Rome, for they mark the historical and doctrinal position of the Church of England.'[3]

Notably, and in contrast to other commentators, Thomas concluded that:

> if, moreover, there should be any question as to the meaning of the Prayer Book on matters of doctrine, the Prayer Book is to be judged by the Articles rather than the Articles by the Prayer Book. The language of the Prayer Book is that of devotion; the language of the Articles that of doctrine, and for exactness, balance, and fullness we naturally look to the latter rather than to the former.[4]

He was adamant that

> ... there is no likelihood of any one finding a discrepancy between the Prayer Book and the Articles on points of

essential doctrine. They were all compiled or drawn up by the same men, and convey their own uniform, clear message of Christian truth.⁵

More recently, Richard Turnbull, the Principal of Wycliffe Hall at Oxford University, lamented that the Articles:

> have become obscured in the life of the Church, in preparation for ministry and in general awareness among both worshippers and decision-makers. EJ Bicknell's major theological treatment of the Articles is dated, dry and obscure, affected by the author's liberal Catholic presuppositions. Thus a veil is being drawn over the Protestant heritage of Anglicanism, which needs to be drawn back.⁶

Turnbull thought the English Reformation:

> shows again its uniqueness by its adoption of the principle of a confession (it is simply inaccurate to claim that the Thirty-Nine Articles are not a confession of faith), but to do so with a distinctive Englishness in tone and content.⁷

He contended that the Articles were:

> unmistakably Protestant. They are also shaped by the uniqueness of the English Reformation. The Articles show some influence of early Lutheranism but also, significantly, of continental Reformed Protestantism. The Articles strike a tone of moderate Calvinism.⁸

For Turnbull, the Articles drew an important distinction between first and second order issues; first order issues related to salvation and could claim a direct biblical mandate. He claimed that an 'overemphasis on the patristic period' began with Bishop Lancelot Andrewes (1555–1626) in the seventeenth century and was accelerated by the Oxford Movement in the nineteenth century which 'contributed to a lessening of emphasis upon the Reformation'. He said the modern Evangelical identity was based on 'moderate Calvinism' which was expressed in the 'Protestantism of the Thirty-Nine Articles'.⁹

Modern Evangelicals from Thomas to Turnbull have traditionally rejoiced in the Articles' Reformed doctrinal content, have resisted any redrafting of the content and have wanted to see the Articles' theological commitments occupy a more central place in the belief and worship of the Church, including greater loyalty to the Articles' doctrine in the preaching and teaching of the clergy. Evangelicals feel that the Articles embody the Reformation spirit of Anglicanism, preserve the insights of English Christianity and anchor the Church's outlook most closely to the witness of Scripture. They tend to be suspicious of anything and anyone wanting to revise or abandon the Articles, fearing innovation in the direction of Romanism or Liberalism.

Anglo-Catholics and the Articles

Anglo-Catholics have never shared the Evangelicals' reverence for the Articles, believing them to be either a restriction on, or distortion of, the Church's continuing life and witness. While many would not join those who disparage the Articles as 'forty lashes less one', they would contend that the Church of England went too far in the direction of embracing the doctrines of Reformed theology and accommodating the tenets of European Protestantism in the sixteenth century. They claim that the balance in the Church's teaching and practice began to be restored as a consequence of the 'Oxford Movement' which was launched after the Reverend John Keble (1792–1866) preached a highly controversial sermon, entitled 'National Apostasy', to the Oxford Assizes on 14 July 1833. A man of culture and learning, Keble declared his objections to secular control of the Church and outlined the damage that government interference had visited upon English religious life. Clergy touched by the 'Oxford Movement' were known initially as 'Tractarians' after the Reverend John Henry Newman (1801–90) began to publish *Tracts for the Times*. These pamphlets were ostensibly devised to oppose the encroachment of 'Popery and Dissent' in the Church of England. The first three were published on 9 September 1833. A number of others appeared in close succession. Although the immediate impetus behind the 'Oxford Movement' was the suppression of Irish bishoprics by the English Parliament in 1832 (the Tractarians believed that episcopal supervision was a matter for the Church, not the State, to determine), its leading figures were convinced the Church of England was a corrupt institution in a state of serious decline.

In contrast to perceptions of the Church as yet another 'department of state', the Tractarians held that it was a Divine Society founded by Christ in history and that it was charged with conveying God's grace to every person in each new age. The Movement did not seek to give the Church of England a Catholic character, because its leaders were convinced the Church was already Catholic. Rather, the Movement wished to revive or recover the Church's grasp of its Catholic identity, and raise the standing of Anglican clergy and the status of the episcopate. Its leaders emphasised the place of the sacraments, the necessity of the Church's social mission, the call to personal holiness and the importance of its pastoral (rather than penal) authority, and re-asserted the Church's spiritual independence and ecclesiastical autonomy. In its earliest days the Movement was reactionary, its ideals having strong similarities to what the English sociologist Peter Berger has called the 'de-modernising impulse'. But its long-term significance should not be underestimated. As historian Hugh McLeod observes, the Movement attracted those 'searching for authority at a time when old authorities were collapsing ... it also appealed to those who longed for a sense of "the Church" and its true grandeur, and those who wanted a religion freed from the respectability and the Puritanism of the churches in which they had grown up'.[10] The English sociologist WSF Pickering argued that 'no movement within the Church of England has so changed its overall ethos'.[11] It was an appeal to mind and heart through ascetic yearnings and spiritual discipline.

Although one of its founders, Dr Edward Pusey (1800–82), 'had no wish to encourage party-spirit [because] he believed in the Catholic nature of the Church of England and it was this he was concerned to defend and make manifest',[12] the 'Oxford Movement' created a number of separate entities. High Churchmen were sympathetic until 1836, when they began to fear the Movement was embracing erroneous, meaning Roman Catholic, doctrine. In many instances, as historian Peter Toon observes, High Churchmen joined hands with Evangelicals, believing they had more in common with them than with Tractarians. The Oxford Movement also spawned the 'Anglo-Catholics' and the 'ritualists'. Those claiming to be Anglo-Catholics later divided into conservative, Anglo-papalist and liberal wings. The traditionalists sought to dig down within Anglican tradition to uncover a Catholic system of faith and practice which was complete in itself within the 'Catholic Church of England'. The Anglo-papalists, sometimes known as 'Reunionists', were not convinced that Catholicism could ever exist securely outside obedience to the Roman Curia, and they remained within the Church of England in order to facilitate Anglican return to papal obedience. Liberal Catholics were unwilling to make superior claims for their system of belief and were willing to cooperate and learn from other parties.

The Evangelical clergy were until 1836 ambivalent towards the Oxford Movement, when they began to share broader fears expressed about the Tractarians' ultimate objectives. There was a growing belief that the Tractarians would try to take the English Church back to Rome. In that year the leading Evangelical and Church Missionary Society (CMS) secretary, Edward Bickersteth, published *Remarks on the Progress of Popery*, in which he took aim at the general trend of the Movement. While acknowledging that the Tractarians opposed the 'most glaring part of popery', he alleged that 'the very principles of popery are brought forward by them under deference to human authority, especially that of the Fathers: overvaluing the Christian ministry and undervaluing justification by faith'.[13] When Dr Pusey published his tracts *On Baptism* in 1836–37, one reviewer suggested his ideas would be welcomed in the Vatican and asked how he could remain a clergyman of the Church of England.

In the twentieth century, Catholic Anglicans continue to assert that the Articles did not discount or disqualify many of their defining beliefs. In a popular work on the Articles published in 1957, the Reverend Kenneth Ross, Vicar of All Saints Margaret Street in London, explained that 'just as Queen Elizabeth made few very significant changes in the Prayer Book which enabled a Catholic to accept it, so when the Forty-Two Articles were revised and became the Thirty-Nine Articles, anti-catholic teaching was skilfully removed'.[14] While conceding that the 'language of the Thirty-Nine Articles is markedly Lutheran and Calvinistic, and because whole phrases and even paragraphs are taken from continental confessions, it is often been supposed that the Church of England is therefore committed to those particular errors' he claimed that the Articles 'always stop short of the characteristically Lutheran or Calvinist doctrines, and they were subjected to bitter attack by Protestant extremists, who objected especially to Article XVI.'[15] He felt that 'there can be no objection to the use of Lutheran or Calvinistic expressions so long as they are controlled and kept in balance by the orthodox counterweight.' He contended that:

> they are far from being a complete conspectus of religious teaching. They are no more a final exposition of Anglican teaching than the Elizabethan Prayer Book was the last word in Anglican liturgy. Unlike the Catholic Creeds, the Articles of any part of the Church have only a temporary value, being concerned with disputes and controversies of a particular country in a particular age.'[16]

Ross was therefore adamant that the Articles contain:

> nothing which the Churchman who values the name Catholic cannot accept. I would go further, and say that they are still of value as giving a sketch of the general position of the Church of England. But the vexed questions of today are not the same as those of the sixteenth century, and in emphasis and balance the Articles leave a good deal to be desired. Scholarship and study have advanced in the last four centuries, and we can now see that the difficulty of finding the right answer to certain problems four hundred years ago was due to questions being formulated in the wrong way.[17]

In his account of the Articles, Ross located and then interpreted the Articles within a number of contexts: the period in which they were written, the limitations of the best learning of the day, the controversies they attempt to settle, the ambiguities they preserved and the ambivalence thought desirable in relation to some beliefs and practices, the possible reinterpretation of the Articles as a consequence of the Church's experience and the deliberations of theologians not bound by the social and political structures of the day. He understood justification in a Reformed way so long as it does not exclude effectual sacramental grace – and he concluded that it does not diminish this belief if the teaching of one article is considered in the light of another. He agreed that medieval Catholicism taught beliefs and encouraged customs that were far removed from the teaching of the New Testament. He also took a minimalist view of predestination, claiming that 'rightly understood, is an assertion of the sovereign will of the merciful God. Salvation depends on Him and not on our turning to Him'.[18] He was disappointed that the Articles do not contain a comprehensive statement concerning 'the ministry of the Church' and the ordering of its life.[19] He said 'it cannot be disputed that at the Reformation all explicit prayers for the dead were struck out of the service books from 1552 onwards, and one of the Homilies goes so far as to deny their legitimacy altogether'. But Ross appealed to earlier editions of the Prayer Book and several notable court cases to contend that prayers for the dead were permissible, citing the actual wording of the article and the New Testament as the basis of intercession for 'the Church Expectant'.[20] He thought the 'question seems in general to have been deliberately left open, and the dead would seem to be included in the prayer that 'we and all Thy whole Church may obtain remission of our sins'. The practice was generally discouraged, but not forbidden'.[21] He concluded, in another echo of Newman, that the Church of England's teaching on prayers for the dead and purgatory was a reaction to dangerous and deluded medieval Catholicism rather than the purer form of such beliefs.

On the Sacraments, he thought the Articles were drafted 'decisively on the side of the Catholic faith as against the errors of Protestantism' in the forms of Lutheranism, Zwinglianism and Calvinism. The Articles acknowledged five 'lesser' sacraments noting that the wording of the article – 'those five commonly called Sacraments' – implied no condemnation of the common custom, any more than 'commonly called Christmas Day' [a phrase used in the *Book of Common Prayer*] means that the Feast of the Nativity of our Lord is wrongly so called'.[22] He understood that article to teach a doctrine of baptismal regeneration because this conviction appeared to shape the Prayer Book liturgy. He moderated his position by insisting that the Church should refuse to sanction the 'indiscriminate administration' of baptism and refuse to baptise any child who is 'unlikely to receive Christian education and Confirmation'.[23] The most detailed treatment of any of the Articles addressed those concerned with Holy Communion. He agreed with the Articles' condemnation of the medieval understanding of transubstantiation, accepting that there is 'no local movement and there is no physical change' in the bread and wine. But he insisted that 'Christ is in the sacrament and Christ is in the believer: neither presence is local.'²⁴ Therefore, he contended, Article XXVIII 'in no way denies but rather asserts the doctrine of the Real Presence of our Lord in the Holy Sacrament.' He then defended the reservation of the sacrament for the purpose of communicating the sick, and used this as the platform for advocating the reservation of the Sacrament for devotional purposes for which he sought greater latitude within the Church. This latitude would be consistent with the Church's asserted authority to sanction ceremonies and customs that meet its needs.

On the legal Establishment of the Church of England, Ross stood firmly in the Tractarian tradition in remarking that:

> no Churchman can be happy about the restrictions which are placed on the life of the Church of England as a result of its connection with the state. It is an odd state of affairs, to say no more, when the Church is unable to choose its own apostolic rulers, but is obliged under threat of heavy penalties to accept those whom a perhaps anti-Christian prime ministers chooses to nominate.'²⁵

He accepted that State control of the Church might appear to be 'as bad as any exercised by the Pope' but was relieved that 'state control in England is becoming progressively weaker, and further improvements in the situation may be expected.'

In the latter part of the twentieth century, Canon Arthur Middleton offered a view of the Articles that drew greater attention to Patristic influences in the shape and substance of Anglican theology. He explained that:

> within the contemporary disputes of reform, the Thirty-Nine Articles provided an agreed body of teaching in the Church of England, but not a complete conspectus of religious teaching, and are no more a final exposition of Anglican teaching than the Elizabethan Prayer Book is Anglicanism's final word on liturgy.

He claimed that the 'value of the Articles is temporary, being concerned with disputes particular [to England] in a former age.' He thought an appeal to the Articles is to 'that which is much wider than its own particular age or place, it is to the faith of the universal Church of Christ contained in the Holy Scriptures as interpreted by the

Church from the beginning'. Middleton claimed the Articles embody a return to the religion of the Fathers and undivided Christendom and went on, with the aid of a number of seventeenth and eighteenth century Anglican theologians, to interpret the Articles, the teaching of the Homilies and the doctrine contained in the Prayer Book in the light of Patristic more than Reformed lines.

Anglo-Catholics have generally not shown a great deal of interest in either interpreting or defending the Articles. They have tended to think that the Articles are not a crucial element in the Church's identity nor have Anglo-Catholics traditionally regarded them as an integral part of the Church's outlook. As the Anglo-Catholic theological mentality is not restricted to nor dominated by the sixteenth century, convinced that the entirety of Church history is able to provide valid if not compelling insights that shape both belief and practice, thoughts of reviewing or reforming the Articles are minor concerns. The preference of Anglo-Catholics has been to reinterpret the Articles rather than to revise them, conscious that Evangelicals will oppose the inclusion of Tractarian emphasis in any new wording. Having a different view of the Reformation and its legacy, Anglo-Catholics have consciously ascribed to the Articles a less prominent place in the Church's life and witness and promoted a less rigorous application of the Articles to the teaching and preaching of the clergy. They have been more interested in recovering lost treasures from earlier epochs of Christian experience than abolishing the Articles altogether – which those of more advanced Anglo-Catholic sentiment would prefer.

Broad and Liberal Anglicans and the Articles

Less conspicuous in its origins, the 'Broad Church' or 'Liberal' tradition claimed its origins in Richard Hooker's appeal to human reason, to the policy of comprehension of the Cambridge Platonists in the seventeenth century, to the Latitudinarians in the latter part of the seventeenth century and to eighteenth century philosophers such as Bishop Joseph Butler (1692–1752) and Bishop George Berkeley (1685–1753), who commended Christianity as a rational account of the universe. This Anglican tradition generally disliked what had been referred to as 'Enthusiasm': pious individualism and emotional exuberance. The publication in 1860 of *Essays and Reviews* (a collection

Chapter 4   Assertions, arguments and articles

of radical writings from seven leading theologians) gave the Liberal tradition:

> a focus with an appeal from convention to the freely functioning reason and conscience of the individual, both of which were agents by which humanity could gain a clearer understanding of the divine character and purpose, and the superiority of the character, teaching and accomplishments of Jesus Christ.

As a consequence of this appeal, theologians like FD Maurice found that notwithstanding the new knowledge and enlarged freedom offered by biblical liberalism there was no reason to abandon the essentials or even the peripherals of Christian orthodoxy.

The Liberal Anglican attitude towards the Articles was expressed in the popular work, *An Introduction to the Articles of the Church of England*, which was published by two clerics, George Maclear and WW Williams, in 1896. In contrast to the works by WH Griffith Thomas and Kenneth Ross, this book attempts to steer clear of partisan controversy and to deal only with the matters that were in dispute during the sixteenth century. It is a broad Anglican account reflecting the affiliation of the authors with St Augustine's Missionary College at Canterbury. They do not cover subsequent debates which are, in many respects, of equal importance. Unlike other authors, Maclear and Williams are concerned with the translation of the Latin text of the Articles into modern English and to show other possible renderings. The book also explores variations in translations of the Greek New Testament into English with some commentary on the reliance of Reformation theology on superseded ancient parchments. The authors mention contemporaneous objections to the Articles but refrain from personalising them or attributing them to particular theological parties. In an effort to stand above what they perceived to be theological partisanship, they contended:

> The guiding principle of the Church of England in the sixteenth century was not any wish to found a new church or a novel system of her own, but to return to the old paths; not to make a new, but to bring back the old national church, not to break away from the rest of Christendom, but only to extinguish the unlawful jurisdiction of a proud and bold usurper,

and by following the footsteps of the primitive church to eliminate the distinctly Roman but not Catholic element which has intruded itself into her.[26]

There is, however, an element of unreality to their treatment of the Articles, buffeted as they have been by competing claims and counterclaims which go to the heart of the Articles' meaning.

A number of twentieth century Broad and Liberal Anglican theologians have expressed very different attitudes towards the theological content of the Articles and the place they should be accorded in the Church's life. The Reverend Hensley Henson (1863–1947), the Vicar of Barking and later Bishop of Durham, told readers of the *Guardian* that the 'half-abrogated Articles "cracked and strained by three centuries of evasive ingenuity" are rather a trashy foundation for anything'.[27] During his brief tenure as Archbishop of Canterbury (1942–44), William Temple remarked that 'the movement of my own mind is not towards the rewriting of the Thirty-Nine Articles or the Westminster Confession, but towards the dropping of them all, and the concentration upon such statements as the classical creeds regarded as standard formulations'.[28] WR Matthew, the Dean of St Paul's London (1934–67), declared that the Articles 'do not represent the present mind of the Church'.[29] When he concluded his term as Executive Officer of the Anglican Communion in 1964, Bishop Stephen Bayne described the Articles as 'a kind of monument to an attempt on our part, centuries ago, to show how far we could go in the direction of a confessional attitude without actually adopting one … In any case, they are museum pieces now'.

More recent commentary has been a little more generous towards the Articles. The English theologian and ecumenist Paul Avis contended that Broad Anglicanism, as apart from Liberal Anglicanism, achieves a combination of restraint and affirmation which are held in balance. Concerning restraint, Avis explained that the historic Anglican formularies such as the Prayer Book and the Articles 'conspicuously avoid giving hostages to fanaticism, fundamentalism and dogmatism. The spirit of restraint inhibits these affirmations from becoming instruments of ideological oppression'. Conversely, 'in their character as affirmation they are equally inhospitable to relativism, indifferentism and pragmatism. They do not convey the impression that the truth of the Christian faith and life is either unattainable or of secondary importance'. He suggested that:

> A cursory glance at the Articles will show that they are not a complete account of Christian doctrine, even less an Anglican systematic theology. They are in fact a response to matters of controversy in the sixteenth century. They make certain central affirmations directed against several specific targets: anti-trinitarianism, Roman Catholicism and radical Protestantism.[30]

He also noted opposition to 'a more extreme form of Calvinism than was acceptable in the Church of England is referred to in Article 17 on predestination and election. The approach here encourages speculation and encourages humble trust and practical obedience.'[31]

Judging claims to genuine Anglicanism

Although an advocate for their retention, O'Donovan accepted that the Articles needed some work. He has suggested a number of ways in which the Articles are inadequate and incomplete, and ways in which they might have been extended and enhanced. He noted that the cause of clarity and precision would have been assisted by another approach or a different set of words. But he had great regard for their theology because he understood their context and recognised the questions they were attempting to answer. He did not derive these things from the Articles but from study of the historical documents from which the Articles draw (one might even say plagiarise) and the people and places that had a bearing on the doctrines that were included in the Articles, the order in which they were considered, and why certain matters were overlooked as being either unimportant or uncontroversial – at that time. O'Donovan noted the old textbooks on the Articles, some of which are canvassed above,

> ... were conceived as manuals for induction into a party tradition, comfortably reassuring about what it was permissible for an Anglican parson of the right persuasion to believe, uncomfortably challenging to the doubtful convictions of the other party. They inculcated minute scholarship on details, disagreeable prejudices on generalities. The picture they gave

of the Articles was lopsided, preoccupied by the polemical concerns of the late Victorian age.[32]

He went on:

> It is certainly true that Protestant Anglicans who have championed the Articles have sometimes made claims for their role as a norm of Anglican belief which are too extensive. This has sprung from a desire to interpret the Anglican church as a church of the Reformation, based, like other Reformation churches, upon a great confession. But although the Anglican church is indeed a church of the Reformation, it does not relate to its Reformation origins in quite the same way as other churches do, and its Articles are not exactly comparable, in their conception or in the way they have been used, to the Augsberg or Westminster Confessions or the Heidelberg Catechism ... One might say that Anglicans have taken the authority of the Scriptures and the Catholic creeds too seriously to be comfortable with another single doctrinal norm.[33]

In his observation of the prevailing mood across the Anglican Communion, the American theologian William Sachs noted 'a cacophony of voices with equal claim to being normatively Anglican has risen without a means to mediate between them'. Consequently, the 'history of modern Anglican life reveals a bewildering profusion of claims to be Anglican and a pervasive tension between order and community'.[34] This arises from a number of circumstances and conflicts but, in part, from the absence of a standard against which to test claims. In our view, the Articles can serve that function although they have been the subject of sustained and serious criticism as the next chapter will show.

Notes

1. Oliver O'Donovan, *On The Thirty Nine Articles: A Conversation with Tudor Christianity*, Paternoster Press, Exeter, 1986, p. 8.
2. WH Griffith Thomas, *The Catholic Faith: A Manual of Instruction for Members of the Church of England*, Church Book Room Press, London, 1904.

Chapter 4 Assertions, arguments and articles

3. Griffith Thomas, *The Catholic Faith*, p. 197.
4. Griffith Thomas, *The Catholic Faith*, p. 198.
5. Griffith Thomas, *The Catholic Faith*, p. 198.
6. Richard Turnbull, *Anglican and Evangelical?*, Continuum, London, 2007, p. 14.
7. Turnbull, *Anglican and Evangelical?*, p. 17.
8. Turnbull, *Anglican and Evangelical?*, p. 17.
9. Turnbull, *Anglican and Evangelical?*, p. 93.
10. Hugh McLeod, *Class and Religion in the late Victorian City*, Crook Helm, New York, 1974, p. 248–49.
11. WSF Pickering, Anglo-Catholicism: a study in religious ambiguity, Routledge, London, 1989, p. 2.
12. Peter G Cobb, 'Leader of the Anglo-Catholics?' in Perry Butler (ed.), *Pusey Rediscovered*, SPCK, London, 1983, p.349.
13. Edward Bickersteth, *Remarks on the Progress of Popery*, Macmillan, London, 1836, p. 17.
14. Kenneth N Ross, *The Thirty-Nine Articles*, Mowbray, London, 1957, p. 8.
15. Ross, *The Thirty-Nine Articles*, p. 8.
16. Ross, *The Thirty-Nine Articles*, pp. 8–9.
17. Ross, *The Thirty-Nine Articles*, p. 11.
18. Ross, *The Thirty-Nine Articles*, p. 40.
19. Ross, *The Thirty-Nine Articles*, p. 48.
20. Ross, *The Thirty-Nine Articles*, p. 52.
21. Ross, *The Thirty-Nine Articles*, pp. 52–3.
22. Ross, *The Thirty-Nine Articles*, p. 57.
23. Ross, *The Thirty-Nine Articles*, p. 65.
24. Ross, *The Thirty-Nine Articles*, p. 69.
25. Ross, *The Thirty-Nine Articles*, p. 87.
26. George Maclear and WW Williams, *An Introduction to the Articles of the Church of England*, Macmillan, London, 1896, p. 2.
27. Hensley Henson, *Guardian*, 24 August 1892, p. 1251.
28. FS Temple (ed.), *Some Lambeth Letters, 1942–44*, London, Oxford University Press, 1963, p. 131.
29. WR Matthews, *The Thirty-Nine Articles: An Expanded Version of a Lecture Given at Sion College*, Hodder & Stoughton, London, 1961, p. 17.
30. Paul Avis, *The Anglican Understanding of the Church*, p. 52.

31. Paul Avis, *The Anglican Understanding of the Church*, p. 53.
32. O'Donovan, *On The Thirty Nine Articles*, p. 9.
33. O'Donovan, *On The Thirty Nine Articles*, pp. 11–12.
34. William Sachs, *The Transformation of Anglicanism: From State Church to Global Communion*, Cambridge University Press, Cambridge, 1993, p. 4.

5 Conviction and consensus

Criticisms of the Articles

The preceding chapters have given some hints as to the nature and extent of objections to subscribing to the Articles and criticisms of their content. In addition to those who think that the whole notion of codifying belief is a forlorn project and an intolerable intrusion into the reasonable expression of Christian liberty, those of more fervent Evangelical, Liberal and Anglo-Catholic temperament have also found fault with the Articles and identified areas of possible improvement. The amendments or additions proposed by some Evangelicals and Anglo-Catholics have usually reflected the particular emphases shaping their overall theological position. Those suggested by Liberals have often involved a more expansive and less rigorous attitude to doctrinal assertions and a desire to permit theological development over time. But because the majority of Anglican theologians are licensed clergy who subscribed to the Articles when they were ordained, and because the Articles are included in the Church's historic formularies, those who have disagreed with the content of a particular article or the tone of several articles have tended not to personalise their 'difficulties' in the form of an outright denial for fear of being suspended from their ministerial duties. The most common form of objection, other than to advocate a diminished status for the Articles and their rejection as a test of orthodoxy, is to claim that an article is inconsistent with Anglican belief as it is expressed in the Prayer Book. Another is to claim that the members of a particular party could not conscientiously subscribe to an article because it conflicts with some other belief or practice which is (or has become) part of Anglican 'tradition' or an element of many people's experience of Anglicanism. In this chapter we will explore a range of historic and contemporary objections to the Articles as the basis for suggesting in chapter six some possible additions and amendments of our own.

Catholic objections

The most sustained criticism of the Articles has come from Anglo-Catholics with many echoing the sentiments of the Reverend John Henry Newman who published Tract XC entitled 'Remarks on Certain Passages in the Thirty-Nine Articles' on 25 January 1841. It was the last and most controversial of all the *Tracts for the Times*. Newman was condemned by a number of bishops as a consequence of his handling of the Articles and effectively retired to Littlemore near Oxford to live in virtual monastic seclusion with sympathetic friends in 1842. By then, Newman had moved a considerable distance from his Evangelical roots. In 1836 he had confided privately to his friend Arthur Philip Perceval: 'I am not a great friend of [the Articles] and should rejoice to be able to substitute the Creeds for them.'[1] He had earlier attempted to deal with his growing anxiety about the Articles by drawing a sharp distinction between what he called the 'articles of faith' which referred to beliefs essential to authentic Christianity and mandatory for church membership and 'articles of religion' which he thought served only to clarify these essentials and are not required for church membership. It was the role of the 'Episcopal Tradition' to ensure that the 'articles of faith' were handed down faithfully to the next generation with the truth intact and the role of the 'Prophetical Tradition' to ensure the faith is proclaimed in a manner that speaks to the rising generation without deviating from unchanging divine truth. Newman thought the Creeds belonged to the 'Episcopal Tradition' and the Thirty-Nine Articles to the 'Prophetical Tradition'. Critics objected to this distinction on several grounds including the observation that the Creeds were themselves clarifications of what had already been given to the Church. It was a distinction Newman was unable to preserve and he later abandoned it.

In the introduction to Tract XC, Newman explained that:

> while our Prayer Book is acknowledged on all hands to be of Catholic origin, our articles also, the offspring of an uncatholic age, are, through God's good providence, to say the least, not uncatholic, and may be subscribed by those who aim at being catholic in heart and doctrine.

He argued that 'it is a duty which we owe both to the Catholic Church and to our own, to take our reformed confessions in the most Catholic sense they will admit; we have no duties toward their framers.' He thought that in giving the Articles 'a Catholic interpretation, we bring them in to harmony with the *Book of Common Prayer*, an object of the most serious moment in those who have given their assent to both formularies.' He contended that the declaration that preceded the Articles supported the approach he was commending because 'its enjoining [of] the 'literal and grammatical sense', relieves us from the necessity of making the known opinions of their framers, a comment upon their text.' He went on to argue that 'its forbidding any person to "affix any new sense to any article", was promulgated at a time when the leading men of our Church were especially noted for those Catholic views which have been here advocated.' Newman was convinced that the Articles left open 'large questions' but did not explain how they could be answered. For instance, he wrote, the Articles:

> say that all necessary faith must be proved from Scripture, but they do not say who is to prove it. They say that the Church has authority in controversies, they do not say what authority. They say that it may enforce nothing beyond Scripture, but do not say where the remedy lies when it does. They say the works before grace and justification are worthless and worse, and that works after grace and justification are acceptable, but they do not speak at all of works with God's aid, before justification. They say that men are lawfully called and sent to minister and preach, who are chosen and called by men who have public authority given them in the congregation to call and send; but they do not add by whom the authority is to be given. They say that councils called by princes may err;

they do not determine whether councils called in the name of Christ will err.

Newman almost defiantly claimed that Anglican Catholics were:

> the successors and representatives of [the] moderate reformers; and their case has been directly anticipated in the wording of the Articles. It follows that they are not perverting, they are using them, for an express purpose for which among others their authors framed them. The interpretation they take was intended to be admissible; though not that which their authors took themselves. Had it not been provided for, possibly the Articles never would have been accepted by our Church at all. If, then, their framers have gained their side of the compact in effecting the reception of the Articles, the Catholics have theirs too in retaining their own Catholic interpretation of them ... The Protestant Confession was drawn up with the purpose of including Catholics; and Catholics now will not be excluded. What was an economy in the reformers, is a protection to us. What would have been a perplexity to us then, is a perplexity to Protestants now. We could not then have found fault with their words; they cannot now repudiate our meaning.

Conscious of the reactions that Tract XC might prompt, Newman conceded that:

> It may be objected that the tenor of the above explanations is anti-Protestant, whereas it is notorious that the Articles were drawn up by Protestants, and intended for the establishment of Protestantism; accordingly, that it is an evasion of their meaning to give them any other than a Protestant drift, possible as it may be to do so grammatically, or in each separate part.

But he nonetheless insisted that he was not actively anti-Protestant but pro-Catholic.

Newman was reviled for distortion, duplicity and disloyalty after publishing Tract XC. He was accused of interpreting the Articles in a manner that was self-serving and conniving. He was disparaged for holding beliefs and drawing a salary from an institution he obviously wanted to undermine. He was reviled for advancing the cause of the Roman Church while overlooking its sins and shortcomings. The Hebdomadal Board of Oxford University determined that Tract XC promoted a warped sense of the Thirty-Nine Articles and 'reconciled subscription to them with the adoption of errors they were designed to counteract.'

When Newman was received into the Roman Catholic Church in 1845, those who claimed that Tractarian thinking inevitably led to Rome felt vindicated. Scholars are divided largely on party lines in their opinions of Newman's summation of the Articles, with some labelling it 'clever' and others 'courageous'. But even his Anglican admirers think he went too far in claiming for them an exclusive 'Catholic' character. The Anglo-Catholic Bishop of London, William Wand (1885–1977), writing in 1951, thought it 'would be useless to deny the generally 'Reformed' tone of the Articles.[2] The Anglican Benedictine monk, Dom Gregory Dix (1901–52), found difficulty in determining where the Catholicism of the Articles ends and where its Protestantism begins, concluding that the doctrine of justification by faith was the line of demarcation.[3] But Newman's interpretation of the Articles nonetheless prompted a good deal of spirited discussion and debate about their meaning and function.

By 1850, Anglo-Catholics were concerned that their defining beliefs were inconsistent or incompatible with the Articles and fearful that the Articles might be used as a weapon against them. Those who shared many of Newman's views but preferred to work for the English Church's reunion with the Papal See made the Articles the focus of sustained criticism and complaint. A correspondent with the *Church News* writing in 1867 commented that:

> Almost all sincere Reunionists would allow that whatever temporary advantages accrued from the setting forth of the Thirty-Nine Articles three centuries ago, very great permanent disadvantages have followed from their continued retention in the English Church since. They have done little good at home and untold mischief abroad. For there are some Articles which, unless their language is duly weighed and carefully examined, sound very startling in the ears of foreign Catholics, whether Greeks or Latins .... Of late years, however,

so many contradictory explanations of them have been given ... that they might be quietly set aside, to the great advantage of religion and morality in the Church of England.[4]

The *Christian Remembrancer* declared that it was 'impossible to deny that they contain statements, or implications, that are verbally false, and others that are difficult to reconcile with truth. In the times that are coming over the Church of England, the question will arise: what have the Articles of the Church of England ever done? ... Before reunion with Rome can be effected, the Thirty-Nine Articles must be wholly withdrawn.'[5]

By 1870, many Anglo-Catholics had been persuaded that the Articles blighted the Church of England. After referring to Article XXV as 'perhaps the most obnoxious' because of its allegedly dismissive attitude towards Confirmation, Penance, Orders, Matrimony and Extreme Unction, and denouncing Article XXXI because it appeared to be 'denying the Eucharistic Sacrifice', the Reverend Archer Gurney told readers of the *Church Review* that 'the sooner we are rid of the Thirty-Nine Articles the better. We can, and we must, and do put a Catholic interpretation on them as they are, but this is only making the best of a bad matter.'[6] The *Union Review* recommended the 'total abolition' of the Articles as a first step towards the reunion of Christendom. Before complaining that Article VI 'distinctly ignores Tradition' and 'positively affirms private judgement', the *Union Review* alleged that some of the Articles:

> contain statements which are unintelligible; in the case of others, one is tempted to wish that the statements were unintelligible or non-sensical in order to escape the disagreeable impression of their being – well, truly Protestant; others contain contradictions or qualifications which eviscerate or destroy what has gone before; there are statements of facts which are not wholly indisputable, there are trivial points of Christian discipline or of everyday life, which derogate from the importance and value of a confession of faith.[7]

The *Union Review* was angry that 'with all these defects and blemishes, the Thirty-Nine Articles continue to be paraded as *the* authoritative standard of Anglican doctrine, and they are imposed as a heavy yoke upon the consciences of all who would serve in the ministry of the

Church'. The attack continued throughout the nineteenth century as the Anglo-Catholic cause gained momentum and converts.

In his very popular work *The Catholic Religion: A Manual of Instruction for Members of the Church of England* first published in 1893, Canon Vernon Staley (1853–1933) told his readers that the Articles 'are not Articles of Faith like the Creeds, and they are not imposed on members of the Anglican Church as necessary terms of communion.'[8] He explained that the Articles 'would be understood by the clergy who first subscribed to them as Articles of Peace for the preservation of unity.' Because they are not religious tests, 'they were made as comprehensive as possible, and they were to be interpreted and understood in accordance with the general rule of catholic tradition, ie., in the Catholic sense.' Attracted by Newman's approach to the Articles in Tract XC, Staley repeated several of Newman's assertions including the claim that the Articles did not condemn the notion of purgatory, only 'the Romish doctrine' of purgatory. The article was not, he said, focussed on 'the primitive doctrine of the intermediate state as we have stated it.'[9] He took the same view of Article XXII's condemnation of 'the Romish doctrine concerning invocation of saints', arguing that the objection was to a 'system of prayer to the saints which led to their being regarded otherwise than as exalted suppliants.'[10] Staley asserted that belief in 'the saints who have gone before to pray for us has always been the belief of the Church'. Likewise, he alleged that the Articles did not reject the Catholic idea of a Eucharistic sacrifice but the misguided medieval notion that each Eucharist was 'regarded as a distinct act of sacrifice, possessing its own independent value' so that the more Eucharists that were offered for the dead – something the article refers to as 'sacrifices of Masses' – the sooner their suffering in purgatory would end.[11] This was not the most straightforward reading of the article and was a weak basis for building a case for the Eucharist having any sacrificial element. Staley also invoked Article VI 'On the Sufficiency of Holy Scriptures for Salvation' to exhort his readers to buy a Bible that included the Apocrypha because, he explained, 'no Bible is really complete which does not contain these books.'[12] This is not the teaching of the article and Staley's advice is, in fact, contrary to the article's intention.

For the greatest part of the twentieth century, Anglo-Catholics did not want to see the Articles amended, revised or expanded. Their consistent plea was for liberty to read the Articles in a manner that allowed them freedom for the promotion of specific beliefs and the conduct of certain rituals. Their concerns were confined mainly to the doctrine of the Church and the provision of the Sacraments.

Liberal Objections

Anglican Liberals shared the Latitudinarian dislike for formal subscription to the Articles by the clergy although they objected more because they actually disagreed with elements of its doctrine than because they were committed to the expansion of individual liberty. A leading Liberal, Professor GWH Lampe, the Ely Professor of Divinity at Cambridge, suggested in 1964 that the Articles should cease to be treated 'as an official exposition of the doctrinal position of the Church of England'. The Church should not require subscription to them, he said, or 'substitute any new 'articles' for them'.[13] He did not think the Articles have ever been 'regarded as the last word in the interpretation of the Christian revelation within our Church'. Their 'real purpose', he asserted, was to 'provide our Church with an appropriate doctrinal label: to identify the Church of England'. The Articles 'explain the theological reason for the existence of the Church of England as a particular national church in a divided Christendom ... [and serve to] justify its distinctive position as one of the Churches of the Reformation, and hence to clarify the main issues on which it took its stand in opposition to what it held to be the errors of others'.[14] Lampe argued that the 'drafting is sometimes remarkably loose and the language obscure'. He was also concerned that the drafters may not have realised the 'full logical consequences' of the position they had taken. Lampe also disputed Jim Packer's claim that the Articles occupied a position analogous to the Creeds within England, contending that the Homilies were nearer to presenting a systematic theology than the Articles. While he did not think that anyone who ascribes to Roman or Anabaptist teaching can claim, in good conscience, that their position represented a valid Anglican tradition, Lampe concluded that the Articles do not represent 'the 'real' mind of the Church of England today'.[15] He thought they were 'based on a conception of revelation and of authority in doctrine' which no longer met with 'general acceptance'.

Lampe contended that:

doctrinal inferences are subject to reinterpretation from age to age; to confirmation in the light of the continuing experience of the Christian society; to modification and re-expression in different terms in response to fresh insights mediated through God's gift of new knowledge about the world and about ourselves, through the changes which the hand of God brings about in the structure of human society and in the process of what we are pleased to call 'secular' events.[16]

He drew attention to the work of the Holy Spirit who 'guides the Church into all truth. The whole truth is not to be ascertained at any single point in history. It always lies ahead'. Lampe also noted deepening views of biblical inspiration and the development of more sophisticated biblical exegesis, including among Evangelical Anglicans. Because the authority of Anglican doctrinal formulations 'does not rest upon any imposed *magisterium* but upon the free consensus of the Church's membership as a whole', he held that 'the process of interpreting the data of revelation and their implications is dialectical ... It is a matter of hammering out an agreed understanding by the slow process of argument and discussion ... It is a process which must always remain incomplete in this life, always partial, unfinished, and subject to correction, revision and supplementation'. This effectively precluded the possibility of regarding any formulary as final, including the Creeds which he said are 'not necessarily the 'last word'. In principle, they are open to revision'.[17] In the context of ecumenical dialogue, he was not inclined to think they even expressed 'the Church's position *vis-à-vis* other churches'. Nor did the Articles disclose the Church's attitude to 'the religious and moral issues of our time'. He suggested that 'it is very doubtful whether any single document could do this in the present circumstances'.[18]

While he took issue with some of the articles on theological grounds, for instance, disputing their teaching on grace and predestination at several points, he thought the 'real objection to revision is the impossibility of securing agreement on how it should be done'. In what might have appeared a rather pessimistic attitude given his previous preference for theological deliberation being undertaken in dialogue, he thought that differences between Anglicans 'are too great to permit it, and they are likely to increase rather than diminish, unless we can learn how to listen and discuss in a better spirit than we do at present'.[19] Nevertheless, he thought the 'ultimate goal, lying far ahead, would probably be the emergence of a new confession, but this would be more broadly based than the Articles'. He suggested that any new confession ought to have ecumenical agreement but should not serve as a test of orthodoxy. He did not think dispensing with the Articles would weaken the unity of the Church because, he asserted, the Articles were not even then serving to strengthen its unity. Conscious that Evangelicals might have feared the loss of the Reformed character of Anglicanism if the Articles are abandoned, he asked them to have faith because 'if those beliefs are true and if those who hold them are prepared to take their full part in the process of exploration and conversation, there is every ground for confidence that they will prevail'.[20]

Twenty years later, little progress had been made along the lines Lampe had proposed and Liberals maintained their campaign against the Articles. Writing in 1983, the English liberal ecclesiastical historian JRH Moorman remarked that 'two documents of the Anglican Church – the Ten Commandments and the Thirty-Nine Articles – are both very much loved by the laity and the Evangelical wing'.[21] After explaining that the Articles 'represent what was the teaching of the Church in the sixteenth century' and noting that 'things have changed considerably since then', he claimed that 'predestination and election are something which not many members of the Anglican Communion would nowadays accept' nor did he think they would accept the Articles' assessment of 'works done before justification'.[22] He thought the Articles' condemnation of Roman beliefs and practices to be 'a hard judgement' and alleged that those articles dealing with the authority of Scripture and the nature of salvation were 'either Lutheran or Calvinist in their origin'. He appeared pleased that the Articles are 'ceasing to have the authority which was once theirs. They are no longer read by clergy on accepting any position in the Church, nor are they regarded as a test of loyalty and orthodoxy'.[23]

The attitude of contemporary Liberals is largely unchanged. Most seek an end to formal subscription to the Articles and a majority do not generally feel themselves bound to teach the doctrine contained in the Articles or to comply with their disciplinary provisions. Liberals are generally opposed to the development of new or replacement Articles.

Evangelical Defences

Evangelical Anglicans have traditionally been the foremost advocates and defenders of the Articles because, it is claimed, they protect and preserve the Reformed identity of the English Church and provide a faithful Biblical witness to the distinctive features of Anglicanism. The leading English Evangelical, Jim Packer, insisted that the Thirty-Nine Articles supplied 'the only legally valid answer to the question: what version of Christianity does the Church of England hold and, more particularly, where does she stand with reference to Reformation cleavages?'[24] He referred to the Articles as the 'domestic creed of the *ecclesia Anglicana*' and contends that this standing remains. He regarded the Articles as being 'full and exact on all central issues of the Gospel' and thinks the Articles are 'nowhere narrower or more exclusive than they have to be, and their own definitions were, it seems, always made as broad and comprehensive as was thought consistent with theological safety'.[25] He acknowledged that in the first 150 years after the Articles were first promulgated:

> the pendulum of theological opinion was swinging all the time: from the modified Lutheran outlook of Cranmer and his colleagues to the more scholastic Calvinist position of [John] Jewel, [John] Whitgift, [William] Perkins and [William] Whitaker; thence, partly in reaction, partly through Greek patristic and philosophical influence, to the 'churchy' Arminianism of the Carolines and the moralistic Arminianism of the Latitudinarians ... All this being so, it is no wonder that different interpretative traditions grew up, different theologians expounding the Articles from different standpoints and in the light of different estimates of the significance of the Reformation.[26]

Packer acknowledged that none of the major schools of thought within Anglicanism 'can easily be denied the right to exist in the reformed Church of England, whatever our convictions may be about the issues that divide them'.[27] But he contended that every school of thought is obliged to reconcile their claims with the Articles because they have 'the authority proper to a creed'. After explaining why he believed the word 'creed' is a suitable label for the Articles, he defended his position by noting that 'the Articles contain a great deal more than the ecumenical creeds' and deserve the same, if not more, respect. He concluded that the Articles:

> exhibit not only the same doctrine as other Reformation confessions do, but also the same concern to identify the faith they confess with the faith of the Fathers and the New Testament, and the same conviction that the road they fence is, in fact, the highroad to catholicity, from which Romans and Anabaptists alike had gone astray. Like the rest of the Reformation confessions, the Articles are a domestic creed, and their authority must be understood accordingly.[28]

Packer argued that the 'collective authority of the Articles derives from the Scriptures and, in so doing, is in the nature of a universal call to ensure Biblical fidelity and consistency in every time and place'. The Anglican Articles 'come to us as prior judgements, time-honoured judgements, on specific issues relating to the faith of Christ, as set forth in the Scriptures.' They have the authority, he thought, of a 'faithful witness'. They provided for an 'evangelical comprehensiveness' that sought to keep 'doctrinal requirements down to the minimum … allowing the maximum of flexibility and variety on secondary matters'. They were, however, intended to unite the clergy in 'teaching an Augustinian doctrine of sin and a Reformed doctrine of justification and grace'.[29] Together with the Creeds, the Articles are 'reassertions of the gospel in the face of particular errors'. He considered it a 'prime obligation for Anglicans to take full account of the expository formulations to which our Church has bound itself; and to ignore them, as if we were certain that the Spirit of God had no hand in them, is no more warrantable than it is to treat them as divinely inspired and infallible.'[30] Did he believe they were in need of revision? Packer thought the suggestion was 'impracticable (for no revision could command general agreement) and misconceived. You do not revise creeds; instead, you draw up further statements to supplement them'. He felt it 'no more proper to alter the Articles than to alter the creeds' because he feared changing the Articles, assuming they truly teach Catholic doctrine, might give the impression of retreating from Catholic doctrine 'and, to that extent, jeopardise the catholicity of Anglicanism'. What kinds of matters might appear in a supplementary set of articles? There might be a case, he conceded, for dealing with questions about '(for instance) creation, providence, and common grace' because they are matters 'on which the Articles scarcely touch'.[31] It is very obvious, however, that Packer's strong preference is for the Articles to remain unamended and without augmentation. He was convinced that they safeguarded authentic Anglican belief and concluded that any revision was a risky undertaking best avoided.

A similarly conservative view of the Articles has been offered by Broughton Knox (1916–94), the Principal of Moore Theological College from 1959–85, in *The Thirty-Nine Articles: The Historic Basis of Anglican Faith* first published in 1967.[32] This work deserves detailed attention because it is one of the few Australian expositions on the content and function of the Articles in modern Anglicanism. It is likely that the manuscript for this book began life as a set of lectures on doctrine delivered to ordinands. Knox's biographer, Marcia Cameron, described it as a 'short densely written book of 91 pages with sparse footnotes (34 in all)'.[33] While noting that it was intended to 'explain the doctrinal expression of Anglicanism', she claimed it 'somewhat paradoxically' showed 'unmistakable signs that Broughton was becoming less Anglican'. He used this discussion of the Articles to propound his own doctrine of the Church and to stress the place of propositional revelation – a position for which he had become widely known in Anglican circles. Cameron thought that in this small book Knox was 'at his best: clear, intellectually sparkling, reflective, readable and pastorally acute'.[34]

Broughton Knox claimed not only that the Articles were an historic document, but that 'they remain a guide to the doctrines which the ministers of the Church of England are required to believe and teach'.[35] The full title of the Articles, he pointed out, discloses their intent: 'for Establishing of Consent touching True Religion'. Knox understood this to mean that they are normative and not merely descriptive; they are 'to establish and not merely reflect the mind of the Church'[36] although the entitlement of Convocations to devise and prescribe the Articles is not explored. Knox explained that the Articles were 'not designed as a comprehensive survey of Christian belief or a complete theological system'. This explained their 'somewhat eclectic character and emphasis'. They were, he contended, 'intended to control the teaching within the Church of England and to mark the limits of its comprehension'.[37] In terms of the relationship between the Articles and the other formularies, Knox argued that the *Book of Common Prayer* ought to be interpreted in the light of the Articles and not the reverse because to do so would be 'reversing the purposes for which the Articles were agreed upon. The Articles were designed to be the agreed doctrinal basis within which the Prayer Book is to be used and interpreted'. This view was contrary to the conclusion of the Church of England Doctrine Commission in 1968.

In response to those Anglicans who argued that the Articles did not reflect the 'mind of the Church', Knox had this to say:

> It is, of course, highly desirable that the Articles should reflect the common mind of the Church, but that they should be altered to reflect that mind does not follow, for it may be that the mind of the Church should be altered to reflect the teaching of the Articles ... The Articles, then, are to be normative, not merely descriptive; they are to establish and not merely reflect the mind of the Church.[38]

Knox regarded any movement calling for 'cancelling of the requirement for assent' to be consistent with 'the present temper of Protestantism which since the rise of pietism (as exampled by the Quakers) has seen the progressive eroding of the importance of dogma in Christianity'.[39] He warned that there is 'no future for undogmatic Christianity ... because Christianity is essentially, and always has been historically, a dogmatic religion'. Although he did not think that local congregations needed the Articles because they were the venues where the Word of God was rightly preached and faithfully ministered, entities like denominational associations that lacked a biblical prototype were in need of something like the Articles because:

> Scripture itself was not written as a document for a basis of association of churches and it is not suitable for this purpose. Yet a doctrinal basis of association is necessary especially when the association takes a form in which the churches hand over to the central organisation of the association so many vital matters which concern their own continuance as truly Christian churches.[40]

Knox does not admit any inadequacy or failing in the Articles. He makes no concession to any critic of any article other than possible scope for 'a verbal revision ... to remove some of the obscurities of the language in order to make clear their original meaning' although he judged the effort involved to be out of proportion to the benefits. He accepted that 'some matters' have less importance now than 400 years ago but felt even these statements should stand 'since they are in themselves correct'. There may be 'room for a supplementary confession' but he seemed far from convinced. His book inferred that any admission of the need for the Articles to be revised might weaken the Reformed character of historic Anglicanism or diminish the respect properly owed to the Reformers.

But not all Evangelicals have been so content with the Articles. In a set of essays entitled *Liberal Evangelicalism: An Interpretation* published in 1923, a group of prominent English clergy attempted to outline an agenda for change and reviewal within the Church of England.[41] In a chapter entitled 'Religious Authority', the Reverend Guy Rogers, a chaplain to the King, claimed that in the sixteenth century the Articles could be regarded as 'a charter of freedom' but in the twentieth century they had become 'a fetter to progress'. He was adamant that 'no evangelical is likely to under-value the Articles as a whole'. Indeed, he thought the Articles:

> protect the New Testament doctrine of salvation from the abuses of priestcraft. They have preserved the Church of England from the sectarian attitude of the Church of Rome towards questions of Church order. They witness to the necessity of divine grace at every point of human life. They provide a balanced doctrine of the sacraments.[42]

Rogers contended that contemporary gratitude to the Reformers for their work was diminished by submitting the Articles to 'too severe a strain.' He observed that 'some of the controversies upon which they are supposed to adjudicate have either disappeared altogether, or have passed into another phase, in which the particular article which refers to them can be of little service'. He thought that 'no-one accepts the wording of all the Articles now, in precisely the same sense and with precisely the same nuances as those who drew them up'. He did not think it unreasonable after three centuries to expect that the Articles 'might well require supplement or revision'. Rogers, and those of like mind, did not believe the articles were 'fixed' statements of belief in like manner to the Creeds or the Decisions of General Councils. He thought they were open to inquiry and the possibility of modification. This judgement reflected his broader sentiment that 'progress is the law of theology as well as of science, and the truth at which we can arrive at any given moment is only relative'. He thought it contrary to the profession of a dynamic faith in Christ 'to pre-judge a living issue today by what Thomas Aquinas "said" or what the Articles "allow"'. Notably, a copy of the book held by the authors contains a pencilled margin note from the book's initial owner alongside the remarks quoted above. It reads: 'The Articles are an "agreed" interpretation of Scripture. A Minister of the C of E, having subscribed to them, should resign if he ceases to agree to them'.

More recently, Evangelicals have drawn attention to the Articles in an attempt to remind their fellow Anglicans of their Church's historic formularies in the midst of considerable doctrinal exploration and redefinition.

Australian commentaries

Few other Australian commentators have dealt with the Articles in detail. Bruce Kaye has attempted a critique that sets them firmly in their historic context as statements of Reformed English belief. He noted that the Reformers were 'aware of German confessions such as that of Württemberg and Augsberg, particularly on the Eucharist. Only Article XVII gives any hint of the shadow of John Calvin, and that hint really only must rely on an anachronistic reading of the article. The Articles therefore cannot be described as Calvinist or Lutheran. They are in fact Anglican'.[43] He asked his reader to note that the Articles are 'a mixture of positive statements and polemical denial' with the latter 'directed against two fronts, Roman Catholicism and radical Protestantism'. After observing that half of the articles are polemical in content, Kaye pointed out that the 'positive and substantial items are not extensive'. While rejecting the notion that 'everything is absolutely relative', he counselled readers to be aware that 'the nuances and direction of the Articles ... are expressed in the terms of their historical circumstances and of Tudor theology'.[44]

To illustrate his point, Kaye noted that the description of God in Article I as being 'without parts or passions' employs 'Neo-Platonic terms filtered through the perspective of Augustine'. While his knowledge of the period and acquaintance with classical philosophy allowed him to understand what the drafters of the article were trying to say, he explained that 'the difficulty with the terminology [of the Article] if taken simply on its own, as if it were all that might be said, is that its thrust might deceive us into thinking of God in distant, perhaps even deistical, terms'. He noted other articles, such as XIX 'Of the Church' which touches on the visible Church of God, implied a subsequent discussion that never occurs. In effect, the treatment of some subjects was incomplete and, therefore, inadequate given all that might usefully be said about a particular subject. The order in which the articles appear also implied a great deal about Anglican theological foundations, ecclesiastical organisation and Christian discipleship. When taken together, the Articles are 'very strong in their commitment to the Catholic Christian belief about God as Trinitarian, the reliability of Scripture for what it is necessary to believe for salvation, and the central effect of faith in sin and salvation. Yet they are nevertheless strikingly open on the subjects of church, sacraments and ministry'.[45] He contrasted the precision with which they defined the Church with the lack of a 'precise theological definition or rationale offered for the three-fold order of bishops, priests and deacons'. Other than the requirement that ministry in the Church be properly authorised, it is not until Article XXXVI that there is commentary on ministry and it is limited to the efficacy of the Ordinal. Finally, he detected from the Articles a sense in which 'there is such a thing as genuine development which takes place under the providential guiding of the life of the Church by God. In that context the church has the authority to decide'.[46]

In contrast to Kaye's exploration of the Articles and their continuing importance to the Church as an indicator of an Anglican theological method, other Australian commentaries are brief or discursive. In her self-consciously partisan book *The New Puritans*, Melbourne lay-woman Muriel Porter claimed that 'increasingly in Sydney, commitment to the Articles is used as a yardstick of orthodoxy' and claims the Sydney Diocese has elevated the Articles 'to a position just below holy writ'. After noting that the Articles are 'the product of compromise', she declared that 'in my mind', the Articles are 'a quaintly worded, seriously limited summary of Anglican understandings of faith and doctrine, which are scarcely relevant to modern Australian life'. She contended that 'in some areas, they are now directly contradictory to current Christian teaching' but acknowledged that 'theologians who have studied them closely take a more positive view'. In describing the Articles as a 'confession of faith' that was necessary to 'win clarity' in areas not covered by the Creeds 'which were designed to reflect the agreed beliefs of all Christians', the Melbourne Evangelical scholar Rhys Bezzant believed the Articles highlighted 'beliefs which were yet to be reconciled with other Christian understandings'. Consequently, the Articles 'are not structured to list error *tout court*, but to promote sound doctrine, and only then to demonstrate distance from either Roman Catholic or Anabaptist views'.

General criticisms

The most widely expressed criticism of the Articles focuses on the gaps in the treatment of the doctrines that are canvassed and the absence of any reference to doctrines that deserve to be mentioned. The inclusion of some doctrines and the exclusion of others could imply that the beliefs upon which the Articles focus are core beliefs while all other matters are of secondary importance or peripheral to the Christian life. While the doctrine of the Trinity is compressed into one short article, the doctrine of election is four times the length. While the Articles are derived principally from Scripture, there are a number of critical Christian beliefs that could be drawn from Scripture about which the Articles say nothing while several articles deal with events that occurred subsequent to the compilation of Scripture and about which Scripture is silent. For example, the Articles say nothing about creation and almost nothing about eschatology. They embody an opinion on matters such as the place of General Councils, the mandate of civil authority and the ordering of Christian ministry that cannot reasonably claim to be the last or the only possible word on the subject. The character of the Articles' content and the context in which they were written is not without enduring consequences while the vision of social life portrayed in the Articles conveniently reflects the aspirations of the Elizabethan ruling elite rather than anything derived from the Bible. The life and witness of Jesus is almost completely overlooked and we learn nothing about the coming Kingdom of God – the focus of Jesus' preaching and teaching – from the Articles.

We are also entitled to ask questions about the link between the Articles and the Catechism given that the latter does not include the prohibitions and polemics featured in the Articles. Of course, they serve a different purpose but they do not exist in isolation. Nor does the Prayer Book exist as a stand-alone statement of Anglican belief. Another problem is contemporary disputes about the Articles descending into historical arguments about the times and temperament of the Reformers, details of which are beyond our reach. In this respect, the Church finds itself in a similar position to the High Court of Australia which needs to interpret the Constitution in the light of the intentions of the drafters, whose motives and aspirations are not altogether consistent or clear. Unlike the Australian Constitution, the Articles do not contain any means or mechanism by which they might be reviewed, amended or re-worded. This was a serious omission on the part of the drafters who knew that points of dispute in theology change over time and arguments for a particular position improve gradually.

There is also, according to some commentators, an element of literalism and descriptive over-statement in the Articles which they contend make them liable to mislead readers who might be deprived of a proper sense of God's grandeur and glory. An example sometimes cited is Article IV which states that when Christ was resurrected he 'took again his body, with flesh, bones, and all things appertaining to the perfection of Man's nature; wherewith he ascended into heaven'. While the Biblical texts emphasise that Jesus' resurrection was indeed a bodily one, his resurrection body was more than a physical body contained by temporal realities or affected by human mortality. The Reformers wanted quite correctly to affirm the physicality of the resurrection but it is possible, some have contended, that in the minds of believers this article could be misunderstood in a manner that diminishes the glory of the Risen Jesus and which distorts perceptions of the Ascended Christ. In effect, the desire to define doctrine too tightly or too emphatically might obscure the majesty and mystery of God. The concern here is a due regard for the limitations of human language and the capacity of words to obscure rather than illuminate that which they seek to describe. It is this kind of objection that Bishop Stephen Neill has in mind when he contends that the Articles 'state truth in forms which are no longer acceptable to the modern mind'.[47]

Other commentators, such as the compilers of the *Oxford Dictionary of the Christian Church*, draw attention to the 'masterly ambiguity' of the Articles. In 1595, Lord Burghley (otherwise known as William Cecil) noted with some pride that the Articles were deliberately ambiguous on certain points before declaring that there were matters too mysterious for even the Archbishop of Canterbury to comprehend. The English-born liturgical scholar Peter Toon (1939–2009) took the opposite view. He claimed the 'the Articles are certainly not ambiguous (when interpreted historically and contextually) but they are minimal in their requirements, leaving many secondary questions open'. He argued that they were originally laid down 'to secure Catholic faith and ordered life in the Church of England; and they do not seek to go past the minimum. On the central issues of the Gospel they are full and exact. Yet they are as broad and comprehensive as was deemed to be consistent with theological safety'. And yet, on some matters the Articles appear to recoil from answering some of the most pressing questions.

Critics often point to Article VI which explains that Scripture contains all things necessary for salvation and that nothing is to be required for salvation that cannot be proved by Scripture. And yet, they note, the Articles do not disclose the identity of those who will determine what is to be considered necessary and what constitutes proof. Does the individual determine what is necessary and what can be proved by their own reading of the Bible or must they rely upon and submit to the collective judgement of the Christian community? When Article VI is read in conjunction with Article XX, observers are entitled to inquire about the role of the Church and to seek clarification of the force and effect of tradition in settling disputes over doctrine. Some have argued that individuals must read the Bible carefully and prayerfully, and not be swayed by the judgements of their neighbours. Others have contended that the Bible must be read with an awareness of the teaching of the Church and the weight of tradition. Bishop Gilbert Burnet (1643–1715) of Salisbury writing in 1699 argued that Christian believers must read the Bible free from the demands of the Church and the dictates of tradition.[48] JH Newman took a different view, drawing attention to Anglicanism's 'double rule': that 'Scripture is interpreted by Tradition, Tradition is verified by Scripture'. But the question remains: who has responsibility for the verifying? The article seems to suggest that the task rests more with the individual and the exercise of private judgement than the Church and its collective counsel. This implies that the Reformers had a high view of Scripture and great confidence in its Spirit-shaped reception. They were certainly conscious of the dangers of excluding individual interpretation and private judgement, and it was their desire to avoid them that prompted a more positive view of the Bible and its spiritual efficacy.

There was also the emerging debate about historical subjectivity and the presence of identifiably ideological approaches to history. Appeals to the past were also influenced by individual interpretation and private judgement, and had no stronger claim to reliability. There is no evidence that historians agree more in the interpretations of the past than theologians do on the interpretation of Scripture. This is not to say that dominant, persuasive or even accepted interpretations of Scripture are beyond reach. There is evidence of convergence and agreement on doctrine when the Bible is approached in a manner that is consonant with Scripture's claims about itself. But there is no theory of revelation or account of biblical inspiration in the Articles. It accepts that reason and tradition have some part to play but does not determine where and when and how they are operative, other than to insist that the counsel of Scripture is final. The Articles do not discuss the teaching of the Church Fathers but they appeal to the reputation of Saints Jerome (347–420) and Augustine (354–430) to settle disputed points of doctrine. It has been suggested that the Christian faith is revealed in Scripture, outlined in the Creeds, proclaimed by the Church and clarified in formularies. On the matters canvassed in this paragraph, the Articles stopped short of clarity.

The Articles also include an element of provisionality: they are to be believed on the proviso that they accord with the teaching of Scripture. If it can be shown that they are in error or distort Scripture, they are no longer binding. The drafters of the Articles also presumed that they would be amended and augmented. Indeed, they believed themselves entitled to do just that in the process of drafting the document which was approved in 1571. The Articles are not, therefore, set in stone. They are not Scripture nor are they infallible. The whole notion of producing 'Articles of Religion' implied they were working documents that would evolve as theological insights deepened and theological controversies came and went. They were never intended to be complete or comprehensive statements of Anglican belief. There is nothing final about either the Articles or their promulgation. Regrettably, the text was not reviewed or revised by the Church when conditions more conducive to such action prevailed. Consequently, the Articles were tethered to the Reformation period and appeared to be the final word when a range of new controversies subsequently arose that required equally firm clarification of doctrine. The Articles might have been expanded to cover those elements of doctrine in both extreme Protestant and Papal directions that needed to be opposed. As a result the Church was unable to deal with a range of disputes in the nineteenth century and with time orthodox Anglican belief gradually became whatever individual Anglicans claimed it to be.

The Archbishops' Doctrine Commission mentioned earlier noted the number of issues that were as important in the twentieth century as those upon which the Reformers felt the need to comment in 1571 but about which the Articles offer no guidance. For instance, the bishops asked, 'what is the Christian's duty to a secular state? What about developments in urbanisation and technology? Race? Ecumenism? Other religions? Science and religion?' The list could go on. There is, then, no good reason why the Church should not amend a set of statements that relate to questions, issues and concerns from 450 years ago to canvas matters of equal pertinence in this third millennium after Christ. Put simply: the Anglican Church is no longer concerned with many of the subjects that were of such concern in 1571. Certainly for the Australian Church the denial of the Pope's authority in England has never been of much interest while the importance of conducting divine worship in a language people can understand has been a given for some time.

Before proposing some amendments and suggesting some additions to the Articles that deal with some of the more valid criticisms outlined in this chapter, the following chapter will survey a range of modern confessions, declarations and statements in the hope of finding contemporary answers to historic questions, and areas of new

Chapter 5   Conviction and consensus

and emerging difference between Christians within and beyond the Anglican Church.

Notes

1. John Henry Newman to Perceval, quoted in the Henry Parry Liddon (ed.), *Life of Edward Bourverie Pusey*, vol. I, Longmans, London, 1894, p. 301.
2. William Wand, *What the Church of England Stands For*, Mowbray, London, 1951, p. 62.
3. Dom Gregory Dix, *The Question of Anglican Orders*, Dacre Press, Westminster, 1944.
4. *Church News*, 21 August 1867, p. 367.
5. *Christian Remembrancer*, no. 131, p. 188.
6. *Church Review*, 3 January 1863, pp. 9–10.
7. *Union Review*, 1870, p. 289.
8. Vernon Staley, *The Catholic Religion: A Manual of Instruction for Members of the Anglican Communion*, Mowbray, Oxford, 1893, p. 385.
9. Staley, *The Catholic Religion*, p. 194.
10. Staley, *The Catholic Religion*, p. 223.
11. Staley, *The Catholic Religion*, p. 301.
12. Staley, *The Catholic Religion*, p. 342.
13. GWH Lampe, 'The Revision of the Articles' in JC de Satge, JI Packer, HGG Herklots and GWH Lampe, *The Articles of the Church of England*, Star Books, London, 1964, pp. 91–2.
14. Lampe, 'The Revision of the Articles', p. 94.
15. Lampe, 'The Revision of the Articles', p. 98.
16. Lampe, 'The Revision of the Articles', p. 100.
17. Lampe, 'The Revision of the Articles', p. 108.
18. Lampe, 'The Revision of the Articles', p. 107.
19. Lampe, 'The Revision of the Articles', p. 110.
20. Lampe, 'The Revision of the Articles', p. 113.
21. JRH Moorman, *The Anglican Spiritual Tradition*, DLT, London, 1983, p. 218.
22. Moorman, *The Anglican Spiritual Tradition*, p. 218.
23. Moorman, *The Anglican Spiritual Tradition*, p. 219.

24. JI Packer, 'The Status of the Articles', in de Satge et al (eds), *The Articles of the Church of England*, p. 28.
25. JI Packer, 'The Status of the Articles', p. 31.
26. JI Packer, 'The Status of the Articles', p. 32.
27. JI Packer, 'The Status of the Articles', p. 34.
28. JI Packer, 'The Status of the Articles', p. 45.
29. JI Packer, 'The Status of the Articles', p. 50.
30. JI Packer, 'The Status of the Articles', p. 47.
31. JI Packer, 'The Status of the Articles', p. 54.
32. D Broughton Knox, *The Thirty-Nine Articles: the Historic Basis of Anglican Faith*, Hodder & Stoughton, London, 1967.
33. Marcia Cameron, *An Enigmatic Life: David Broughton Knox, Father of Contemporary Sydney Anglicanism*, Acorn Press, Melbourne 2006, p. 211.
34. Cameron, *An Enigmatic Life*, p. 211.
35. Knox, *The Thirty-Nine Articles*, p. 5.
36. Knox, *The Thirty-Nine Articles*, p. 79.
37. Knox, *The Thirty-Nine Articles*, p. 49.
38. Knox, *The Thirty-Nine Articles*, p. 78.
39. Knox, *The Thirty-Nine Articles*, p. 80.
40. Knox, *The Thirty-Nine Articles*, p. 84.
41. T Guy Rogers (ed.), *Liberal Evangelicalism: An Interpretation by Members of the Church of England*, Third Edition, Hodder & Stoughton, London, 1940. The original edition appeared in 1923.
42. T Guy Rogers, 'Religious Authority', in Rogers (ed.), *Liberal Evangelicalism*, p. 42.
43. Bruce Kaye, *Church Without Walls: Being Anglican in Australia*, Collins Dove, Melbourne, 1995, p. 64.
44. Kaye, *Church Without Walls*, p. 67.
45. Kaye, *Church Without Walls*, p. 68.
46. Kaye, *Church Without Walls*, p. 76.
47. Stephen Neill, *Anglicanism*, Mowbray, Oxford, 1958, p. 400.
48. Gilbert Burnet, *An Exposition of the Thirty-Nine Articles of the Church of England*, revised and corrected by the Reverend JR Page, Scott, Webster and Geary, London, 1837, pp. 94–6.

6 Alternatives, amendments and additions

Most organisations are guided by a charter or code that sets out key convictions and core objectives. Churches are not dissimilar. The institutionalisation of Christianity and the federalisation of local congregations has been achieved, in part, by the evolution of declarations of belief and mission statements. In effect, they serve both to confirm identity and to assert a common purpose. In this chapter, and before suggesting amendments and additions to the Articles, we will outline and critique a series of modern statements and contemporary declarations drawn, first, from Charismatic–Pentecostal communities and, second, from emerging Anglican networks. The former were chosen because these groups are among the fastest growing Christian communities in Australia and because their creedal statements are very recent attempts to define belief in a post-Christian society. They show what communities unencumbered with long traditions or complex histories think is essential to Christian belief and the terms in which these beliefs are to be stated. The latter were included because they disclose the areas of theological concern to contemporary Anglicans and demonstrate the difficulties of producing succinct doctrinal statements in the context of continuing conflict. These critiques reveal some of the current disagreements among and between Anglicans and other Christians, and provide some cues for the possible content of clarifying statements and defining declarations. They also show how difficult it is to produce an intentionally succinct statement of belief.

There is always pressure to include more things and to say more about what is actually included.

We recognise that proposing the inclusion of some additional articles is something of a thought experiment. In this sense, we would liken ourselves to a couple of cricket aficionados imagining the players they would select for a World XI team. We recognise the potential for hubris in the exercise were it to be taken as ending rather than starting discussion of what Anglicans might confess. Although we both serve in institutions that provide theological education to the Anglican Church of Australia and would like to think we reflect informed opinion, we do not imagine ourselves here drawing up an agenda that others need follow. Having conceded as much, we believe this kind of reflection is necessary, edifying and most distinctly lacking in the contemporary Church. In that spirit we have devised a list of topics rather than specific articles that we believe are worth wider consideration and perhaps eventual embrace.

Christian City Churches

This cluster of churches has a nine-point doctrinal statement that begins with an affirmation of God as Trinity before moving to the person and work of Jesus, starting with the incarnation and ending with his second coming, and the work of the Holy Spirit whose 'fruit and gifts [are] available in the Church'. It claims the 'baptism of the Holy Spirit [is] a gift available to believers, with the normal evidence of speaking in other tongues'. After affirming the 'sacraments of the Lord's Supper and Baptism', it notes that baptism must be 'by full immersion in water for all believers'. It affirms the authoritative character of the Bible which serves as 'the foundation of all Christian doctrine'. In an unexpected turn, the statement draws attention to the 'existence of an evil spiritual being – the devil' before emphasising the 'resurrection of both the saved and the lost, the one to everlasting life and the other to everlasting separation from God'. The final affirmation touches on the Church and the necessity of 'each member being an active part of a local church, fulfilling the Great Commission'.

Chapter 6   Alternatives, amendments and additions

Apostolic Church – Australia

This family of churches has a ten-point doctrinal statement beginning with the Trinity and an affirmation of the 'divine inspiration and authority of Holy Scripture'. It then deals with fallen humanity and the 'necessity of repentance and regeneration by grace and through faith in Christ alone', before emphasising the 'eternal separation from God of the finally unrepentant'. The statement then moves to the person and work of Jesus, highlighting the 'security' of believers in Christ and their 'future resurrection in an incorruptible body'. After requiring 'Baptism by immersion', it claims the 'baptism of the Holy Spirit' empowers 'believers with supernatural signs'. Following a statement about 'Christ's leadership of the Church through the ascension ministries of apostles, prophets, evangelists, pastors and teachers', it ends with a call to 'the privilege and responsibility of wise stewardship of all that God has given, including the practice of tithing to the local church'.

Australian Christian Churches

The various churches claiming affiliation with the Assemblies of God in Australia gather under an umbrella organisation called the Australian Christian Churches. Unlike most other modern declarations, its statement headed 'What we believe' begins with an affirmation of Scripture rather than God: 'we believe that the Bible is God's Word. It is accurate, authoritative and applicable in our everyday lives'. The second of the ten statements in the declaration affirms the triune character of God and emphasises that God is 'totally loving and completely holy'. Attention then turns to Jesus as the 'only One who can reconcile us to God'. It notes his 'sinless and exemplary life' and that he 'died on the cross in our place, and rose again to prove his victory and empower us for life'. In order to 'live the holy and fruitful lives that God intends for us', the statement's drafters insist that 'we need to be baptised in water and filled with the power of the Holy Spirit'. It goes on to explain that 'the Holy Spirit enables us to use spiritual gifts, including speaking in tongues which is the initial evidence of baptism in the Holy Spirit'. In noting that spiritual gifts are given to individuals for the Church's mission, the statement claims that 'God wants to heal and transform us so that we can live healthy and prosperous lives in order to help others more effectively'.

Depending upon 'our response to the Lord Jesus Christ', the ACC believes that 'our eternal destination [is] either Heaven or Hell'. The final statement is an affirmation that 'the Lord Jesus Christ is coming back again as he promised'.

Christian Revival Crusade

The 'declaration of faith' of the Christian Revival Crusade also begins with Scripture and the claim that the canonical writings 'as originally written, are infallible and inspired by God'. The Bible is 'not to be added to, superseded or changed by later tradition or supposed revelation' because it is 'the complete revelation of God'. After a basic account of the Trinity and the attributes of God and a description of each person of the Godhead, there is mention of fallen humanity which was brought about by 'voluntary transgression through the original sin of Adam and Eve'. The human condition is exacerbated by the devil who is 'a fallen angel' whose 'influence brought about the downfall of man, and now as the god of this world seeks to destroy humanity'. The declaration notes, however, that 'every believer has access to absolute authority in Jesus Christ over all the power of the devil because Christ's substitutionary death has stripped the devil of his power and authority'. Human beings are saved by faith in Christ's death which brings about 'new birth'. Accordingly, there will be two resurrections one for the just and one for the unjust. For the latter, there will be a 'resurrection into judgement' which is consistent with belief in the 'eternal punishment of people who wilfully reject and despise the love of God manifested in the great sacrifice of his Son upon the cross for his salvation'. Rather than speaking of Sacraments, the declaration mentions 'two perpetual ordinances'. The first is 'believers' baptism' which requires 'immersion in water' although it is 'not essential for salvation'. The second is the 'Lord's Supper' constituted by a 'meeting of believers in which bread and wine, symbolising his body and blood, are shared in remembrance of Christ's death, in proclamation of his presence, and in anticipation of his Second Coming'. Notably, 'baptism in the Holy Spirit is distinct from the 'new birth' and is accompanied by speaking in other tongues as the initial evidence'. Consistent with the dispensation of 'the various supernatural gifts of the Holy Spirit', the declaration claims that 'Jesus Christ gave his disciples authority and power to heal all kinds of sickness and disease, and to minister deliverance to those bound by demonic power'.

⁓

Notably, none of these statements contains any description of their origins, the process by which they were drafted and refined, or any indication of their authority and standing. It would seem their drafters believed they were self-evident and self-authenticating. These statements do not seek to respond to objections or to answer critics. None contains a preamble explaining that what follows is a summary of the Christian faith or an inventory of its essentials. They are essentially an amalgam of assertions and contentions that infer rather than identify a number of beliefs and customs that these networks either do not share or believe to be mistaken. Each grants a foundational position and an authoritative status to Holy Scripture. In different ways, they hint at its essential character and the manner in which it is to be approached by Christian believers. There is emphasis on the necessity of 'believers' baptism' (ie., adult rather than infant baptism) and stress on the vital link between baptism, the work of the Holy Spirit and the imparting of spiritual gifts, principally the capacity for ecstatic utterance. The other significant element is belief in the personification of evil in the Devil or Satan and the need for believers to combat demonic influence in their lives and in the world. These statements do not present an holistic vision of Christianity. They rightly emphasise the need for right belief but they seem to deprecate the corresponding need for right belonging – being committed to a congregation of believers and playing an active role in congregational life – and right behaving – being committed to thinking and acting in a manner that reflects the words and works of Jesus and which brings honour to God. They do not give an account of the location, possession or delegation of authority in the Christian community and they are silent on the status and standing of other Christian traditions. In effect, these statements do little more than identify those elements of belief and practice that distinguish Charismatic-Pentecostal congregations from the Anglican and historic Protestant denominations from which they have tended to draw the majority of their members. In our view, Anglicans ought to study these statements because they highlight the pressing need for an article on eschatology and because they remind us that the matters of church practice and Christian spirituality tend to find their way into contemporary statements of faith because they effectively differentiate one group from another. Whether they have sufficient substance to divide groups of Christians is, of course, another matter. We would also point out that these statements include certain beliefs and specific practices that either contradict or are inconsistent with the theology expressed in the Articles and deserve some response.

Anglican networks

Common cause partnership

The Anglican Church in North America was founded in December 2008 to provide a 'separate ecclesiastical structure' for Anglicans who could no longer remain members of the Episcopal Church of the United States or the Anglican Church of Canada. It was formed, in part, by the groups who had earlier become members of the 'Common Cause Partnership' which had been formed in June 2004 when the leaders of six separate Anglican bodies – the Anglican Communion Network, the Reformed Episcopal Church, the Anglican Mission in America, Forward in Faith (North America), the Anglican Province of America and the American Anglican Council – published an open letter to Dr Rowan Williams, the Archbishop of Canterbury, committing themselves to 'make common cause for the gospel of Jesus Christ and common cause for a united, missionary and orthodox Anglicanism in North America'. In 2006, the 'Theological Statement of the Common Cause Partnership' was signed. It identified 'seven elements as characteristic of the Anglican way, essential for membership'.

The first element is a commitment to the canon of Scripture as 'the inspired Word of God, containing all things necessary to salvation'. It is followed by belief in Baptism and the Lord's Supper which are to be 'ministered with unfailing use of [Jesus'] Words of institution and of the elements ordained by him'. After identifying the 'godly historic Episcopate as an inherent part of the apostolic faith and practice', the statement claims the episcopate is 'integral to the fullness and unity of the Body of Christ'. The teaching of the three Creeds of undivided Christendom is then affirmed, there is affirmation of the 'teaching of the first four [General] Councils, and the Christological clarifications of the fifth, sixth and seventh Councils in so far as they are agreeable to the Holy Scriptures'. The partnership members 'receive the *Book of Common Prayer* as set forth by the Church of England in 1662' as the 'standard for Anglican doctrine and discipline' rather than the American revisions of 1789, 1892 and 1928, and accept the 'Thirty-Nine Articles of Religion of 1562 [sic.], taken in their literal and grammatical sense, as expressing the Anglican response to certain doctrinal issues controverted at that time, and as expressing fundamental principles of authentic Anglican belief'.

GAFCON

The 'Jerusalem Declaration' was developed by the Global Anglican Futures Conference (GAFCON) which was held in June 2008. The preamble to the document places the statement in its immediate context and is indicative of the drafters' intent: 'we agree to chart a way forward together that promotes and protects the biblical gospel, and mission to world'. Then follows an inventory of those things that the signatories believe constitute 'the tenets of orthodoxy which underpin our Anglican identity'. It begins with rejoicing 'in the gospel of God through which we have been saved by grace through faith in Jesus Christ by the power of the Holy Spirit'. It goes on to affirm belief in 'the Holy Scriptures of the Old and New Testaments to be the Word of God written'. After restating the Articles' phrase about the Scriptures containing all things necessary for salvation, the declaration requires the Bible to be 'translated, read, preached, taught and obeyed in its plain and canonical sense, respectful of the Church's historic and consensual reading'. The Thirty-Nine Articles are upheld because they contain 'the true doctrine of the Church agreeing with God's Word and as authoritative for Anglicans today'. There is rejoicing in the 'Anglican sacramental and liturgical heritage as an expression of the gospel' and recognition that 'God has called and gifted bishops, priests and deacons in historic succession to equip all the people of God for their ministry in the world'. The declaration 'gladly accepts' the 'Great Commission of the Risen Lord to make disciples of all nations' and of bringing 'new believers to maturity'. It is 'mindful of our responsibility to be good stewards of God's creation, to uphold and advocate justice in society, and to seek relief and empowerment of the poor and needy'. There is mention of the need to build ecumenical relationships although it rejects 'the authority of those churches and leaders who have denied the orthodox faith in word or deed'. In the middle of the statement (statement eight in a list of fourteen) there is indirect mention of the immediate issue prompting the declaration:

> We acknowledge God's creation of humankind as male and female and the unchangeable standard of Christian marriage between one man and one woman as the proper place for sexual intimacy and the basis of the family. We repent of our failures to maintain this standard and call for a renewed commitment to lifelong fidelity in marriage and abstinence for those who are not married.

It is noteworthy that the Declaration goes beyond the Thirty-Nine Articles at a number of points and addresses matters that were unknown to the sixteenth century English Reformers.

Covenant for the Church of England

The 'Covenant for the Church of England' devised by a group of Evangelical leaders in 2006 was predicated by the concern that the 'Church of England and the Anglican Communion, faced with a faulty view of revelation, false teaching and indiscipline' required 'orthodox Anglicans' to set out their position. The document contained two parts: the first was headed 'Our Identity' and the second 'Our Action'. There was mention of the Articles in the first part as one of the 'classic formularies of our tradition'. The recent difficulties faced by the Anglican Communion were a consequence of 'departure from [the] common faith' set out in these formularies. The second part contained five headings: mission, appointments, fellowship, money and oversight which the drafters of the 'covenant' thought gave expression to their commitment to the Gospel of Christ. The document concluded with the statement: 'we are committed, as authentic Anglicans, to praying, believing and working for a restored, reformed and renewed Church of England, holding its traditional convictions: confidence in the truth of God in his Word, the sacrificial death of his Son for this world, and in the power of God's Spirit to fulfil his mission'. It was apparent from this document that the Articles needed to be supplemented with doctrinal statements and theological assertions in order to deal with questions and controversies that did not trouble the Church in the sixteenth century or disputes and disagreements that had taken a different form in the twenty-first century.

⁓

Each of these declarations emerged from disapproval of the actions of one National Church or an individual diocese within the Anglican Communion and discontent over the Church's alleged collective failure to deal with departures from historic belief and practice. Although each document is a reaction to a particular set of circumstances and a specific issue of doctrine, there is an attempt in each to reassert the authority of extant formularies, most pointedly the Thirty-Nine Articles, and the foundational Christian truths on which they claim to be grounded. There is obvious attention given to the supremacy and sufficiency of Scripture and the need for the Church's teaching and witness to reflect biblical principles. These declarations also deal, albeit tangentially, with questions about the spiritual character of the Church and its prerogatives in determining doctrine and settling theological disputes. The emphasis on Christ's uniqueness and the stress laid on his atoning sacrifice are intended to preclude any form of ecumenical compromise or philosophical syncretism. While these statements are not intended to be a supplement to or a replacement for the Thirty-Nine Articles, they reveal the extent to which the Articles do not function as the English Reformers intended and highlight the inability of the Articles to settle many modern disagreements. Of course, the sixteenth century Reformers could not have predicted the range of issues that would divide Christians some four hundred years after their own time. But the existence of these declarations demonstrates the pressing need for new and enlarged Articles of Religion that can, at the very least, point to a means by which competing points of view might be reconciled with the teaching of Christ as the Anglican Church has received and understood it.

Amending the Articles

Anglicans have discussed revising the Articles for centuries but have recoiled from the task, perhaps because they feared that agreement on a replacement text might be elusive. There is no doubting the existence of deep divisions with the contemporary Church and the extent of disagreement about a range of issues, some central to the character of Christian belief. The solution is not to pretend that these disagreements do not exist or to minimise their seriousness. It should not be inferred that a desire for a review of the Articles necessarily indicates substantial disagreement with them any more than attempts at some revision denotes any allegation that they are unorthodox or heretical. Put simply: after more than four centuries the Articles desperately need a 'make over'. Individual articles can be improved from a number of perspectives while their collective outlook can be made more relevant and explicable to a new generation of Anglican believers. To leave the Articles in their 1571 form is to guarantee their drift into obscurity.

The remainder of this chapter is an attempt to tidy up the Articles in a number of ways. We identify those articles that can be deleted because they related in part or whole to the circumstances of the sixteenth century and those articles that are irrelevant to modern Christian living. We highlight articles in need of minor editorial change and those that can be shortened, simplified or combined. In our view the Articles are presently much longer than they need to be. We also focus attention on articles whose meaning or intent might be changed to reflect contemporary theological thinking and identifying several that need to be entirely re-written. We have also suggested a number of matters that ought to be the subject of several new articles. Notwithstanding a natural desire to comment on a plethora of potentially contentious issues, for the sake of consistency we have decided to limit ourselves to Thirty-Nine Articles and the same word length for the entire document. There are, of course, endless possibilities when it comes to what ought to be included in any statement of belief. We are conscious our proposals reflect our own circumstances and outlook and accept that Anglicans of other races, nationalities or cultural contexts would nominate different emphases. So in the same way that we note the historical and sociological captivity of the Reformers, we acknowledge that we too are chained to the time and place in which we see the world and concede that we are fleeting and passing away. However, we offer them in good conscience from a sincere and prayerful reading of Scripture.

Particular amendments

Article I
While wanting to affirm the notion of divine impassibility – that God's character is not subject to pain or pleasure nor are the divine attributes susceptible to fickle motives – the only aspect of Article I that might be amended is the statement that God is 'without body, parts, or *passions*'. A word to replace 'passions', such as 'moods', or a fuller statement of the intention of this phrase would help contemporary readers better to grasp the article's meaning.

Article II
Unchanged

Article III
Given that belief in the descent of Christ into hell is no longer a defining belief, that it is contained within the Creeds and that it might suggest a kind of layered cosmos with heaven above, the Earth around us and hell below us, Article III could be safely deleted in favour of a more pressing matter.

Article IV
Unchanged

Article V
The only possible alteration to be considered in relation to Article V is the potential appeal of changing the first part of the article from stating that the Holy Ghost proceeds 'from the Father and the Son' to 'from the Father *through* the Son' although theologians are divided on this point. This is considered a minor rather than a major change serving only to allow a less theologically problematic reading of the text.

Article VI
There is no need to alter the first part of Article VI although in the section headed the 'Names and Numbers of the Canonical Books', reference to the 'First Book of Esdras' could be altered to its modern name 'the Book of Ezra', the 'Second Book of Esdras' could similarly

be altered to the 'Book of Nehemiah', the book of 'Ecclesiastes or Preacher' could be shortened to simply 'Ecclesiastes', and the 'Cantica, or Songs of Solomon' could be become 'Song of Songs'.

Article VII

Article VII would be improved by the deletion of the now unnecessary and rather opaque second sentence, 'Wherefore there are not to be heard, which feign that the old Fathers did look only for transitory promises'.

Article VIII

With respect to Article VIII, there is a compelling argument for setting aside the Athanasian Creed. The Athanasian Creed does not lend itself to liturgical recitation and, indeed, it is no longer recited in an overwhelming majority of Anglican Churches. The proposal is not to deny or reject the contents of the Creed but not to include it in the Articles.

Article IX

Unchanged

Article X

The only change suggested to Article X is the substitution of the word 'guiding' for 'preventing' to avoid confusion among modern readers. The altered clause in the final sentence would read 'Wherefore we have no power to do good works pleasant and acceptable to God, without the grace of God by Christ guiding us ...'.

Article XI

Articles XI and XII ought to be combined because they refer to the same subject – justification. Article XII is not principally concerned with good works notwithstanding its title. In Article XI, the final phrase 'as more largely is expressed in the Homily on Justification' could be safely removed in part because the homily is incorrectly named in the text. The second part of the combined article would begin 'Good Works, which are the fruits of Faith ...', the words 'Albeit that' being deleted from the beginning of the extant sentence. The statement that good works 'cannot put away our sins, and endure the severity of God's judgement' might be altered to 'or obviate the severity of God's judgement' to make the intention of the drafters a little clearer to modern readers.

Article XII
Absorbed into Article XI – see above.

Article XIII
Article XIII could be deleted because its content is largely subsumed by Articles XI, XII and XIV. It adds very little to reinforce points made earlier or later.

Article XIV
Unchanged

Article XV
The first sentence of Article XV could be relocated to become the second part of Article II. The remainder of Article XV could be deleted because it is devotional rather than theological, and simply repeats statements found in the *Book of Common Prayer*.

Article XVI
Unchanged

Article XVII
The phrase 'as vessels made to honour' could be deleted from Article XVII. It does not add substantially to the article whose first sentence is already very complicated. The remainder of the article commencing 'As the godly consideration of Predestination …' could be trimmed because it is essentially a piece of pastoral counsel rather than a dogmatic statement. While recognising that other doctrinal statements of this period also reflect pastorally on predestination, the aim here is to restrict the text to theological principles rather than spiritual counsel.

Article XVIII
Unchanged

Article XIX

The second sentence in Article XIX could be changed from 'As the Churches of Jerusalem, Alexandria, and Antioch have erred' to the observation that 'All churches have erred'.

Article XX

The existing wording of Article XX would remain unchanged but the article could be expanded to include all of Article XXII which is, given the broad range of concerns, inadequately named 'Of Purgatory'. Article XXII contains examples of the things which are the essence of the complaint made in Article XX.

Article XXI

The first part of Article XXI from 'General Councils ...' to '... not governed by the Spirit and the Word of God),' can be deleted. The start of the following phrase, which begins with 'they', would be replaced with 'General Councils' and the remainder of the article shifted to the end of Article XIX. This would bring the statements on ecclesiastical authority together.

Article XXII

Absorbed into Article XX – see above.

Article XXIII

Unchanged

Article XXIV

Article XXIV refers to a matter that is no longer controversial or the cause of division and can be deleted. The importance of the congregation hearing the voice of God and understanding the text of Scripture is now adequately covered in Article VI.

Article XXV

The final paragraph of Article XXV can be deleted because it simply repeats stipulations that also appear in Article XXVIII where their inclusion makes more sense.

Article XXVI

The final sentence of Article XXVI can be deleted because the Church now has a comprehensive set of policies and procedures applying to the disciplining of ministers and we have proposed a stand-alone statement on the conduct expected of the ordained.

Article XXVII

Unchanged

Article XXVIII

The Articles' teaching on the Lord's Supper would be clearer and made more concise if the text of Article XXVIII were slightly rearranged to achieve a more logical sequence of ideas and enlarged by the inclusion of Article XXX. The third paragraph of the article which begins 'The Body of Christ is …' needs to be moved and become the second paragraph and then be followed by the unaltered contents of Article XXX. The rejection of 'Transubstantiation' should follow the positive content in the Articles. The final sentence in the existing article would retain its location as the final statement on the Lord's Supper.

Article XXIX

The contents of this article can be deleted and covered in a new combined article on church discipline.

Article XXX

Absorbed into Article XXVIII – see above.

Article XXXI

Unchanged

Article XXXII

Article XXXII which concerns the 'Marriage of Priests' needs to be retained given the Roman Catholic Church's continuing promotion of, and insistence on, sacerdotal celibacy.

Article XXXIII

The contents of Article XXXIII could be included in a new article which would deal specifically with Church discipline.

Article XXXIV

Unchanged

Article XXXV

Article XXXV can be deleted. The article applies to the period in which they were promulgated. The Homilies are no longer read and rarely consulted. They are very much 'period pieces' that address the social, cultural and economic conditions of the sixteenth century. Proposing the deletion of the article does not imply any specific disagreement with the Homilies but a recognition that they no longer serve the function they once did.

Article XXXVI

Most of Article XXXVI can be deleted because it relates specifically to the sixteenth century. Although the Anglican Church does not profess a continuing need to assert the legitimacy of its Ordinal, the basis of any claim for the validity of Anglican orders could rely on a revision of this article which need only state: 'The Book of Consecration of Archbishops and Bishops, and Ordering of Priests and Deacons, doth contain all things necessary to such consecration and ordering: neither hath it any thing, that of itself is superstitious or ungodly.'

Article XXXVII

The first three paragraphs of Article XXXVII are no longer applicable because the politico-legal context in which the Church conducts its mission and ministry has changed, and because each national church is autonomous (although being in fellowship with) the Establish Church of the English realm. The final two statements in the article – the first asserting the permissibility of capital punishment and the second allowing conscription – are controversial and ill-suited to demonstrating instances of legitimate exercise of civil authority.

Article XXXVIII

Article XXXVIII can be deleted because it touches on a matter – the right of private property – that is no longer a subject of dispute among Christians.

Article XXXIX

Article XXXIX can be deleted for the same reasons as the deletion of the previous Article.

Summary

In sum, ten of the articles – II, IV, IX, XIV, XVI, XVIII, XXVII, XXXI, XXXII and XXXIV – should be retained in their current form although each would benefit from being 'translated' into contemporary English with modern grammar and sentence construction.

Six of the articles – III, XXIV, XXIX, XXXV, XXXVIII and XXXIX – could be deleted because they address matters that are no longer defining of Anglicanism or the cause of division between Christians.

Eleven of the articles – II, XI, XII, XIII, XV, XIX, XX, XXI, XXII, XXVII and XXX – could be combined so as to reduce the number of Articles by four.

Four of the articles – XVII, XXV, XXVI, XXXVI – could be substantially reduced in size to exclude material that is not strictly doctrinal or which involves concerns that are no longer current or pressing.

Four of the Articles – I, VI, VII and X – should be retained with minor editorial amendment to reflect changes in the meaning of English words and phrases.

Changes in content are suggested for only two of the articles – V and VIII. The first change affirms that the Spirit flows from the Father *through* the Son; the second change proposes dropping the Athanasian Creed. These changes are of different kinds.

Two completely revised articles drawing together contemporary insights and practices are proposed in the areas of ecclesiastical discipline (subsuming XXXIII) and church-state relations (subsuming XXXVII).

Given our prior commitment to the Articles numbering no more than 39 (the current number), the revision we have proposed has reduced the number of articles to 22. This gives us scope to propose up to 17 new articles. What might the Anglican church of the twenty-first century seek to confess?

Adding to the Articles

As we have seen, the Thirty-Nine Articles of 1571 both express theological truths that are meant to hold for all times and places *and* are an articulation of those truths in a particular polemical context. Whatever shortcomings they have, they give expression to a coherent theological vision that the drafters of the Articles believed applied to situations vastly different from their own. We know this because they were ready to acknowledge that some things – like liturgical forms – were context specific and ought to be varied. Yet, the drafters made no such concession regarding the doctrinal framework of the Articles. They asserted the prime authority of a particular source for Christian doctrine – namely, Holy Scripture; and they subjected the teachings and practices of the Church of England to the norm of Scripture. What is more, they professed a particular and distinct soteriology: the Reformation teaching that a person is justified by faith in the atoning blood of Christ alone.

In trying to envisage what a contemporary Anglican church might confess, it is important to keep the sense of the Articles as a whole theological vision. The details emanate from the core convictions about the authority of Scripture and the dependence of humankind upon the grace of God for salvation. From this central conviction, the original articles do not shy away from matters of church order, liturgical practice, ethics and politics even as they allow enormous freedom within them.

Confessing the same historic faith as the Reformers is not a matter of saying the same words as they did. That would merely be an exercise in antiquarianism, like playing Baroque music with the original instruments. It goes without saying that we live in an entirely different historical context, and in a very different place. Just as the

Chapter 6 Alternatives, amendments and additions

Church of England in the sixteenth century sought to distinguish its confession from available alternatives, so also a contemporary confession of faith ought to look to the particular issues that are impinging upon the churches in its own time, and be unafraid to address difficult and controversial matters. Furthermore, a confession of faith is not merely a list describing the current consensus of the thinking of the denomination. While it certainly ought to be broad enough to command agreement, it ought to aim (in all humility) to be a statement of the truth, as unfashionable as that may sound. A confession of faith can serve a didactic purpose as well.

The Anglican Church in contemporary Australia needs to recognise that it lives in a largely post-Christendom context. This means that it confesses the gospel of Jesus Christ in the midst of those who have no affiliation to any church or any belief in a deity whatsoever. Likewise, it lives increasingly among people of many other faiths. It will need to state, respectfully of course, how it differs from these. The entire Christian world-view is no longer a given in the way it once was. Furthermore, the state is increasingly more self-conscious so that 'secular' means 'not religious at all'. Although there are genial and co-operative relationships between the churches and the state (more so than in the United States, for example), these relationships are now being questioned and some may dissolve. A modern-day confession must be conscious of the witness it is offering to the non-believing world. There is a need to direct its confession over the Church walls to the world that Christians inhabit.

Yet it is still the case that there are enormously controversial issues between Christians themselves. Since the 1960s the presenting issues for Anglicans and others have been issues of church order and ethics: namely, the ordination of women to the priesthood and the blessing of same-sex relationships. However, there are controversies that lie more deeply embedded in the Church's teaching, and on which many Christians are unclear.

Granted that we inhabit a very different situation from the sixteenth century, it would also be wrong to overemphasise the differences between the sixteenth century and today. It is a sloppy intellectual habit of the present time to imagine that there is such a radical discontinuity with the past that we have nothing in common with it. While we inhabit a time and place greatly removed, it is also the case that we stand in continuity with that world. We speak the same language, for example. In many ways, the society that contemporary Australians enjoy is a product of the world which produced the Articles. The point is this: that in imagining what an association of churches such as the Anglican Church of Australia might choose to confess today, we need not imagine any new statements as a matter of 'starting all over again'.

Faith and reason

Belief in God is not a given in the contemporary world. It seems that there is a great opportunity in these circumstances to make some confession about the nature of Christian faith itself. Reason and Christian faith are not opposed to one another. In fact, just as 'the fear of the Lord is the beginning of wisdom', so faith in the God of Jesus Christ is a sound basis for a rational knowledge of the world. Particularly since the rise of the so-called 'New Atheism', a banal but common perception is that faith is absolutely contrary to reason. There is also an intra-church version of this understanding. There has been a tendency within Christian theology of the last century or so to see reason as an opponent of faith. Rightly, there was in this theology a critical response to Enlightenment rationalism on the one hand and, on the other, to the prominence of ideas based on the thought of Thomas Aquinas in Roman Catholic circles. This comes out, for example, in the work of the great German New Testament scholar Rudolf Bultmann (1884–1976), who applied his immense scholarly ability to show how (in his opinion) a rational grounding for Christian faith was actually impossible, as well as being contrary to the nature of that faith itself. But Bultmann goes too far in our view. The knowledge of God is not merely rational nor is it attained through a process of reasoning. It is indeed given as gift from God. And though it is in many ways a challenge to the pride of human reason, it is not *unreasonable* or *irrational*. Anselm of Canterbury's maxim *fides quaerens intellectum* ('faith seeking understanding') has a particular relevance for the current moment.

The existence of God

The current form of the first article assumes the existence of God, although it does distinguish God as a single entity (*contra* polytheism). It might be that affirming the Creeds is enough to witness to the existence of God. However, given the context in which the Church confesses, it perhaps ought to remind itself that it does indeed witness to the real existence of a God. Anglican Christianity is *theistic*, in other words. The testimony of Holy Scripture is that there is a divine being, God, who exists independently from the world and independent of our experience of him. To testify thus would also mean rejecting the so-called 'non-realism' of Cambridge Anglican theologian Don Cupitt (1934–), who argued that our theological statements are not claims about objective 'out-there' states of affairs, but ways of coping with and experiencing the world. It would seem hard to reconcile this with almost any orthodox doctrine of God.

God the Creator

The Articles say nothing at all about God as the creator and the nature of the creation that he creates. Once more, we might be happy enough that the Nicene Creed asserts that God is 'maker of heaven and earth, and of all that is, seen and unseen.' But there is an intense interest in what orthodox Christianity has to teach about the created world, especially given the findings of modern science and the environmental crises that many feel is looming. Many people within and beyond the Church believe that the theory of evolution by natural selection is irreconcilable with belief in a God who creates.

A confession to God the Creator ought to affirm that God created *ex nihilo*. This is not strictly speaking a directly biblical affirmation, but it is consistent with the teaching of the Church since the earliest times. That God created from nothing means that nothing other than God precedes the creation of all things. There is nothing on which God is dependent for his action in creation. The Anglican Church ought also to bear testimony with Scripture to the goodness and order of the creation as it was made. This is not to say that this goodness and order is completely describable or even ultimately perceptible to human beings. But it is to say that the world is not chaotic, or governed by chance. It is not haphazard. The importance of this insight made possible the scientific discoveries of the last few centuries on which our society so heavily relies.

It would be worthwhile also affirming the calling of humans to tend and care for the creation, although technically this ought to be under the heading of 'theological anthropology' (of which more below). A misreading of the theological notion of 'dominion' has meant that this idea has been frequently blamed for the violation of the planet's natural resources. The biblical testimony to the human responsibility for creation is needful. But it is also necessary to witness against the tendency in some environmentalist circles to see human beings as a great carbuncle on the earth, a pest needing to be eradicated. Though we might share the wonder of it with the Psalmist (Psalm 8), Anglicans ought to affirm that human beings are endowed with authority to act on the creator's behalf within his world.

All Christians are creationists of one kind or another. It is tempting to add an explicit denial of that type of creationism which, on the basis of a literalistic reading of Genesis 1 and 2, insists that Christians are committed to believe in a 'young Earth'. Though this position claims Scriptural warrant, it relies on almost a complete denial that the created order in front of us is, according to overwhelming evidence, millions of years old. The problems with this position are legion, and few Anglicans in Australia would hold to it – even those who call themselves conservatives. However, it is enough to say that, unlike other church associations, the Anglican Church does not insist upon a 'young Earth' reading of the Genesis accounts.

The doctrine of Scripture

Many Protestant confessions have said a great deal more about the doctrine of Scripture than is confessed in the Articles. The Westminster Confession, for example, is far more thorough and places Scripture in a more prominent position. The Articles are, it could be argued, too vague about the *character* of Holy Scripture, as much as its authority in the Church is asserted. More recently, many Evangelicals have wanted to affirm the *inerrancy* of Scripture in all it teaches (see for example the 1978 *Chicago Statement on Biblical Inerrancy* which leading Anglican Evangelical theologian Jim Packer helped frame). While many Anglicans would perhaps want to insert a statement on inerrancy today in order to strengthen the authority of Scripture in a new confession of faith, it would not gain wide consensus even among Evangelicals. It would, however, be useful to clarify the common misperception, based on a nineteenth century misreading of the Elizabethan divine Richard Hooker, that reason and tradition are parallel sources of authority for Anglicans. This is the oft-repeated but misleading 'three-legged stool' analogy. Hooker himself is quite clear that reason and tradition serve as auxiliaries in the interpretation and application of Scripture.

Human worth

We have already suggested that something needs to be affirmed about the calling of human beings to tend and serve creation as God's ambassadors. Following the New Testament, Christ himself is to be seen as the model for this role as the 'firstborn over all creation' (Colossians 1:15). It is he, after all, who is 'the image of the invisible God' fulfilling and realising the designation applied to the original human beings in Genesis 1:26–28. Alongside this testimony to the calling of humans within the creation to serve and to respond to God must come a statement about the worth of human beings in the sight of that same God.

The Church could usefully affirm its view of the nature and purpose of human life over and against a brash humanism, which exalts in the human ability to master and control the world and which hopes that human ingenuity will be remarkable enough to save the race from every predicament. But there is also a strain of anti-humanism in contemporary culture. Economic and political interests are repeatedly allowed to crush human individuals and to diminish the human spirit. The utilitarianism of contemporary moral thinking leads inexorably to the legalisation of abortion and the push for legal euthanasia, even though the rhetoric of human freedom is used disingenuously to bolster these claims. Even the technocratic, democratic liberal state is capable of treating human individuals as expendable.

The anthropology of the Bible is the basis for a remarkable testimony to the worth of individual human beings grounded in the Creator's high regard for what has been made. The incarnation of the Son of God further enables the Church to assert the value of each person, even when that value is not externally apparent. Human equality, which the American political philosopher Ronald Dworkin (1931–) calls the 'sovereign virtue', has a theological foundation. The British economist RH Tawney (1880–1962) once wrote: 'in order to believe in human equality it is necessary to believe in God'. It is not accidental that those societies most influenced by Christianity have been at the forefront of establishing social equality in the last two centuries. The Anglican Church can and must affirm the complete and fundamental equality of human beings of either gender or whatever race by looking to the gospel it preaches (see Galatians 3:28). Such an affirmation would perhaps go some way to demonstrate repentance for such actions in the Church's history that have denied this.

The life of Jesus

In addition to the anthropological statements that might emerge from a discussion of the issues above, it would be worth confessing the importance of the perfect human life of obedience lived by Jesus. It is a lacuna in almost all creedal statements that nothing or very little is said about the life of Jesus of Nazareth even though the four Gospels present to us this life, and not merely as a superfluous narrative. The German theologian Jürgen Moltmann (1926–) is among those who have suggested that the Creeds should be revised to include a statement about the life of Jesus – not only as the exemplary human life, but as a life lived for others. It was divine life, humanly lived. There is not perhaps some explicit error that such a testimony would speak against, but it could be argued that adding such an affirmation might correct a tendency to neglect the significance of the life of Jesus. It has also the benefit of reminding us that Christianity does not boil down to a set of values or principles, but it is a faith deeply embedded in the history of a particular nation (Israel) and a particular individual (Jesus).

The uniqueness of Christ in salvation

Just as the Anglican Communion must reckon with the global context that it now inhabits, so the Anglican Church in Australia cannot ignore the presence of other religions among its neighbours. Anglicans have learnt in their history to tolerate a diversity of beliefs within society, and to recognise that the freedom of religious belief is of enormous benefit. It is imperative to repudiate the use of coercion in extending the faith. Likewise, the members of other faiths ought to be accorded the greatest respect. Nevertheless, respect and tolerance do not equate to relativism regarding theological truth claims. It is possible to engage in respectful discussion and dialogue without having to concede or accept that two completely contradictory propositions about the divine person are both true in some way. Christians ought to be able to testify, as they did in the earliest times, that 'there is salvation in no one else [than Jesus], for there is no other name under heaven given among mortals by which we must be saved' (Acts 4:12). The scope of the gospel is universal – Jesus Christ is Lord for and of all. Finally, '*every* knee shall bow and every tongue confess that Jesus is Lord' (Philippians 2:10–11) (emphasis added). That gospel is not only a declaration of the universal Lordship of Christ, it is also a critique of human worship that does not recognise Christ as Lord. The Anglican Church has long been and remains today a missionary church, sending missionaries to proclaim the gospel of Jesus Christ throughout the world. This has been true of both Evangelicals and Anglo-Catholics. While not everything in this history has been glorious, there is far more of which to be proud than is often recognized. The fruit of the missionary endeavours of a previous era lies in the extraordinary numbers of Anglican Christians now worshipping in what is sometimes called the 'Global South'.

The person and work of the Holy Spirit

The Articles say nothing about the work of the Holy Spirit, although the Creeds affirm the divinity, personality and Lordship of the third member of the Holy Trinity. In the light of the extraordinary spread of Pentecostalism and the charismatic movement across the globe and within the Anglican Communion itself, it would be important for pastoral and theological reasons to make some clarifications about the Holy Spirit's work, including Anglican disagreement with any claim that a person was not fully Christian when they accepted Christ as Lord and Saviour or that some kind of 'second' conversion was needed for the believer to know and experience the fullness of the Holy Spirit.

The Holy Spirit is God's second agent in creation, bringing to perfection all that is made through the Son. This includes human beings. The Spirit of Christ has vivified the Church since its first day, when it filled the apostles and empowered them for the proclamation of the gospel to the nations (Acts 2). The Holy Spirit is given to every believer as the promise or seal of their salvation (2 Corinthians 1). Every Christian is as such 'baptised in the Holy Spirit'. This baptism is not an event subsequent to a person's conversion to Christ; and it is not evidenced by some external miraculous sign, such as speaking in tongues. While there are scriptural examples of people being 'filled' with the Holy Spirit for special tasks, it is not an indication that they were somehow lacking the Spirit beforehand. Anglicans would want to affirm the Holy Spirit's gifting of members of the Church for the task of building up the Church (as in 1 Corinthians 12–14); but would not want to overemphasise the so-called supernatural gifts at the expense of the less spectacular ones. The gifting of the Spirit means that the work of ministry in the Church is not confined to the office-bearers of the Church. In the light of some extraordinary practices of exorcism among contemporary Christians, an Anglican would want to confess that a Christian having the Holy Spirit need not fear possession by a demonic spirit.

Marriage

For sound Scriptural and theological reasons, the Anglican Church in Australia ought to be unafraid and unembarrassed to testify to the pattern of marriage as a lifelong and exclusive commitment between one man and one woman. Not only that, such a statement ought to affirm that marriage between husband and wife is the context ordained by God for the mutual expression of natural sexual desire. Alternative positions on this subject can only be established by rejecting the normative and authoritative grounds for Anglican thinking – namely, Holy Scripture. What is more, this view of human sexuality reflects the view of the vast majority of Anglicans globally, of the church down the ages, and of the modern day Roman Catholic and Orthodox churches. Under enormous pressure from within and without, the Anglican Church would be courageous in making its teaching explicit in this way. Making such an affirmation does not deny the call of churches to care pastorally for those who may for the strongest of personal convictions feel that this pattern of marriage is not for them.

Christian hope

The original list of articles numbered forty-two and included some statements about eschatology – the Christian teaching about 'the last things'. These were removed in 1571, and so the Articles as they were finally established do not commit the Anglican Church to a particular eschatology. The problem this presents is that, as has been seen by a number of contemporary theologians, the faith promoted and commended in the New Testament is thoroughly eschatological. A lack of a clear testimony to the end time can tempt the Church to become somewhat self-congratulatory, imagining that it in some way embodies the totality of the Kingdom of God, or allowing it to imagine that it is not ultimately subject to the judgment of God. The perversity of this triumphalist version of Christianity was exposed by the calamity of World War I, as the Swiss theologian Karl Barth (1886–1968) and others observed.

The Church of England has not been quite so unguarded in its thinking about eschatology. If anything its besetting vice is a kind of suburban complacency rather than a sabre-rattling pride. Yet, to prevent the Anglican Church in Australia being caught in the same triumphalist trap that snared the European Protestant Churches, it ought to remind itself that God's future is not yet with us. While the substance of the future lies behind us in the resurrection of Christ, the full scope of the future lies in the hand of the saving God. The divine will is to save. It is crucial to affirm the triumph of God's chosen king as the ruler of this world. But it is a triumph achieved through self-sacrifice. The sign of God's kingdom is a life characterised by self-sacrifice, as illustrated particularly in the martyrdom of Christians. The focus of God's will is the glorification of the Son as Saviour. But it is also God's intention to vindicate the Son against the enemies of salvation. God will exact justice against the enemies of the Son. The most vehement words in the New Testament are levelled by the Lord Jesus against those who presume and rely upon their own righteousness.

The Anglican Church ought to remain reserved about some features of Christian eschatology. It is not a millenarian faith. Nor does it have patience for those who make specific predictions about the dating of the return of Jesus. It ought not to commit itself to a particular ordering of the events that will transpire. But it does heed the New Testament warnings to be alert, so as not to be surprised when the end comes (Mark 13:32).

Church workers are subject to the laws of the land

As we have seen, the original articles made some strong affirmations about the relationship of the Church to the authority of the State in the form of the English Crown. These articles read the most awkwardly for the contemporary Australian context. The next three topics put forward here recognise the usefulness of making some common commitment to a form of relationship with the state in our own day while recognising the difficulty and provisionality of doing so.

The Christian Churches in Australia have in recent times been engulfed by terrible scandals to do with child abuse. The Anglican Church has not been chief among these but it has not been innocent. The taint of abuse has damaged the standing of all Christian churches. Paedophilia is not solely an ecclesiastical problem by any means. However, there has been in the Christian churches a craven disregard for the processes of law and the protection of children in the care of church workers. The scandal has been not that child abuse occurs, but the ecclesiastical authorities have not acted with due vigilance against church workers, including priests and bishops, who have abused children. In part, some distorted theological notions have enabled this situation to develop. While priestly celibacy (often blamed, rightly or wrongly, for the crisis in the Roman Catholic world) is not the rule in the Anglican Church, the view that orders are in some way indelible has made church authorities reluctant to remove perpetrators from positions of responsibility. A sense that if a person is genuinely repentant and claims to know divine forgiveness then they are not beholden to secular processes of law seems to have determined the policies of some bishops. The Biblical provenance for this is perhaps Luke 12:57–59 where Jesus exhorts his followers to seek justice among themselves rather than from civil courts. Interestingly, the debate in its structure is not new: prior to the Reformation there was a tense struggle in the English Church about the lack of accountability to the Crown of ecclesiastical workers.

It is in keeping with the political arrangement envisaged in the Reformation that Anglicans might now testify that we are subject to the laws of the land and to the demands of justice. As an act of repentance we ought to confess publically that church workers who commit offences against children and vulnerable people will be subject to the Church's discipline which includes the deposition of clergy (sometimes known as 'defrocking') as well as being brought to the notice of the legal system. The Church ought to commit itself to the short and long term pastoral care of the victims of abuse. Having such a statement within the Church's confessional document would signal to Australian society a determination to act justly and wisely. It is not too much to say that this is an issue of gospel significance. Will the Anglican Church act in a way that demonstrates the truth of the gospel that it confesses? This may indeed be a beginning.

Social justice

The Thirty-Nine Articles is not a moralistic tract. Indeed, the Reformers stood against a version of Christianity which was too easily confused with a system of morality. That said, the call to Christian obedience is articulated. Only Article XXXVIII ('Of Christian Men's Goods, which are not Common') which includes a comment about alms-giving to the poor directs this to the general society. A far stronger and more stirring affirmation could be made about the Christian desire to see the justice and peace of God reign on earth, committing Anglican Christians to pursue the good of the disadvantaged and the alienated.

It would be vital not to politicise such a statement in a worldly sense. If ecclesiastical bodies too readily aligned themselves with a conservative social vision in the past, then it is too often the case today that church statements about social issues reflect not biblical teaching and theological reflection but the most fashionable progressive social policies. Care for the poor and disadvantaged is a Christian given – a conviction that stems from the gospel of Christ itself. The means by which this is delivered must not be confused with it, nor must it be enshrined in the confession of the Church. Furthermore, it is imperative that a commitment to a more just society is eschatologically modest. The final consummation of divine justice always remains for the end of history. Though it may be anticipated by social action in the present, it is not finally to be brought about by it. That remains for God alone to do. The careless alignment of much 1970s 'Liberation Theology' with a now-outmoded and discredited Marxist social vision is a salutary reminder of the temptation here to be avoided. The Church's expertise is not contemporary social policy; it is Christ and the Scriptures.

The public sphere

Anglicans of all theological dispositions have always felt that they must speak in 'the public square'. Contemporary secularism, however, has attempted to make Christian speech a matter of private communication only. The public sphere must not be the venue for theological reasoning. What replaces theological reasoning is the language of technological expertise and statistical data – namely, a discourse which pretends to being beyond mere opinion. But the Christian Churches proclaim a public gospel. The Lordship of Christ is not merely a matter of internal conviction but, they confess, a matter of the public record. The resurrection of the Christ is not confessed as a matter of inward experience only, but rather as the declaration of Jesus himself as the Son of God (Romans 1:1–5). Anglican Christians can affirm that the gospel has ramifications for all people everywhere. The mode of discourse that Christians may employ in the contemporary public forum will of course be radically different from what it was even a few decades ago. For example, Anglican bishops can no longer command attention and respect in society by the mere fact of their office alone. Speaking in a way that is both specifically theological *and* communicates in public is extremely difficult. Even though this is the case, the Church ought not accept the secularist invitation to remain mute about matters of common concern. Furthermore, the assumption that there is a value-neutral public speech which can act as a common currency is a dangerous myth that needs unmasking. Again, the memory of Christian martyrs ought to be a guide as to the character of Christian public speech.

There are many other topics and questions that might be deemed worthy of definition or clarification in an updated or expanded set of Articles for the worldwide Anglican Communion. Our hope is that by identifying the prospects and possibilities that exist to alter and amend the Articles, Anglicans might ponder the body of belief that effectively defines the Christian faith in the context of other religions and the cluster of convictions that distinguishes their particular experience of Christian discipleship in contrast to that of other denominations. While we recognise the importance of identifying what is essential to Christian faith and separating these beliefs and practices from those that might be deemed secondary or subordinate, we realise the perilous nature of any discussion that implies the existence of a hierarchy of doctrines or customs. Such hierarchies are ordered according to a scale involving preference and prejudice more than evidence and argument. The range of matters that might be included in any revision of the Thirty-Nine Articles must be limited to those that warrant inclusion because they are in need of more detailed definition or precise clarification rather than because they embody whatever might be deemed the essence of Christianity. The amendments and additions we have proposed are intended to indicate the directions in which we believe the discussion ought to be heading in the context of continuing conversation with the watching world and the persistence of disunity among those claiming to profess the one name by which humanity is saved – Jesus Christ.

Closing remarks

It might seem to some observers of the Anglican Church that it requires little doctrinal integrity from its clergy and is disinterested in theological precision. This is far from true. That the Church has survived heresy trials and controversial schisms shows it is capable of holding together a great many Christians of different temperament but not at the expense of truth. The dissenting parties have remained in dispute over contested points of doctrine but they continued to be in sufficiently close proximity that continuing conversation was possible and there have been notable instances when superior arguments prevailed and minds were changed. The most unwelcome factor has been the intrusion of legal processes and recourse to the secular courts. Then and now, civil law should not be used to secure compliance with theological positions.

History shows that the Thirty-Nine Articles are an unreliable weapon during litigation. As we have explained in earlier chapters, the Articles attempted to clarify the Church's position with respect to a number of controversial issues. Some of these issues remain contentious more than four centuries on. The Articles are a reflection of a not unreasonable desire for unanimity in key areas of conviction and they help with differentiating right from wrong belief. They point to some distinctive Anglican doctrines and hint at an Anglican theological method. Although some Anglicans see them as the basis of a teaching syllabus, the Catechism is better suited for use as an instructional resource. Similarly, there are Anglicans who want them to serve as a statement of minimum belief although the Creeds also serve this function. These purposes are somewhat removed from the original intention of the drafters but this does not make these expectations unfair or unreasonable. Using the Articles for these purposes needs, however, to be tempered by an appreciation of what the Articles were and were not drafted to do.

Quite apart from a number of institutional purposes, we believe that the Articles are a source of spiritual insight and pastoral wisdom when read with the right attitude – an attitude we have attempted to describe in this book. Those who drafted the Articles never intended that they should be used to encourage self-righteousness or to imply that mere intellectual assent to a set of theological statements amounted to a proper grasp of the Christian faith. The English Reformers hoped the Articles would promote spiritual maturity among those who subscribed to them and might help to bring nearer the Kingdom of God. They presumed that those who assented to them were followers of Jesus who were committed whole-heartedly to personal transformation into the likeness of Christ.

We also believe that the Articles need to be read and interpreted alongside the *Book of Common Prayer* and the Ordinal. They are complementary expressions of the Church's mind and, when taken together, give a fuller sense of what Anglicans believe about themselves and the world they inhabit. While we wholeheartedly agree that the Church must listen to eminent voices from the past and respect the convictions of those who laid the foundations of modern Anglicanism, this does not preclude judgements being made about the present standing of the Articles or the cogency of the belief they commend. Those who drafted the Articles never implied that they could not be improved, expanded or augmented as biblical exegesis and theological reasoning advanced – as inevitably it would.

Nevertheless, we believe that the Articles still serve the purpose for which they were intended although we acknowledge that they do so now imperfectly and inadequately. We concede that they are poorly understood, widely neglected and regularly disparaged. The whole notion of producing a statement of belief and obliging the Church's leadership to teach and preach only those things contained within it requires a change of heart and mind among Anglicans who have become accustomed to promoting their own beliefs and proclaiming their own insights rather than, as the Ordinal puts it, 'the doctrine, sacraments and discipline of Christ, as he has commanded and as this Church has received them'.

Closing remarks

What, then, would we like to see happen within the Church with respect to the Thirty-Nine Articles? We hope for closer study of the history and content of the Articles within parish communities, serious attempts among Anglican clergy to understand the period in which they were written and the commitments and convictions that inspired them, consistent attention to the content of the Articles by ordinands throughout their preparation for ministry, honest reflection of what subscription means and why adherence to a statement of belief remains important, open debate about where and why the Articles might be amended, and sincere efforts to apply the Articles to contemporary claims and current assertions.

But our foremost hope is not an increase in doctrinal rigour among Anglicans although this would be a laudable aspiration in itself. We long for every man, woman and child to enjoy personal fellowship with the living God through Jesus Christ. Good doctrine will express and extend that fellowship; bad doctrine will hinder and curtail it. If we help one person to experience a deeper knowledge of God and a closer relationship with Christ, we will be well satisfied.

About the authors

Michael Jensen

A native of Sydney, Michael Jensen is the rector of St Mark's Anglican Church, Darling Point. Following his ordination in 2000, he served as a school chaplain and then a church planter before returning to Sydney's Moore Theological College to teach theology. He gained his doctorate in Moral Theology from Oxford University in 2008. He is the author of twelve books, including *Martyrdom and Identity: the Self on Trial* (2010) and *Subjects and Citizens: The Politics of the Gospel* (2024). He is passionate about cricket, conversation, and black coffee. Michael and his wife Catherine live in the Eastern suburbs of Sydney and have four adult children.

Tom Frame

Tom Frame was born in Sydney in 1962. After service in the Royal Australian Navy (1979–92) he was ordained at Goulburn in 1993 and held several parish appointments in Australia and England. He was Bishop to the Australian Defence Force from 2001 to 2007. A graduate of the Universities of New South Wales (UNSW), Melbourne and Kent, he is the author or editor of 50 books including *Anglicans in Australia* (2007) and *Losing My Religion: Unbelief in Australia* (2009). He was Director of St Mark's National Theological Centre and Professor of Theology at Charles Sturt University from 2007–2014, and then a research professor at UNSW until his retirement in 2023. He received the Centenary of Federation medal in 2002 for services to the Anglican church and was made a Member of the Order of Australia in 2019 for his contributions to higher education. Since 2010 he has lived and ministered in the village of Tarago, NSW.

Index

'13 Articles' (1538) unpublished, 24
'42 Articles' (1553), 24
   Elizabethan Settlement, 25

A

A Prayer Book for Australia (APBA), 10
   Articles in Supplementary Material, 113
Act Against Puritans 1593, 27
American Anglican Council, 164
American Church and the Articles, 114
An Australian Prayer Book (AAPB), 10
Anabaptist, 75
   church-state relations, 91
   common ownership of goods, 92
   swearing of oaths, 93
Andrewes, Lancelot, 121
Anglican
   belief, 117
   doctrine
      atonement, 36
      continuing conversation and conflict, 29, 30
      life and witness, 95
      networks, 164
      validity of orders and rites, 89
Anglican Church in North America, 164
Anglican Church of Australia
   Articles and the Constitution, 10, 112
   assent to the Articles, 113
   status of the Articles, 10
Anglican Communion
   hostility to the Articles and subscription, 108
   status of the Articles, 9
Anglican Communion Network, 164
Anglican Mission in America, 164
Anglican Province of America, 164
Anglicanism
   distinctiveness, 117
   genuineness claims to be judged, 131
   identity crisis, 6
   modern disagreements, 168, 177
   problems defining beliefs, 118
   'young Earth' reading of Genesis, 180
Anglo-Catholic Revival, 103. *see also* Oxford Movement
Anglo-Catholicism
   Anglo-Papists, 123, 124
   and the Articles, 122, 128
      objections, 136, 140
   beginnings, 123
   defining beliefs inconsistent with the Articles, 139
   Liberal, 124
   missionary minded, 183
Anselm, 178
   Satisfaction, 81
antinomianism, 45, 53
anti-subscription movement, 98
   petition to repeal legislation, 100
Apocrypha, 43
Apostle's Creed- descended into Hell, 36
Apostolic Church – Australia doctrinal statement, 161
Aquinas, Thomas, 178
Arianism, 66
   minimal assent to the Articles, 98
Article I: Of Faith in the Holy Trinity, 33, 34, 35
   proposed amendment, 169
Article II: Of the Word or Son of God, which was made very Man, 35
   Latin translation, 31
   placement of redemption, 105
Article III: Of the going down of Christ into Hell, 36, 37
   proposed deletion, 169
Article IV: Of the Resurrection of Christ, 38
   criticism, 153
Article V: Of the Holy Ghost, 39, 40
   proposed amendment, 169
Article VI: Of the Sufficiency of the Holy Scriptures for Salvation, 30, 41, 42, 43

general criticisms, 154
ignoring tradition, 140
proposed amendment, 169
Vernon Staley's view, 141
Article VII: Of the Old Testament, 44, 45
   proposed amendment, 170
Article VIII: Of the Three Creeds, 46
   proposed amendment, 170
Article IX: Of Original or Birth-Sin, 47, 48, 49
Article X: Of Free-Will, 49, 50
   proposed amendment, 170
Article XI: Of the Justification of Man, 51, 52
   proposed combining with Article XII, 170
Article XII: Of Good Works, 53
   proposed combining with Article XI, 171
Article XIII: Of Works before Justification, 54
   proposed deletion, 171
Article XIV: Of Works of Supererogation, 55, 56
Article XV: Of Christ alone without Sin, 56, 57
   proposed amendment, 171
Article XVI: Of Sin after Baptism, 57, 58, 125
Article XVII: Of Predestination and Election, 58, 59, 60
   proposed amendment, 171
Article XVIII: Of obtaining eternal Salvation only by the Name of Christ, 60, 61
   hint of Calvin, 150
Article XIX: Of the Church, 62, 63
   Bruce Kaye commentary, 151
   proposed amendment, 172
Article XX: Of the Authority of the Church, 30, 64, 65
   and Article XXXIV, 85
   general criticisms, 154
   preamble added, 25
   proposed amendment, 172
Article XXI: Of the Authority of General Councils, 65, 66, 67

proposed amendment, 172
Protestant Episcopal Church (USA), 10
Article XXII: Of Purgatory, 67, 68
   Latin translation, 31
   proposed combining with Article XX, 172
   Vernon Staley's view, 141
Article XXIII: Of Ministering in the Congregation, 69, 70
Article XXIV: Of speaking in the Congregation in such a tongue as the people understandeth, 70, 71
   proposed deletion, 172
Article XXV: Of the Sacraments, 71, 72, 73
   Anglo-Catholic attitude in 1870, 140
   proposed amendment, 172
Article XXVI: Of the Unworthiness of the Ministers, which hinders not the effect of the Sacrament, 73, 74
   proposed amendment, 173
Article XXVII: Of Baptism, 75, 76
Article XXVIII: Of the Lord's Supper, 76, 77, 78
   proposed amendment, 173
   Real Presence, 127
Article XXIX: Of the Wicked which eat not the Body of Christ in the use of the Lord's Supper, 79
   late inclusion, 25
   proposed deletion, 173
Article XXX: Of both kinds, 79, 80
   proposed combining with Article XXVIII, 173
Article XXXI: Of the one Oblation of Christ finished upon the Cross, 81, 82
   Eucharistic sacrifice, 140
Article XXXII: Of the Marriage of Priests, 82
   proposed amendment, 173
Article XXXIII: Of Excommunicate Persons, how they are to be avoided, 83, 84
   proposed amendment, 174
Article XXXIV: Of the Traditions of the Church, 30, 85, 86
Article XXXV: Of Homilies, 87, 88

Index

proposed deletion, 174
Protestant Episcopal Church, 10
Article XXXVI: Of Consecration of Bishops and Ministers, 89
   Bruce Kaye commentary, 151
   proposed amendment, 174
Article XXXVII: Of the Civil Magistrates, 90, 91
   proposed amendment, 174
Article XXXVIII: Of Christian men's Goods, which are not common, 92
   proposed deletion, 175
Article XXXIX: Of a Christian man's Oath, 93
   proposed deletion, 175
Articles I - V teaching on the persons of the Trinity, 8
Articles I-VIII, 33
Articles VI -VIII character and exercise of faith, 8
Articles IX - XVIII
   life of faith, 47
   personal dimensions of belief, 8
Articles XIX - XXIV, 62
Articles XIX - XXXIV duties and responsibilities in community, 8
Articles XXV - XXXI, 71
   ministry of the sacraments, 86
Articles XXXII - XXXIX, 82
Articles XXXV - XXXIX religious and civil life in England, 8
Assemblies of God. *see* Australian Christian Churches
assent to the Articles. *see* subscription to the Articles
Athanasian Creed, 47, 170
atonement, 81
Augsberg Confession, 106, 150
Augustine, 155
   human will, 50
   original sin, 48
Augustinian Doctrine, 146
Australian Christian Churches doctrinal statement, 161
Australian theological colleges and the articles, 10, 11
authority. *see also* Scripture

issue for the Reformation, 4
reason and tradition, 180
Avis, Paul, 130

B

Baden Powell, Robert, 102
baptism
   Article XXVII, 75, 76
   full immersion, 160, 161
   and the Holy Spirit, 58
baptism of the Holy Spirit, 160
   believers' baptism, 163
   speaking in tongues, 161, 162
Barth, Karl, 185
Basil of Caesarea, 40
Batty, Francis, 112
Baxter, Richard, 11
Bayne, Stephen, 130
Berger, Peter and de-modernising impulse, 123
Berkeley, George, 128
Bezzant, Rhys, 152
Bickersteth, Edward, 124
Bicknell, EJ, 9
   Richard Turnbull's review, 121
   subscription to the Articles, 104
'Bishops Book' (1537), 23
Blackburne, Francis and the anti-subscription movement, 98, 99, 100
Book of Common Prayer 1662
   authentic Anglicanism, 6
   baptism, 76
   in conjunction with the Articles, 192
   stressing the need for confession, 49
   translation of some liturgies from Latin, 31
Bramhall, John, 21, 97
Broad and Liberal Anglicans and the Articles, 128
Broad Anglicanism, 30
   and the Articles, 128
   modern attitude to the Articles, 130
Broad Church. *see* Liberals

broad churchmen. *see* Broad Anglicanism
Brook, Stella, 30, 31
Bull, George, 98
Bultmann, Rudolf, 178
Burghley, Lord, 154
Burgmann, Ernest, 112
Burke, Edmund opposing Blackburne, 100
Burnet, Gilbert, 154
Butler, Joseph, 128

C

Calvin, John, 26
   atonement, 37, 81
   authoritative theologian, 28
   Holy Communion, 78
Cambridge Platonists, 30
   origins of Liberal tradition, 128
Cameron, Marcia, 147
Canons 1604, 97
Cecil, William. *see* Burghley, Lord
celibacy, 83
chantry houses, 68
   prayers for the dead, 43
Charismatic-Pentecostal doctrinal statements, 159
Charles I, 97
child-abuse scandals, 186
Christ holding together New and Old Testaments, 45
Christian City Churches doctrinal statement, 160
Christian convictions, 2, 3
Christian hope. *see* eschatology
Christian Revival Crusade doctrinal statement, 162
Christology definition, 35
Church Discipline Act 1840, 103
Church Missionary Society, 119
Church of England. *see also* Anglican
   authority, 64, 65
   ceremonies and liturgies, 85, 86
   factions. *see also* Anglo-Catholicism; Liberals
      diversity of belief, 30
   nature and character, 62, 63
   reformed with historical continuity, 21
Church Pastoral Aid Society, 119
church-state relations, 91
   church workers and laws of the land, 185, 186
Clayton, Robert
   anti-subscription movement, 99
   Athanasian Creed, 98
Clerical Subscription Act 1865, 103
Colenso, John William, 102
Coleridge, Samuel Taylor, 118
Confession of Augsberg, 17, 20
   inspiring Cranmer, 24
Confession of Basel, 20
confession of faith needed in contemporary Australia, 177
Confession of Würtemberg, 25
Continental Reformation, 19
convictions of belief, 1, 2
   importance of, 7
Convocation, 24
   members subscribing to the articles, 95
   presenting of the Articles, 25
   'Three Articles', 96
Cooper, Anthony Ashley, 119
Council of Chalcedon, 35
Council of Constance, 80
Council of Jerusalem, 46
   General Council model, 66
Council of Nicaea, 35
Council of Orange, 48
Council of Trent, 25, 65
   Decrees, 18
   extra books as canonical, 43
   Mass in the vernacular, 71
   purgatory, 68
   transubstantiation, 77
   withholding the cup during Communion, 80
'Counter Reformation', 22. *see also* English Reformation
Covenant for the Church of England, 166
Cranmer, Thomas, 100, 119

Index

atonement, 81
'Bishops Book', 23
Confession of Augsberg, 24
General Councils, 66
Homilies, 88
marriage, 82
martyrdom, 8
'New Learning' Party, 19
reformed Church, 22
sermon at accession of Edward VI, 91
work on the Articles, 5
creeds as summaries of the teaching of Scripture, 46

D

Darwin, Charles, 101
Decian persecution, 55
devil as the personification of evil, 163
Dix, Dom Gregory, 139
Doctrine Commission, 156
   (1922), 106, 107
   (1967), 108, 109, 148
      presenting report, 111
      suggestions, 110
Dworkin, Ronald on human equality, 181

E

Eastern Orthodox Church, 21
Ecumenical Council. *see* General Council
Edward VI, 5
   accession, 24
   clerical marriages, 83
   First Book of Homilies, 88
Elizabeth I
   embrace of Reformed theology, 24
   excommunication by Rome, 22
   opposing Puritan ecclesiology, 27
'Elizabethan Settlement', 26
   1552 Prayer Book, 25
   theological debates, 29
English Monarchy and Papal authority, 90
   excommunication of Elizabeth I, 95
English Reformation. *see also* 'Counter Reformation'; Reformation
   debates and declarations, 22
   episcopacy and Establishment, 28
   Henry VIII, 20
   key principles, 21
   origins, 18
   personal faith and social order, 69
   political aspirations, 21
   Reformed Catholicism, 25, 46
   responses to Luther, 19
episcopate, 164
Erasmus and Luther, 50
eschatology, 184, 185
Establishment of the Church, 101
   subscription to the Articles, 9
Evangelical Movement, 119
Evangelicalism
   and the Articles, 119, 149
      defences for, 145
      Spirit of the Reformation, 122
   fundamentalist, 119, 120
   missionary minded, 183
evolution, 179
existence of God, 178

F

faith and reason, 178
filioque clause, 40
First Helvetic Confession, 20
Forward in Faith (North America), 164
free-will, 50

G

GAFCON, 165
Gardiner, Stephen and the 'Old Learning' Party, 19
General Council, 66
General Synod Doctrine Commission, 13
Gibson, ECS, 9
God the Creator, 179
good works, 53

Goodwin, Charles Wycliffe, 101
Grace
    not hindered by human lack of holiness, 74
    sacraments, 72
Gray, Robert, 102
Gregory of Nazianzen, 66
Griffith Thomas, WH, 9, 55, 129
    Evangelicalism, 120
    sin, 48
Grindal, Edmund, 27
Gurney, Archer, 140

H

Hale, Stephen, 12
Hammond, TC, 112
Henry VIII, 3
    'Bishops Book', 23
    religious reform for political and personal reasons, 20
Henson, Hensley, 130
high churchmen, 30. *see also* Anglo-Catholicism
    Oxford Movement, 123
Holy Spirit, 183
Homily on Justification, 52
Homily on Salvation, 52, 87
Hooker, Richard
    Anglican understanding of the Reformation, 117
    appeal to reason, 128
    Church, 65
    reason and tradition, 180
    sacraments, 72
    theological response to Puritanism, 27
Hughes, Thomas, 104
human worth, 181
Huxley, Thomas Henry, 102

I

imputed righteousness, 51
indulgences, 56, 65, 68
Institutes of the Christian Religion, 37

intercession of the saints, 23

J

James I, 28
Jerome, 43, 155
Jerusalem Declaration, 165
Jesus' life of obedience, 182
Jewel, John, 25
Jones, John (Vicar of Alconbury)
    revision of *Book of Common Prayer*, 98
Judaism, 46
justification by faith, 4, 47
    separating Catholicism and Protestantism, 139
    soteriology, 176

K

Kaye, Bruce, 150, 151
Keble, John, 122
Kierkegaard, Søren, 53
'King's Book' (1543), 23
Knox, Broughton, 147, 148, 149
Knox, John, 27

L

Lambeth Conference 1888, 10
    new Church Constitutions, 114
Lambeth Conference 1968 and the report of the Doctrine Commission, 109, 111
Lambeth Quadrilateral, 110
Lampe, GWH, 142, 143
Latimer, Hugh, 119
    martyrdom, 8
    reformed Church, 22
Latitudinarianism
    definition, 100
    dislike of subscription, 142
    origins of Liberal tradition, 128
Laud, William, 97
liberal sentiment, 100
    Darwin, Charles, 102
    French Revolution, 101
Liberals, 106

Index

and the Articles, 128, 129
  contemporary attitude, 130, 144
  objections, 142
  origins, 128
Liberation Theology, 187
Lindsey, Theophilus and the Unitarian chapel, 99
liturgies in the language of the people, 70
Locke, John, 61, 99
Lollards, 19
low churchmen, 30. *see also* Evangelicalism
Luther, Martin, 4, 19
  antinomianism, 45
  authoritative theologian, 28
  dispute with Erasmus, 50
  negative attitude to the Old Testament, 44
  sin, 49

M

Maclear, George, 129
Marcionite heresy, 44
marriage, 184
Matthew, WR, 130
Maurice, FD, 47, 105, 129
McFadyen, Alistair, 50
McLeod, Hugh, 123
Middleton, Arthur and Patristic influences on the Articles, 127, 128
Mill, John Stuart, 101
Moltmann, Jürgen, 182
monasticism, 56

N

Neill, Stephen
  Anglican belief, 117, 118
  criticism of the Articles, 154
Nestorianism, 66
New Atheism, 178
'New Perspective on Paul', 52
New Testament political theology, 91
New Zealand Church and the Articles, 114
Newman, John Henry, 68
  Anglo-Catholicism, 138
  Articles, 136
  received into the Roman Catholic Church, 139
  Scripture and Tradition, 155
  teaching on purgatory, 68, 126
  Tract XC, 136, 137, 138
    Vernon Staley, 141
  Tracts, 122
Nicene Creed, 3
  filioque clause, 40
  work of the Spirit, 39
Nietzsche, Friedrich, 1
Null, Ashley, 85

O

O'Donovan, Oliver, 73
  Articles as a church document, 118
  Articles in need of work, 131
  Old Testament political theory, 91
  orthodoxy and the creeds, 46
Oxford Movement, 121. *see also* Tractarians
  restoring balance in Church teaching, 122
  reviving Catholic identity, 123

P

Packer, Jim, 142
  inerrancy of Scripture, 180
  revision of the Articles, 146
  view of the Articles, 145
Paley, William, 100
Papal authority
  in England before the Reformation, 18
  English rejection, 23
  limited by the articles, 66
Paton, MJM, 104
Paul III, 65
Pearson, John, 7
Peasant's Rebellion, 69
Pelagians and original sin, 48
penance, 68
  resumption of fellowship, 84
Pentecostal-Charismatic, 7
Perceval, Arthur Philip, 136

Pius V, 22
Pope, Alexander, 55
Porter, Muriel, 151
Prayer Book (1552), 24
prayers for the dead, 23, 126
predestination, 59, 60
    Catholic view, 125, 126
    Liberal viewpoint, 143
Prophetical Tradition, 136
propitiation, 81
public square, 187, 188
purgatory, 23, 65, 67
    appealing to grieving relatives, 69
    challenged by the Reformation, 44
    objections to the doctrine, 68
    prayers for the dead, 43
Puritans, 26, 27
Pusey, Edward, 123

R

Ramsey, Michael, 118
reconciliation, 36
redemption, 81
Reformation
    Continental Reformation. *see* Continental Reformation
    'Counter Reformation'. *see* 'Counter Reformation'
    creeds, 17
    disagreements among reformers, 19, 20
    in England, 4
    English Reformation. *see* English Reformation
Reformed Episcopal Church, 164
Religion Act 1539, 23
Resurrection, 38
Reunionists, 139, 140
Ridley, Nicholas, 119
    martyrdom, 8
    reformed Church, 22
Robinson, John, 108
Rogers, Guy, 149
    revision of the Articles, 150
Roman Catholic, 7
    emancipation in England, 101
    papal agents, 27

Roman Catholic Church extra-scriptural tradition, 42
Ross, Kenneth, 125, 129
    defence of Articles and Catholic belief, 124, 127
Royal Supremacy, 96
Ryle, John Charles, 76

S

Sachs, William, 131
sacraments, 22, 23
    Catholic view, 126
    definitions, 72
salvation
    and predestination, 60
    theories in medieval times, 4
    uniqueness of Christ, 182
Sanderson, Robert, 28
Sandys, Edwin, 28
Scotus, Duns, 50
Scripture. *see also* Apocrypha
    authority, 4
    challenged, 120
    for determining Doctrine, 43
    doctrine of, 180
    the Old Testament, 44
    primacy, 22
    sufficiency for salvation, 41
    testimony to God, 179
Secker, Thomas, 99
Second Vatican Council, 71
Shaftesbury, Lord. *see* Cooper, Anthony Ashley
Simeon, Charles, 119
Simeon Trustees, 119
sin
    Christ's sinlessness, 57
    original sin, 48
'Six Articles' (1539), 23
    clerical celibacy, 82
social justice, 186
soteriology, 4
    scripture, 42
Staley, Vernon, 141
subscription to the Articles, 24, 96
    in Australia, 113
    by clergy, 8, 11

Index

diversity of belief, 103
Doctrine Commission (1922), 107
in the Established Church, 9
made mandatory by the English Parliament, 96
members of Convocation, 95
modified by 1865 Act, 104
not necessary for the Lambeth Quadrilateral, 24
not required by some National Churches, 114
Puritans, 97
strengthened requirements, 97
Sykes, Stephen, 118

T

Tawney, RH and human equality, 181
Temple, William, 130
'Ten Articles' (1536), 22
The Articles of Religion, 3
    Anglican Belief, 33, 131, 147
    apologies, 25
    authority from Scripture, 6, 146
    Covenant for the Church of England, 166
    defining doctrine, 18, 106, 107, 112, 114
        as a creed, 146
        statement of faith for the sixteenth century, 5
        tests of orthodoxy and belief, 105, 106, 144
    Doctrine Commission (1967), 109
    first and second order issues, 121
    general criticisms, 135, 152, 153, 155
    inability to settle modern disagreements, 167
    modern purposes, 191, 192, 193
    and morals, 187
    originally drafted in Latin, 30
    Patristic influences, 127, 128
    questions about their future, 110
    Reformation Spirit, 122
    relationship to Prayer Book, 120
    revision, 146, 150, 167
        intended as working documents, 156
    proposed alternatives, amendments and additions, 159, 175, 176, 189
    status in the Australian Church, 12
    what they are and are not, 7, 8
'The Blogging Parson', 12
Thirty-Nine Articles. *see The Articles of Religion*
'Three Articles' (1583), 96
tithing, 92
Toon, Peter, 9, 123
    criticism of the Articles, 154
Tract XC, 137, 138, 139
Tractarians, 122. *see also* Anglo-Catholicism; Oxford Movement
traditions of interpretation, 9. *see also* Anglo-Catholicism; Evangelicalism
translation of the Latin text of the Articles, 31, 129
transubstantiation, 77, 126
Trinity, 39
    doctrine, 34
Trollope, Anthony, 102
Tudor, Mary, 22, 24
Turnbull, Richard, 121
Tyndale, William, 70
    translating the bible into English, 19

U

Unitarian, 30
    Blackburne campaign, 100
    first chapel in London, 99
    minimal assent to the Articles, 98

V

Venn, Henry, 119
Vidler, Alec, 118

W

Wand, William, 139
    Anglo-Catholic view of the Articles, 112
    subscription to the Articles, 108
Waterland, Daniel, 98

Westminster Confession, 17, 180
   scripture, 42
Whitgift, John, 27, 96
Wilberforce, William, 119
Williams, Rowan, 164
Williams, WW, 129
Württemberg Confession, 150
Wycliffe, John, 19

Y
Yeats, WB, 1
Young, Frances, 46

Z
Zwingli, Ulrich, 4, 19
   Confession of Basel, 20
   Holy Communion, 78

www.ingramcontent.com/pod-product-compliance
Lightning Source LLC
Chambersburg PA
CBHW020409080526
44584CB00014B/1248